COACH
LEE ROSE

COACH LEE ROSE

ON FAMILY AND BASKETBALL

A Memoir

LEE ROSE

With Eleanor Rose & Joe Barry Carroll

Copyright © 2019 Lee Rose

All rights reserved. No part of this book may be reproduced, stored, or transmitted by any means—whether auditory, graphic, mechanical, or electronic—without written permission of both publisher and author, except in the case of brief excerpts used in critical articles and reviews. Unauthorized reproduction of any part of this work is illegal and is punishable by law.

Joe Barry Carroll Publishing
Atlanta, Georgia
joebarrycarrollpublishing.com

ISBN-13: 978-1-7332144-1-4 (paperback)
ISBN-13: 978-1-7332144-3-8 (ebook)

Managing Editor: Tara Coyt
Cover Design: Vanessa Maynard
Interior Design & Layout: Madison Lux

Library of Congress Control Number: 2019919023

The paper used in this publication meets the minimum requirements of the American National Standard for Information Sciences—permanence of paper for printed library materials ANSI Z39.48-1992

CONTENTS

In the Beginning... 1
   Coal.. 3
   Young Lee... 5
   Family.. 8
   Young Athlete.. 14
   Lexington.. 17
   Work... 19
   Transylvania College... 25
A Perfect Girl... 29
   More Family.. 31
   Marriage... 33
   A Father... 39
Coaching.. 47
   Transylvania... 51
   The Places You Go.. 57
   Moving Up.. 60
Theology.. 63
   Race... 66
   Broken Hearts.. 71
   Whole Person, Whole Education.. 73
   Discipline... 77
   Preparation.. 79

 Game Day 81
 Conditioning 83
 On Fairness 84
 Humility 85
 Cheating 86
 Coach-Player Relationships 90
 Helping 91
 Tragedy 92
 Communication 93
 Everybody In 98
 Networking and Relationship Building 99
 The Right Assistant 103
 Always Learning 106
Cincinnati 109
University of North Carolina, Charlotte 113
 Bite of The Big Apple 116
 Getting Better 121
The Boilermakers of Purdue 129
 Something to Consider 131
 The Other 132
 The Seven-Footer 134
 Left and Right 137
 From Deep 139
 International Play 142
 The Final Four, Again 144
 So Close 150
 A Mystery 151
 Regrets, I Have a Few 153
University of South Florida 157
 What I Liked 159
 The Good and the Bad 161
 Season of Change 166
San Antonio Spurs 169

New Jersey Nets 175
    The Captain 178
Milwaukee Bucks 183
    The Senator 185
    Wheat From Chaff 186
    One and Done 189
    The GOAT—Greatest of All Time 191
    Style and Substance 193
Charlotte 195
    Further On 200
    Behind the Scenes 202
    An Ending 203
Golden Years 205
    Forward in the Fifth 208
The Long Goodbye—Lee 217
The Long Goodbye—Eleanor 221
    A Cruel and Vulgar Visitor That Will Not Leave 225
    Normal? 240
    A Team 243
    Writing a Memoir 247
In Gratitude 249

IN THE BEGINNING

I WAS BORN in 1936 in a small house in the small town of West Irvine, Kentucky, at the base of the Appalachia Mountains. Kentucky is not just where I am from; it is who I am. It doesn't really matter that I lived in West Irvine for only nine years before moving to Lexington, or that I have lived in many other places in my eighty-plus years on Earth. It is hard to determine the reasons for the emotional tug that this *place* has on me.

We are all aware of our five senses—sight, hearing, taste, smell, and touch. Kentucky is my sixth sense. I filter everything through those early experiences in those mountains of Appalachia, then later when my family moved to Lexington. When I am successful in my career and life, my homeland is the backdrop of that success. I consider that area and my family and friends in Kentucky as the foundation from which any of my success springs. In many ways, I feel I am paying tribute to this place and my people when I do well. The stuff I learned, the experiences I had, the lessons that the experiences taught me, leave me forever grateful. Even events that appear as failures, I am able to survive because of the values embedded in me as a result of this early life. The memories of my small-town Kentucky have branded me in a way that is eternal.

When I was growing up in West Irvine, it was a small community of just a few homes located close to the Kentucky River in clear view of the Appalachia Mountains and Sweet Lick Knob. For those not so refined to hill living, a "knob" is this land formation not as tall as a mountain but higher than a hill. Sweet Lick Knob was a beautiful natural landmark. West Irvine was at the base of the mountains, and there were fields and open green spaces all around. As a kid, I wandered freely in these areas. I remain puzzled at how such scenic terrain could, at the same time, hold so much pain for some of the people who lived there.

Appalachia is a mountainous region in the eastern United States that runs through Kentucky, Georgia, South Carolina, North Carolina, Tennessee, Virginia, and all of West Virginia. Appalachia has a history of being one of the most impoverished regions of the United States. These are my people, yet my loyalty to them does not require me to overlook that in this part of America, people tend to be disproportionately poor and often undereducated. Life in Appalachia can be as hard and cold as the coal deposits that tunnel under those mountains.

Strangely, one of my most vivid recollections is that of a huge graveyard close to the church in West Irvine. It always seemed to me that there were more headstones in that cemetery than there were people walking around. I guess it would make sense that there would be fewer people above ground in this very small town than below, given that the area had been settled in 1812. That and the area was tightly tied to the ups, downs, and dangerous outcomes of the coal industry. Perhaps one wasn't necessarily connected to the other, but both details gained my attention. In addition to plenty of grave markers, there are other monuments scattered around as testimony to a time gone by. In some way, these markers allow recognition that the person was here and mattered.

I was like most children of my generation and the generations before me, whereby a day would come that I would need to decide to either leave Kentucky for good or stay there forever. At some point, a person is faced with making a deal either with the devil that you know or the one that you do not. Does one stay in this imperfect place that holds the relationships you want to maintain, with the family and culture that you love, or do you choose to strike out for any place else in hopes of something better? Or, if not better, then just different. Those who leave to pursue a life unknown elsewhere often seem to go and never come back. Years later, I would relate to the song by Hal Ketchum that offers, "the world must be flat, cause when people leave town, they never come back." That was the way for me, my kin, and friends. Sometimes, the natural flow of life events will decide for you. Like when a boy meets a girl who becomes a wife, then he and the wife have a baby, followed by (sometimes) being held captive by the eternal demand of the cycle of food, shelter, and clothing. Even if you want to pursue someplace better, it is just not that easy. These decisions are a complicated matter, further complicated by the possible move to a place unknown.

COAL

The Appalachia region has long been a major resource of coal. West Irvine, because of its location convenient to the mines and waterways, became a mining center for extracting and transporting coal. The Kentucky River runs along the side of the neighboring town, Irvine, allowing it to act as a center of commerce and transportation. Irvine was a coal-car exchange town, where the coal was staged prior to its move to places near and far.

In many ways, the coal mines that tunneled deep under the mountains were bigger than the people above. People would come and go, but there was always another layer of coal to be found. The coal industry was the economic support for the region—it was many families' way of life and financial support. It seemed to guide all things large and small, though we remained conflicted about this hazardous industry in many ways. In our unguarded moments, I think that most folks knew that coal was a dirty and unhealthy business. In present times, I have heard coal referred to as "clean coal" in response to environmentalists' attack on the hazards of the fuel on the environment and its citizens. I am still not sure how "clean" any coal can ever be, but that black and dusty rock always appeared green like money to us because it was how most families supported themselves in these closed communities. I have heard politicians and corporate folk glorify the coal industry, suggesting that workers just love everything about working coal. I disagree. I doubt that loving coal has ever entered their thoughts. My family and friends worked the ill-fated mines because the pay was good, and it would allow them to provide for their families. This was especially so back in the 1930s.

I have always been a fan of the popular biographical movie *Coal Miner's Daughter*, on the life of country singer Loretta Lynn, portrayed by Sissy Spacek. The film centers on the mountain culture of Kentucky. It was so realistic to my own life in Kentucky that, at some point, while watching the film, I began to look for my family and friends, expecting them to be among the actors on the screen. One of the many memorable lines during the movie is when the father tells Loretta that he long ago stopped measuring his body weight because he was unable to tell how much was his and how much was the lifelong deposit of coal that he had ingested. The coal profession is populated by lean men—men with a grayish color to their skin caused by most of their daylight hours being spent underground in the mines. Many of the men who chose to stay in our small and very poor community usually found, at road's end, a chest full of dust as they sat, waiting for the next phlegm-filled cough, each one a consequence of a career in the coal mines. Inhaled coal dust is likely to cause lung and breathing problems, though some die young before they suffer the symptoms of black lung disease.

More immediate dangers included when miners were injured by heavy equipment, vehicle collisions, explosions, gas leaks, and collapses. For those men who worked underground, there was a daily brush with doom. There were always somber, hard-faced women who waited above ground, hoping against hope that the person they loved had somehow managed to find a pocket of air when the tunnel collapsed, that somehow, the rescue would happen in time. When the men die, the women move forward—they have to.

YOUNG LEE

As a young boy, I grew up with railroad tracks close to most of the roads I traveled, and almost all of the train-cars were piled high with black coal. The trains lumbered along slowly with their heavy loads, carrying cargo that would be used as heat and power for homes and businesses near and far. The trains created a rhythmic clacking sound as they moved along the tracks, as though they were trying to tell you something. The long blow of whistles accompanied that clacking sound and became part of the soundtrack of our lives. The sound of that whistle remains for me as clear today as it did all those years ago. It continues to tie me to the culture of the lonesome towns dotted along those mountains.

As a boy, I had the freedom to be outside all day in the summer and play with my friends. This is the freedom that comes with growing up in a community where most folks know your name and you theirs. Like many children, I played jacks and red rover and walked fence rows. Walking those fence slats was a daily, competitive challenge to see who could go the farthest along the top of a fence rail without falling. When jacks became broken or lost, we would play the game with rocks instead. I learned to swim in the Kentucky River, but most of the time, I played a variety of games that involved a ball. I loved to compete.

West Irvine had a population of a few hundred people at that time. We had an elementary school, a church, a grocery store, a filling station, and a few homes scattered around. There was no particular center or hub to the community. I suppose when everything is so small and near, everything is the center. In nearby Irvine, there was a courthouse in the square, a movie theatre, and a few small businesses, including a dry goods store. That kind of place generally sold a mix of things like clothes, utensils, canned goods, and odd items, but not necessarily fresh meat and milk like a grocery store. There really wasn't a lot of class or economic distinction between the small towns of Irvine and West Irvine, but still, people always made it clear which one they called home.

I walked the railroad tracks to Irvine and the courthouse on Saturdays. West Irvine was just a mile removed from Irvine, which was the county seat of Estill County. Saturdays were always festive in some way. It was like everybody found a reason to come to the center of town. I remember the music: the sounds of fiddles, banjos, guitars, and harmonicas, and the clicking sounds from those few who could play spoons. I was always fascinated by the sound of those spoons, like a tap dance and a drumbeat combined. Somewhere in history, someone discovered that two spoons held in opposition to one another and at just the right angle became a percussive instrument and a brilliant source of music.

My elementary school had four classrooms, a furnace, and a coatroom. Since there was no indoor plumbing, the school had outhouses. I am guessing they are called outhouses because they are put out and away from your house because of the unpleasant details. They were basically an enclosed stall with a wood bench that had an opening and a deep hole dug out under that opening. Everyone, from the principal to the youngest student, had to visit the outhouse if nature called during school hours.

There were four teachers who each taught two grades per room in our little schoolhouse. During my first four years of school, the Broadus sisters were my teachers. They were really good yet strict. They were of the era when if you were caught talking without their permission, you had to stay after school and write "I will not talk in

IN THE BEGINNING

class" over the whole blackboard—only to wipe it clean after you were done and begin again until the teacher was satisfied you had learned your lesson. That was if you were lucky. This was also a time when children were struck by teachers with rulers and paddles. Whether the "whuppin" took place at school or home, it was assumed that the child had it coming. These were not my challenges—I was known as a good boy because I was. I really did not struggle very much with behaving myself; I have always wanted my family to be proud of me. I was always concerned with what I could do to help my family, even at a young age.

Our little 1942 schoolhouse sat atop a hill, and our water came from a well that was down the hill, on the other side of a fence four slats high that ran across a big field. A slat is technically a strip of wood measuring six inches wide, but "slat" is also used generally as a rule-of-thumb measurement. Over time, a child of Kentucky is likely to add the word "slat" among that group of words that were estimates of measurement like "down the road" and "knee-high." Each day, two students—a boy and a girl—were picked to take a five-gallon bucket on the journey to get our drinking water for the day. It was an exercise in balance and speed because that field and hill became an imaginary obstacle course for young kids. We carried the bucket carefully by its handles, but it never came back as full as it started. I'm not quite sure how children were coached into feeling that the carrying of the bucket was an honor and not a grinding chore, but that was how we felt.

Students who could not afford to pay for their lunch received a free lunch. We all ate lunch together in our classroom or maybe outside in the schoolyard if the weather was nice. I probably qualified for the free lunch based on financial need, but I brought my lunch from home in a brown sack each day. I was never sure if bringing my lunch was a matter of my family's pride or just my grandmother's wanting me to eat her cooking. To this day, I don't see how Mama and Grandmama covered the expense of food, clothing, and shelter for all of us on what little they earned.

FAMILY

I never knew much about my father or his side of my family other than a random reference to him here and there. My parents split up very early on in my life. I can never remember being in the same house with my father, or my parents standing side-by-side in any place or at any time. My mom, Elizabeth Hyden Rose—known by us as Biddy—rarely spoke about the details of their marriage and our family. I do think it is characteristic of people from her era to be less prone to talk about personal issues than in today's world, with its constant sharing of photographs and telling of tales that perhaps should remain private. I think there was also something in Mom—maybe stubbornness, maybe pride—that made her feel that they'd failed at the marriage, and she did not want to be reminded of that failure.

For whatever her reasons, Mama rarely spoke of my father to me. Our mountain culture feels that most family matters—even the good things—are personal in nature, and we just don't talk about them. Sometimes, the silence is for a particular reason, and then there are other things folks feel require no explanation. When someone does bad, everyone is embarrassed, and so things should go unspoken. If discussed, bad news is usually mentioned in hushed tones and reserved for certain folk. I guess that unless you are there to witness a thing for yourself—good or bad—you are likely to miss it. You can't rely on the news being posted. In most instances, all we had to work with were bits and pieces.

It seemed that the word father was supposed to have some meaning, but I was not sure what at that time. My memories of Lee Crawford Rose, are very limited. I am not sure if I really understood or knew very much about him beyond his being referred to as my father. I do remember that he appeared out of the blue one day and picked me up in an old truck after school when I was five years old. He and another man took me a half-hour away to Booneville, Kentucky, to a farmhouse. Perhaps it was a family gathering on his side of the family for some reason or none at all. I do not remember very much about that day. I was never sure why he picked me up, or whom the other man was in the truck, or even whom the people that I met that day were supposed to be to me. The stranger and my father dropped me off afterward.

My father died of tuberculosis when he was thirty-eight years old, and I was six. I remember attending his funeral in Booneville, but little else about that time.

My mother and I moved in with my maternal grandmother after my father's death. I cannot recall if his death was coincidental to our move or the cause of it. My grandmother's house in West Irvine was a one-story, red-brick house. This was the home that my grandfather had built with his own hands for Grandmama. Whenever someone referenced Grandmama's house, they often included that detail in the same breath. My grandfather, William Hacker Hyden, had been a timber surveyor for the U.S. government and was killed while driving home on those curvy mountain roads in 1936, the year I was born. Part of my grandfather's outsized, Paul Bunyan-type reputation was that he could measure the amount of timber on a mountain on sight. I am not sure how that was ever verified, but it is fun to accept it as so.

This little red-brick structure housed Grandmama, my mother, me, occasionally one or more of my mother's five sisters, and however many of my extended family might be passing through from time to time for one reason or the other. It was the centerpiece of my family's comings and goings and social interactions. Sometimes that was for good and other times for chaos. On good days, the scene might be our front porch with a swing and card-playing. Perhaps Mama and Grandmama could be seen tending the garden of corn, lettuce, tomatoes, and huge cucumbers next to the shed. I call it a shed instead of a garage because garages are for cars, and we did not have a car. Then, there were the lean and difficult times that neither gardening nor card-playing could make better.

The image of all those women around is prominent when I recall my growing-up years. They were loud and sometimes contentious as siblings can be. This group of women could be overwhelming and too much for a little boy to fully understand. When those times arose, I was motivated to slip out to play ball, to create another world for myself. Over time, I may have become drawn to the culture of my sports teams as family and my teammates as strange siblings. Perhaps they provided some type of familial supplement for me.

I suppose that I am like many people when it comes to the emotional recall of a time gone by. As many of us stroll down memory lane, we become torn as it relates to our loved ones. Was my mother emotionally unavailable, or was she just shy? Was my grandmother warm and loving, or was I simply her leverage with my mother? Is someone remote and deep thinking, or are they just mean? I am sure that the answer is yes to either and all of the above. When we are born, we inherit an already-complicated world, and then we add our own layer to that very complication. I heard someone refer to a situation in which they found themselves as being perfectly flawed, meaning it was not necessarily how they would have designed the circumstance, but it worked, nonetheless. I would use that term to describe my family dynamic. I am okay with accepting that each of my family members are whole people, and they are likely to be different things at different times. What I am sure of is that I cared deeply about my mother, my family, and the community where I grew up.

I regret that my brother Gene (seven years older), sister Mary (two years older), and me (the baby of the family) never lived together. This was one of the great mysteries of my life. Often, the details of family history like that are lost when all the older family members are buried. I did not see very much of them growing up. We may have all been together at some point when I was a baby, but I have no memories of Gene and me playing ball together on the cinder surface in West Irvine. Cinder is the result of partially burned coal, and there was certainly plenty of that around. There was no walking to school together for the three of us. There was never a time that I remember us kids sitting together at the table. That is a puzzle to me, especially since Mary was almost my age.

My brother and sister had been sent to aunts and uncles to live before they were later both placed in mission schools. I am guessing that we became part of the tradition common in poor communities for children to be sent to live with relatives or attend mission schools in an effort to relieve some of the economic pressure and expenses that large families with small resources can bring. These mission schools were part of outreach efforts by churches and governments to combat the lack of education and welfare resources in Appalachia. I assume that attending the mission schools did not involve very much money, if any, because none of us had any.

I remember hearing talk that Gene had been "sent away"—and that was the only way I ever heard that said—to a mission school in Blackey, Kentucky. The school in Blackey was Stuart Robinson School and was of a type known as a settlement school. They were part of the Presbyterian Church Mission established back in 1913 in Letcher County, Kentucky. Settlement schools dotted this area of the state. Without them, the children in some of the very isolated areas had no schooling available to them at that time. The school had a work-study program through which students could earn all or part of their tuition, room, and board. I knew that Gene "stoked" the furnaces with coal in some of the school buildings so that may have explained how he was able to attend. I suppose that our family was destined to be in the coal business one way or the other.

Mary Elizabeth was sent to the parochial school Cardome Academy of The Sisters of Visitation in Georgetown, Kentucky. Perhaps she received a scholarship because, again, we had no finances to contribute. I never offer that as a sad song—it simply just was what it was.

My mother worked in some type of clerical position at the Blue Grass Army Depot in Richmond, Kentucky. It was a forty-eight-mile round-trip from West Irvine to Richmond each workday. She caught a ride with several other people who also worked at the depot. During the workweek, they left before daylight and got home after dark. That left me largely supervised (or not) by my grandmother, engaging in whatever activities I chose. My grandmother basically tended to and raised me while my mother was away at work—which seemed like all the time. It was Grandmama who prepared most of our meals. It seemed to always be oatmeal for breakfast. Our meal selection was not intended to be necessarily sensitive to appetites but rather practical. If you didn't like certain staples like oatmeal and white potatoes, you were out of luck. A side note: As a child, I thought that the white potatoes known as Irish potatoes were somehow named "Arsh potatoes." I didn't understand until I learned to spell properly that the word I was pronouncing as "Arsh" was actually Irish, distorted by the local dialect.

Life always seemed hard for Mama. She was born without a hip socket, so even walking was a struggle for her because one of her legs was actually shorter than the other. This resulted in a very pronounced limp. At some point after we moved to Lexington, Mama had an extra measure of sole put on one shoe to allow her to balance her stride, but the limp was still present throughout her life. I could always hear my mother coming or going around the house with the rise, gentle forward movement, and drop of the shorter leg.

My mother was a pragmatic person who took the facts of life and lived with them. For the most part, she did that without a great deal of drama. If it is possible to inherit a trait or characteristic from a parent, I may have inherited my pragmatic nature from Mama. I can't be sure of exactly what I inherited from my father—perhaps some of his athletic ability.

When we were in West Irvine, my mother was taking care of her mother, holding down a job, and taking care of me. This eventually took its toll on her. Even as a young child, I could recognize that she was always struggling to make ends meet, and she seemed to carry the weight of the world on her shoulders. She worked long hours, was gone most of the time, and seemed worn down. I gained my work ethic

IN THE BEGINNING

and discipline from her. Mama said and demonstrated by example, that only through hard work would any money come into our home. The silver lining in being exposed to my mother's difficulties was that it became a motivating force in my life to always want better for her, me, and eventually, my own family.

I am not sure how to fully describe my mother's personality, except that it was necessary for me and anyone else to accept her as a whole person, instead of being distracted by her parts. Our relationship was challenging. Like many children, I always wanted a warm relationship with my mother. I am not quite sure just how warm our relationship was, but it was rewarding. I love my mother, and when I consider her hard work and dedication to me, I know that she loved me, too. Even now, as I reflect on our relationship after all of these years, I am still trying to figure out all of the pieces. She was complicated, but for better or worse, I will always respect and love her—and that is mostly what I want to say about that.

In communities like ours, there is a lot of bartering and borrowing over staples like flour, sugar, eggs, and such until you can pay your neighbor back. Grandmama Hyden would often send me to neighbors to borrow something as neighbors had done with us. Each time I returned home from my errand, she would ask me if I remembered to thank the neighbor. I was pretty sure that I had, but if my wandering child's mind revealed any doubt about that, she would have me turn right around to go back and thank the person.

Grandmama had this fascination with the mythology of Abraham Lincoln and why they called him "Honest Abe." As the story goes, Lincoln was working in a general store when one day, a customer accidentally received incorrect change. That evening, when the store closed, Lincoln walked five miles to return the pennies owed to the family. Grandmama told that story many times, with great emphasis on honesty in dealing with other people. Who can really be that certain if Abe was honest or otherwise, but it is interesting to me how those lessons on values, ethics, and good manners were so ingrained in me with such a simple story. Since my grandmother told me that it was so, I generally accepted it was. Besides, she was the one fixing my breakfast. I was young but old enough to recognize that I should not disagree with the hand that feeds me.

One of Grandmama's favorite sayings was the Golden Rule: "Do unto others as you would have others do unto you." This is something that I try to live by. Over the years, I have added to that, "Do unto others as they would have you do unto them." We are all so different in so many ways, and doing unto somebody by my rules might not fill their prescriptions. I may need to take it a step further in consideration of what that person also thinks is fair for them.

My early exposure to church and religion was limited to observing my grandmother as she read her Bible and listened to services on the radio. Later, I did most of the church-going for our family. I attended Calvary Baptist Church, pastored by Reverend Owens in Lexington, Kentucky. I joined church one night when they had "the call to service." I can't say that there was thunder, drum rolls, and burning bushes, or even that Jesus spoke to me. Mostly, I just saw Reverend Owens up there by himself and decided not to let him stand there alone. I am unable to say exactly why, but I did not wait on other family members to join me—I just went when I felt it.

YOUNG ATHLETE

Football, basketball, and baseball all gave me something different and good. I liked the fact that there was never a clock in baseball—everything in its own time. I enjoyed the stop-and-go rhythm of football and how that contrasted to the constant movement of basketball. Early on, I recognized sports as a place with rules and order, a culture all its own. A society within a society. I was drawn to all of that. I liked that the rules had been pretty much the same since the game began

IN THE BEGINNING

long ago. That made it feel that this society within a larger society was predictable and reliable. In order to be successful, I would just need to learn the rules and work hard.

My love affair with basketball began when I was in early grade school with my best friend, whose name was Norman Taylor but who answered to "Taterbug." In the mountains, almost everyone has a nickname. I often wonder how I escaped being branded with one. Perhaps in some way, "Lee" fit me really well, so there was no need to try to improve on it. You were usually branded by some aspect of your appearance or even sometimes by some imperfection. I guess that Norman caught the name of Taterbug because he was so small that he brought to mind the small bugs that landed on potatoes. He was about three years older than me, but Taterbug and I were the same size—both small for our age. I do not recall how tall I was before any growth spurt, as there simply didn't seem to be the awareness of height in particular at that time. Weight and how fast a person ran a 440-yard dash was a greater measure in those days. That is unless a person towered over the rest of us and was quicker than any other person on the field or in the neighborhood—which I was not. In pictures, I was generally at least a head shorter than the other guys on my teams.

I cannot recall exactly the time or place that Taterbug and I met, but initially, I associated him with picking berries with his dad and then later sports, basketball mostly. Mr. Taylor would allow me to go with them to harvest berries at the base of the hills, and then we would take them to the market to sell.

Somewhere along the way, we found a bushel basket and cut the bottom out. We nailed it onto the side of a shed about nine feet above the ground, and our games began. For Taterbug and me, this was our arena. Dribbling was easy because we were playing on a hard, cinder-based foundation. Every day after school, we played a game to eight baskets. For two months, Taterbug won every game. Each time afterward, I felt like I could have cried as I walked into my house, defeated—I wanted to win so badly.

November came with its rain, snow, and cold weather, so we put away our basketball as we moved on to the next sport until spring. When the warmth finally returned, we would begin our daily competition again. This had a really big influence in my life. Looking back, those competitions on the cinder-stone surfaces of West Irvine was the place that revealed my competitive intensity and desire. I had been introduced to this intense desire to win and learn about myself. Regardless of the frustration I experienced being on the losing side of our proposition, it was somehow always about the game and trying to win. Taterbug was always my friend—the competitive games didn't change that. It seemed to me it was not personal, and I kept my mind focused on my goal. I suppose that I have always been this way. I found myself constantly reaching inside myself to get better. Some athletes need someone to hate in order to gain inspiration. For me, instead of creating an enemy out there, I turned inward to try to get better. I never found any advantage to making it about personalities; I needed to remain focused on the matter at hand, which was the contest. This value would appear time and again throughout my career as a player and later as a coach. I've always tried to stay focused on the goal of winning and not be distracted as I move toward that goal.

During the winter of fourth grade, I grew a little and got stronger, and the scores got closer. Just about the time I felt I had exhausted every strategy for victory, I finally won a game. I don't know if any one thing finally worked, or if it was just that everything eventually came together, but it involved work and sweat all along the way. My first win on that makeshift court made me realize just how much I had missed not winning. From that moment on, we would go back and forth. Taterbug would still win some, but I won my share, and every game was close. At that point in my life, winning gave me something that I had never experienced before. Winning gave me this self-affirming thing to look forward to. I am not completely sure where my very deep desire to win comes from. Since it has always been there deep inside of me, I assume that I was born with it. I have come to regard my desire to win as a virtue. Whether it was winning those games on my homemade court or competing on the world stages that I later walked onto, it was always an incredible experience.

I sometimes wonder what a life could be like without this thing planted so deep into some of our souls—the desire to be victorious, especially since the joy of victory is so temporary. No matter how many times you win, the victory is never permanent and lasting. For competitive souls, each victory is followed by another trip to the well to do it again. No matter how joyous a victory is in the moment, that joy seems to pale in contrast to the dark emotion that losing brings. I feel it—I can sense the foul taste in my mouth, smell it in the air. When you win, you are right, at least for that moment. Yet winning seems never to feel as good as losing feels bad. I am much more likely to replay each loss of my career than to recall the victories, tick by tick, sliding into the pain and regret of what I could have done differently.

LEXINGTON

I was just finishing the fourth grade when we moved forty-seven miles north to Lexington, Kentucky. I am unsure of the details that led to our move but move we did. My mother's sisters pooled their modest resources and helped Mama borrow enough money to get a house there in Lexington, which my mother used as a boarding house. Mama, my grandmother, and I moved into a home on Maxwell Street, which had nine single rooms upstairs that she rented primarily to University of Kentucky students. This new position as the landlord did not deliver us to the land of plenty, but it did help. The house was a three-story frame house, not in the best of condition when we bought it, and it would slowly continue its slide into decay as time went by. Over the years, we held it together with paint, putty, and hope.

Moving to Lexington expanded my athletic horizons in ways I couldn't have imagined. I discovered Woodland Park, a large sports park about six blocks from the house. Woodland Park had a swimming pool, tennis courts, and an outdoor, covered basketball court—a perfect trifecta.

Maxwell Elementary was an easy four-block walk from my house. I made good friends with a set of twins named Odie and Phillip Spears, who lived just a block from me. They came to my house, and we walked to school together every day—that was our routine, rain or shine.

The wooden gymnasium floor at my school was right up there at the top of my list of brand new, modern, unimaginable luxuries. An indoor floor removed all of the limits created by bad weather. I could now play anytime. I had gone from playing basketball on the dusty, gravel spaces of West Irvine to the smooth, predictable wood foundation of Maxwell Street Elementary in Lexington. The smell of that gymnasium, the sound of basketball meeting wood, remains one of the world's great sensations for me.

There was a fifth-and-sixth-grade basketball team. Even though I was the youngest player on the team, I soon became a starter and a major contributor. From that point on, throughout my basketball-playing career, I was always a point guard. I loved the decision-making and athleticism that the position drew upon. I suppose all of my frustrations with Taterbug paid off. He had challenged me athletically and mentally, and it had made me a better player.

At the end of my first semester, my grades were good enough (credit to my mountain schoolhouse teachers, the Broadus sisters) that my fifth-grade teacher placed me in the second half of the sixth grade. I was moved up because I was smart, but I was still not tall, so this created a situation where I was the smallest player trying out for the seventh-grade team. Even at my small size, I still had enough athletic ability and talent to go along with my huge desire to play, whatever the sport or the season.

Morton Junior High presented a totally different challenge as several elementary schools filtered into Morton. With seventh, eighth, and ninth graders from all over the place trying out for the team, the competition was fierce. When the final list was posted, I had made the roster, still the youngest and the smallest on the team. I didn't become a starter until the ninth grade, but I loved every minute of my process getting there. I felt that I was a contributing member of the team, no matter my role. I had fallen in love with the culture of sports and would do almost anything legal to earn my place there.

WORK

I always tried to work at whatever job I could find to help with money for Mom and me. I told one of the guys I played sandlot ball with that I was looking for a way to earn some money, and he suggested that I see the man at the auditorium at Woodland Park. It's still a bit amusing to me as I visualize this other boy and me talking about work in such a mature and serious way at such a young age.

Professional wrestling matches occurred every Thursday night at Woodland Park. Cokes and popcorn were sold at the concession stand and out in the bleacher seats. I went to the man in charge to see if I could work there, and he gave me a job hawking cokes in the stands. I wish I could remember his name now or even where to find him to shake his hand. He was good to me and for me. Not only did he give me a job, but he would recommend me for a future spot among the older guys who worked the stands at the Memorial Coliseum doing the same thing.

When I sold a case of twenty cokes, I'd make a dollar. The first couple of nights that I worked, I made five bucks, which felt pretty good to me, given that often, I had no dollars or cents to my name. Five dollars is worth something even now, but I will leave to you to imagine how much that was to me back in the fifties. I asked if I could also include popcorn on my menu to sell, and the man said yes, which led to me earning a whopping ten dollars per night. I would give my mother five, and I'd keep the other five. I did this all throughout high school. I saved my money and would use some of it to buy my lunch or bus tokens when I would take the bus to school. This was one of my early lessons in self-reliance and entrepreneurship, one of many that would serve me well throughout my life. Then, as well as now, I associated money with hard work.

I was frequently away from home with no particular curfew or real limitations. I must have been a good enough child that my mother and grandmother trusted me either to stay out of trouble or to protect myself from the trouble I might find. It probably helped my case for freedom that I was always willing to share the bounty of my adventures.

Wrestling matches were very popular at Woodland Park. This world of wrestling (pronounced locally as "rass-lin") was a very different world for me—it certainly wasn't West Irvine. In addition to the money, my favorite part of the job was when I went into the wrestlers' dressing room. They used the term "athlete" loosely. I was amazed at the amount of smoke and liquor these men consumed before their matches. It was generally understood that wrestling can be fixed, and I assumed that it had to be. How could anyone truly be competitive if they were filled to the brim with liquor and smoke? How could they even tell the difference between their opponent and the referee?

I became a fixture at the park in general and the wrestling matches in particular. Mostly, the wrestlers paid no mind to a little guy hawking cokes and popcorn. Once in a while, one of them would ask me to get them a coke and would add a little tip for my troubles. In Kentucky, a coke specifically means the soft drink Coca Cola, soda is the ingredient you add to biscuit dough, and a pop is when you hit someone. My favorite wrestler was Big John. He called me Lil' Fellah and always gave me a tip for bringing him a coke, which he added to another cup that already had something else in it. While I found them entertaining, I made little association between this brand of an athlete and my own athletic training. I was amazed at their size, though, and have never forgotten that one of them wore a size twenty-one shoe. That shoe appeared to me as a log stretched out across the floor.

IN THE BEGINNING

I worked concessions for a number of years. I carried over selling cokes and popcorn to the University of Kentucky's Memorial Coliseum, where the Kentucky Wildcats played basketball, and also sold ice-cold soft drinks at Stoll Field, where the Wildcats played football games. Both of these facilities were just a few blocks from our house on Maxwell Street, which made them convenient jobs for me, as I had to walk to and from work. But the appeal of the jobs wasn't just the proximity; it was the fact that I got to see the University of Kentucky games!

I was the kid who hawked his way through enough wrestling matches and athletic events to at least take care of my financial needs outside of the home—lunch and bus tokens. I especially liked being able to contribute something to my mother and our household. I was able to do this for several years. I'm not sure where my initiative came from. Perhaps being surrounded by family and neighbors who were always working and hustling to make ends meet led me to think of work as simply what a person does, normally. I wonder if, in some way, witnessing the courage of my mother and how she handled her physical and emotional challenges compelled me to do something, anything to make a contribution.

I worked jobs during the school year and all summer long while I was in high school. I worked for two years milking cows for a man who had a farm on the outskirts of the city. Each school day around 4:30 a.m., I headed to his barn. A couple of other guys and I would round up the cows, get them into the barn, and milk them by hand. I returned home in time to shower and get ready to meet my friends to walk to school.

I also worked in the tobacco fields in the summer for Coach "Baldy" Gilb. Coach Gilb— my high school basketball coach—had a long-lasting effect on my life. He lived on the outskirts of Lexington and had several acres of land. He would sometimes ask me to come to help him cut tobacco. It might be just for half a day, but five dollars was five dollars. Later, I realized that he absolutely knew I needed any extra cash I could get for my family and me. I worked in the icehouse one summer, loading large blocks of ice, which were picked up by different companies around the city. I also worked loading, carrying, and stacking bricks for a building under construction not too far from my high school.

I attended the legendary Henry Clay High School in Lexington. Over the years, Henry Clay would develop an athletic reputation in the state of Kentucky that remains legendary. It was a large high school for grades ten through twelve. I walked the three-mile round trip daily. There was no cafeteria on campus, so we always ate at Clay's sandwich shop just across the street from the school. I could get lunch for just under forty cents a day. Lunchtime at the sandwich shop was also a great opportunity to visit and get to know my friends and teammates. Kids seem to know certain things about each other—what the next one has or doesn't have doesn't go unnoticed. I don't think that they necessarily thought I was poor, but rather, they looked at me more as self-reliant. My friends were aware that I was paying for my lunches with money I had earned, not money that my parents had given me. I always felt that elevated their respect for me in some way.

My family never had a car when we were growing up. Because of that, my mother never saw me play any high school games. I would return home after each contest with the excitement and single focus to report to Mama what happened and how I did. She was not easily impressed and rarely animated but was polite and patient as she tried to sort through what a double-double or a single-wing offense was.

Henry Clay didn't have any school-sponsored transportation for athletics, which meant that several of us had to manage our own transportation to practice and games, usually with teammates who owned a vehicle. Dickie was a guard on our team, and his dad worked as president of Citizens Union Bank. I assume that's why they could afford to provide Dickie a car. We all chipped in a dime to pay for gas, which was twenty cents a gallon at that time. I'm not totally sure why, but sometimes Dickie didn't charge me the dime.

IN THE BEGINNING

I went out for football my sophomore year. I discovered that I was initially too small for the game that I loved. My first two years on the team were spent on the scout squad as a backup player. I didn't care what my status was; I mostly cared that victory was within reach. I didn't play one minute in a regulation game against another team during that time. Over the summer before my senior year of high school, I adopted an unusual conditioning program. I had caught on as a bellboy in a lodge that had no elevators, so I carried luggage up and down several flights of stairs for nine weeks. That made me much stronger, and I also seemed to hit a growth spurt and grew a few inches—or at least I felt taller. Those factors combined to make my senior year in football a very different experience. I started as both a linebacker on defense and a blocking back in our single-wing offensive set. Coach John Heber was a tough, no-nonsense coach who demanded discipline. I was always drawn to that plain-speaking kind of leadership in coaches and teachers. His personality seemed to match the raw honesty of competition. We ended up with a winning season but lost to our cross-town rival Lafayette High School, who went on to become the state champions.

Throughout the first twelve years of my schooling, I played football, basketball, and baseball, and was a letterman in all three sports my senior year. I was particularly fond of baseball. Baseball is one of those sports where size is not the determining factor of success. Skill is the great separator, and I had the skill to play a number of positions. I played second and third base, any of the outfield positions, and best of all, as a pitcher, I could throw strikes. For three years, I was a starter, and in my senior year, we beat our arch-rival, Lafayette, as we advanced to the state tournament. I really liked this winning thing.

On a rare occasion, Mom would dispatch bits of information here and there about our past. One of the very few facts that I know about my father was that he played semi-pro baseball for at least one summer. Years later, she would offer that in a double-header, he pitched and won one game right-handed, then turned around and pitched and won the second game left-handed! I have very few true regrets in my life or wonderings about what-ifs. However, I do wish that I could have had the opportunity to sit with my father and hear him tell me every detail of that game.

Basketball tryouts began immediately following our last football game. Coach Gilb allowed those of us who played football and basketball a week off while the basketball coaches began tryouts. As a sophomore, I always played the first half of the B-team game and then dressed for the varsity game. This worked well as I got important experience playing a few minutes in some of the varsity games. In one game, just before Christmas of my sophomore year, a starting guard was sick, and his replacement fouled out at the end of the third quarter. That gave rise to the moment I had been waiting for—playing time. I played the entire fourth quarter, hitting eight-straight free throws against Newport Catholic at the end of the game for a win. This solidified my position on the team. I played more as a junior and then started my senior year. More importantly, that course of events taught me the value of getting ready and staying ready.

By the time I was finishing high school at Henry Clay, I knew that I wanted very much to go to college and was aware that athletics was the only way I could get there. I was competitive and felt that I had enough talent to obtain some kind of scholarship to go somewhere. By this time in my life, I realized that if I wanted something—from a college degree to a new pair of jeans—I was going to have to get it through my own determination. I worked hard and tried desperately to remain honest in all things. That determination and drive were guided and encouraged by several coaches, teachers, and the principal at Henry Clay. Those men looked out for me. I was never sure why, really. Perhaps I reminded them of something good in their own lives, or perhaps they saw something in me that I didn't know existed. Whatever the reason, I am glad they did. Their encouragement helped me believe in my ability to achieve a dream—a college degree.

IN THE BEGINNING

TRANSYLVANIA COLLEGE

As I entered my senior year of high school, I started thinking seriously about going to college. I had prepared academically, but the biggest obstacle was that I had no money, and an athletic scholarship had not yet materialized. Not knowing how to resolve my fiscal dilemma, I just inched forward in hopes that something would materialize before my clock ran out. During the last week of my senior year, Dr. Sharpton, the principal of my high school, called me to his office. He had recommended me for the Transylvania College Community Scholarship. I had received a scholarship not tied to my participation in basketball and baseball, but rather, one based more on my academic performance and citizenship. I was overwhelmed. One day I had nothing, and the next day I had a bona fide opportunity. It was truly beyond anything I had ever imagined. I could now turn my attention to obtaining a college degree, not just dreaming about it.

Transylvania College was a small college right there in Lexington, living in the shadow of the hallowed University of Kentucky. There were several players from my high school who were student-athletes at "Transy" at that time, and I hoped that would add to my comfort level in attending. It also seemed that it would be good to be in Lexington, where my mother lived. For as independent as Mama had been, I always felt she needed my help.

In addition to the scholarship, Dr. Sharpton also offered valuable advice. He pointed out that Transy had fraternities and sororities on campus. He explained how they provided social activities that were important for some students, but he didn't think I would need that social outlet. He asked me not to consider joining a fraternity for at least one year so that I could concentrate on my studies and the additional hours that would be required for me to maintain my scholarship. I had no interest in anything or anybody that could potentially interfere with my getting a diploma, besides I didn't know what a fraternity was anyway.

Dr. Sharpton was accurate about the popularity of the fraternities and sororities, and his counsel would prove wise. The coursework required much more time than I'd ever imagined, and besides, there was no way I had the financial means necessary to join a fraternity. I discovered that being a member of the athletic teams I belonged to provided plenty of social interaction. The campus enrollment was small enough that I was involved in most of the gatherings anyway. I knew everyone, and everyone would come to know me.

I attended Transylvania College as an undergraduate student from 1954-1958. During that time, I played baseball for Harry Stephenson each of my four years. I am not exactly sure what motivated some of the people that looked out for me to do so, but I am grateful that it happened. They saw something in me that fueled their concern and moved them to give me a helping hand. It happened again with Coach Stephenson. He had already been involved in my life during summer league baseball and was very helpful in getting me to Transy. He was my academic advisor and baseball coach there for four years.

Back in those days, there was this rule that freshmen were not allowed to play varsity their first year of college basketball. Freshman players were limited to playing on the freshman team. As with many other National College Athletic Association (NCAA) rules, I never understood why, but it was so. My freshman year, I played basketball for Hugh Jones, and then I met Coach Charles Martin (C.M.) Newton, when I became a player on his basketball team as a sophomore. I had met Coach Newton earlier as he had played high school ball with my brother Gene, and now he would be my basketball coach for three years at Transylvania.

I am proud of those three years. I started every year and was captain of my team senior year, scoring a total of 1,039 points during my tenure. There are people that we meet along the way who can influence us for a specific reason, a season, or a lifetime. I did not know it at the time, but C.M. Newton would become a lifelong relationship. He was my basketball coach for just three years, but even now, I call him Coach Newton.

IN THE BEGINNING

I received great support and direction in both academics and sports programs from these men in one way or another. It takes a village to raise a child, and these men were the beginning of the village that raised me. I remain grateful to them.

After my sophomore year, my good friend Odie Spears and I worked all summer at Milprint Paper Company in Milwaukee, Wisconsin. My older brother and his family lived in Milwaukee at the time. We'd heard that the money was good up there, so we went and got us some. Our job consisted of ten-hour shifts stacking wooden slats and moving the materials to the proper cutting machines. I took all the overtime I could and saved every penny possible. We had taken the Greyhound Bus to Milwaukee but returned in a baby blue, two-door Plymouth convertible, which cost me three hundred dollars. My family had never owned a car while I was growing up, so this was a huge deal for me. It had lots of miles and seemed to use more oil than gas to keep it going, but it was mine. As comical as the Blue Goose (her nickname) was from time to time, she remained popular among my friends. However challenging the maintenance was, she ran. Sometimes, to keep gas in the car, I'd loan it to reliable students who had to fill the tank upon its return. Blue Goose lasted throughout my college days.

College brought with it many changes in my life. While I am proud of all of my achievements, I am really proud of being voted Mr. Pioneer as a student at Transylvania University in 1958. That was a campus vote by the students for the senior male who exemplified the traits that the college held important. I had lettered in basketball and baseball and was fairly popular on our small campus. This honor created an additional layer of comfort and confidence. I suppose that Dr. Sharpton was right about my not having to join the fraternity—I ended up building my own social infrastructure.

A PERFECT GIRL

ONE NIGHT DURING my senior year, there was a dance on the tennis courts for all the incoming freshmen. As a student leader, part of my responsibility was to help with freshman orientation. While serving refreshments at this dance, I noticed this particularly beautiful, young freshman. Although she had clearly captured my attention and imagination, I didn't meet her that night. I am not sure why I did not go over and introduce myself then, but I did have the presence of mind to get her name from someone standing nearby.

The name of this perfect girl was Eleanor Lollis.

After that night, it seemed to me that everything became a little different. When I returned to the dormitory, I told my roommate, Bobby, that I had just seen the woman I was going to marry. I did not have a premonition, and there were no fireworks, no thunder, or lightning strikes. Yet, there she was.

Early each year, the school held a Sadie Hawkins dance. This old-fashioned dance originates straight out of Lil' Abner comics and other fables of mountain culture. On this fall date each year, the traditional roles are reversed—the girl asks the boy to the dance and pays for everything. Eleanor had a date with someone else that night, but I "cut in." During that evening, I told her friend, just as I had told my friend, that I had just danced with the girl I intended to marry.

For all these years, it has been a bit of a joke that I made my proclamation to everyone that I had met the girl that I was going to marry with such confidence and certainty. Following the dance, Eleanor and I walked over to the Old Morrison building on the campus and sat on those grand, historical steps. We talked for a long time. We knew after that night that we would rather spend time together than with others. Afterward, we began to take our meals together. We genuinely enjoyed each other's company. We talked about our lives and our families. We discussed our future together, what job I might have, when we would marry, and many other details.

It all seemed so natural. We were certain that we would continue our lives together. We didn't speak of falling in love but very quickly realized that we were.

One spring evening, we parked at Calumet Farms, a historic horse farm. In the old days, you could roll right up to this place with its beautiful, evenly cut grass on palatial rolling hills, shadowed by horses. It was all so incredible; it seems like it should be named something more superlative than what it is at the root—a horse farm. As we talked, Eleanor suddenly became teary-eyed. I was hoping that I had not done or said anything to upset her, so I asked if there was something wrong. She turned to me and said that she couldn't imagine her life without me in it.

I am unable to fully explain how and why, but I knew Eleanor Lollis and I were beginning our life together. It seemed the most natural thing for us to do. I remember inviting her to go to church with me on a warm October evening. Following that service, we went to Frisch's Drive-In for a root beer float. Over the next sixty years, we continued to order root beer floats in celebration of that time—they always taste good enough but are never quite the same as that evening when we were falling in love.

Falling in love, for me, meant that I just wanted to be with her. It is that simple. The magic of falling in love at first sight may be judged as improbable by some intellectual folks, like finding unicorns or the fountain of youth. That you actually see someone that you have never seen before and suddenly, there is love—on sight. Though it's difficult to explain fully to the uninitiated, you just do. I believe in love at first sight because I lived it. I met this young woman whom I had never seen before and found her compelling from the very start, and still do now, sixty years later. Eleanor and I have never had one moment that our marriage was in jeopardy. As each life challenge arrives, we determine a solution, and no part of any solution can contain any element that does not have us in each other's life at our road's end.

MORE FAMILY

Eleanor and I never got engaged—we just knew we were going to get married. I am glad that neither of us felt we had to do what was usually done like promise rings, engagements, and elaborate ceremonies.

We had what appeared at first glance to be more differences than similarities. She was well-traveled and had even lived for five years in Germany and then Japan because of her father's military service. I had traveled very little beyond Lexington and the train tracks that separated Irvine and West Irvine. Eleanor came from a stable family of Mom, Dad, and what seemed to be perfect kids all in tow, while my family was a long and complicated tale.

Eleanor and I had been dating for over a year when I drove her home for a visit. It was my first introduction to Colonel (and Chaplin) George Lollis and Eleanor's mother, Marjorie "Omi" Lollis. Elo's family lived in Elizabethtown, Kentucky, and her father was stationed at Fort Knox. We arrived and got settled in, going through the whole meeting-the-family-for-the-first-time thing.

In addition to its being Christmas, we had come to get her parents' blessings or to announce that we wanted to marry in June. Her family met us with their own announcement that Colonel Lollis and the Lollis family (including young Eleanor) had received orders to deploy to Germany. The urgency of that moment made me realize right then and there how absolutely important Eleanor was in my life. It was just clear that either I was going to Germany with the Lollis family, or Eleanor was going to stay with me. We knew that we were going to get married; we just didn't plan for it to happen so soon.

During our visit, Colonel Lollis gave me one of the most gracious gifts of hospitality that I'd ever received. The next morning when I got up, I couldn't find my shoes. As I opened the door, there they were, shining as if they were new. I knew, at that moment, that I had been given this as a gift of hospitality and welcoming. The welcome was one that I never forgot and was the beginning of our friendship as two men who both loved Eleanor. Elo's father became one of the most positive forces of my life. He remained so for the forty years of our life together before he passed away. His family knew Colonel Lollis as Opa. In addition to its meaning as grandpa, it also means "to be revered and loved by family." Opa was both. As a soldier and chaplain, he lived with the reality of getting orders to move at any time—sometimes with and other times without the family. I believe seeing her parents' handling of these rigors and quick changes prepared Eleanor to deal with the demands of the coaching profession.

We both look back and can't believe that she had two final exams on the day of our wedding. We had this whirlwind of scheduling conflicts for our family and friends. Our wedding was not optimal for everyone's timing. Eleanor's parents were being deployed by the United States Military, and our friends and significant others were about to be scattered around the country. Eleanor got her first taste of the impact basketball would have on our life when we had to plan around the Kentucky State High School finals to accommodate the schedules of two very important men in my life—Coaches C.M. Newton and Harry Stephenson—who would have been away at those games.

Eleanor and I were torn between just wanting to be married and wanting to be sensitive to our family and other significant relationships.

We were married during what was her sophomore year in college. I had graduated already. Our wedding was small and simple, held at the chapel at The College of The Bible Seminary in Lexington.

After the wedding, Eleanor and I settled into our married life. When most couples first marry, everything feels romantic, but there's always some practical matter that needs attention. The practical is what can break a couple apart. It is one thing to speak in romantic lyrics about this wonderful life that we wanted with and for each other, but the living out of all those lyrics is another matter. The chores and heavy lifting of life have fortified our union. At each successful turn, we are reminded that we made the right choice in each other.

Eleanor still has the copy of *The Prophet* by Kahlil Gibran that I gave to her in 1958. It is inscribed: "For Eleanor, I hope the words in this book help to bring our love closer than these pages in this book." Some of our magic is that Eleanor has struck this wonderful balance of being available to me and for me while having a life that feeds her own as well. In some ways, this unique collection of essays on a variety of life subjects has guided us over the years. One of my favorite poems in *The Prophet* is entitled "On Marriage":

> *Fill each other's cup, but drink not from one cup.*
> *Give one another of your bread but eat not from the same loaf.*
> *Sing and dance together and be joyous, but let each one of you be alone,*
> *Even as the strings of a lute are alone though they quiver with the same music.*

I signed that book on Nov 8, 1958, and it has traveled with us everywhere we have lived since.

MARRIAGE

Eleanor and I have always been a great team. The short of our very long tale is that after sixty years, she has remained my partner in all that I do or consider doing. She has always done what was best for us without complaint. It was early on in our union when Eleanor and I first discovered ourselves taking out the long yellow legal pad to highlight the pros and cons of life and career decisions. During our decision-making exercise, Elo drew a line down the middle of the page and wrote "pros" at the top of one column and "cons" at the top of the other. At that time, we were not aware of what rituals we were putting into place. Even though it was my job offers that took us places in our years of marriage, we both had equal input into those moves. We are partners. The legal pad was, in many ways, a symbol of that partnership.

In this current day, everyone is impressed by marriages of great lengths, lasting forty, fifty, sixty years. Many people from our generation expected marriage to last as long as you lasted—if you had a long life, you had a long marriage. Few spoke to the quality of life, good or bad, that people inside the marriages were experiencing; everyone simply aimed for the greatest number of years, which suggested success.

Eleanor and I have always focused on our quality of life. I often hear people refer to their marriage as something that they have to work on like they have a problem that needs resolving or a broken thing that needs fixing. I prefer to think of the energy I put into my marriage as nurturing. We nurture each other. We long ago identified something in each other, and each of us determined it was worth giving the other our best. Maybe that is what anyone is talking about when they speak about love and being in love. It is the way you feel about someone that motivates you to rise to the occasion to serve that person in all the ways required for the moment and their betterment. Throughout our journey, we have committed to being the difference for each other. Eleanor has shown up in my life in ways that I have lost count of by now. I hope that I have been successful in doing the same for her. I certainly have tried.

At times, I do not fully capture the texture of our magic; I just understand that it works. I know that she is a photographer, but I do not understand the full detail of what she sees when she composes her wonderful images. Elo is a poet, and so am I, but I just can't get my arms all the way around the kind of poetry that does not rhyme. She does, though. For me, when Jack fell down, it had to break his crown, because crown rhymes with down. In some of my poetry, I just ignore the spelling and pronounce words in a certain way. I may choose to rhyme "man" with the word "friend," and I can get away with it if I hold on to the last part of the word long enough. I am sure you get my point.

Elo has studied at Columbia Seminary and taken jobs in different NBA cities where we've lived, working in a photography shop or the kitchen of a great catering place. She also has taken writing class upon writing class. Whatever her enterprise may be, I always try to be supportive. Even now, I am thoroughly amused to see Elo amid these hulking men in the CrossFit training regimen. CrossFit is this Navy-Seal-style workout that includes moving around large tires and heavy iron objects. I always feel sorry for the younger people in the photo of her CrossFit class, thinking how difficult it must be to explain why they are unable to keep up with this lady of a certain age.

Every couple has a deal. A deal is an agreement, spoken or not, about how they will live. The deals that any of us make are personal to our own taste and predispositions. What works for my marriage may not work for the next person, but all deals are reflections of the people taking part in them. When asked, I often encourage others—my sons included—to make peace with their very own deal. I am glad that after all of our years together, we still dance in the kitchen, love to hear live music, go to plays, and read poetry aloud to each other.

In 1992, Elo's brother George was brutally murdered in still-unresolved circumstances. This happened just as our basketball season was starting, but I knew when we got that wretched call that I had to, wanted to, and was going to be there for her and us. Then there are other parts of our lives together that continue to be everything good that we ever dreamed. I have always loved her and felt that we would forever be together. Whatever spark of magic that started our union has held us together as we have wept, laughed, and stayed through the years.

Life for the spouse of a person who earns the family bread by coaching can be a lonely journey, even when that spouse enjoys the sport. Earning your living as a professional sports coach, player, or administrator is so different from being a fan. One's enthusiasm for anything can be lost if that thing comes in bunches. Like a thirsty person drinking from a fire hydrant—you can be thirsty but not that much. It is just so different when there are these never-ending, grinding details of preparation and performance for the coach, athlete, and spouse. Something is always happening or about to happen. Over time, I have come to know the unperfected reality of the family life of a coach, but I struggle with it nonetheless.

Even in later years, after our children had children of their own, I remember her picking me up one day from the airport when I returned from somewhere doing something. We were so glad to see each other as we laughed and talked like old friends. Nothing was really that funny; we were just glad to see each other. It felt good to know that all roads led back to this woman. Whenever we recount the details of our narrative, we can often find joy within them. I am not proposing that we have some sort of divine perfection; we are living in a world that treats us like it does everyone else, but we make an effort to recognize our joy. What we both agree upon is that we are grateful for whatever happened, when it happened, that brought us together.

I have always had a very tender and intimate relationship with my wife. It seems so natural for us to touch, to dance, to sing. We still hold hands and remain affectionate with each other. I heard it said, and I believe it to be true, that the greatest gift that a father can give his children is to love their mother. I hope I provided that expression for my sons. I would add to it that a father should be free and open with affection to the mother of his children while around said children.

Affection is a simple thing to do, and it removes the doubt of whether you care, but sometimes we can take it for granted that our loved ones know.

When our children were young, my son, Mark, told Eleanor that he and Michael would follow the music in our house to discover the two of us lying on pillows in the den. At that time, we had record players, which would hold six vinyl records at a time. We might put our feet up on the hearth of the fireplace and sing along to the music of James Taylor and Carole King. Not knowing what the kids might have seen, I told Eleanor to circle back around to Mark to determine the extent of what they had observed. Her report back to me was that he said everything was fairly tame, but a little "juvenile," in his words. Mark said that we were singing to each other and carrying on. Our record collection then, as well as our compact disc collection more recently, reflects that music was always important to us: Roberta Flack, Sinatra, Almond Brothers, Everly Brothers, Willie Nelson, Louie Armstrong, songs by Kern, Porter, and Gershwin—the great American Songbook. We still have a collection of records from that era—the music that we often fell asleep to and love.

Eleanor and I have always loved the arts and carried that lifestyle into our later years as well. Being there for the final tour of James Taylor and Carole King was special to us. We heard Lynn Harrell playing the entire Bach cello suites, Edgar Meyer on his bass at the Aspen Music Festival, and Itzhak Perlman in concert. There've been many memorable evenings with the symphony, as well as concerts with Steve Martin's banjo and the Steep Canyon Rangers. We have always been fans of most of Mark Twain's writings, and we saw Stacy Keach in the one-man play *Mark Twain*. Wendell Berry, the Kentucky author of novels such as *The Memory of Old Jack*, and poems like "The Contrariness of the Mad Farmer," have a special place in our home and on our bookshelf. We both constantly have books lying around to read. Mysteries by Grisham and Baldacci (and more non-mysteries for Elo). One of my favorite non-fiction titles was *The Nine* by Jeffrey Toobin, his take on the United States Supreme Court. We went to Chautauqua twice when the theme for the week was about the Supreme Court. Our list of theaters covers the waterfront: from our first, splashy musical, *Irma La Deuce* at the Palladium in London in 1961, to Judy Dench in *Romeo and Juliet* at the Old Vic that same summer. We were hooked. Local, regional, and national touring productions, as well as Broadway plays, have been priorities in our lives.

We also found enjoyment in expanding our knowledge of philosophy, history, literature, and religion. We made it part of our summer routine to spend a week in places like Aspen and Chautauqua. Elo had family who had gone to this beautiful space in western New York for decades.

Elo's association with a spirituality program at Columbia Seminary in Georgia exposed us to a very diverse group of theologians. We even spent our fiftieth wedding anniversary at that seminary, taking a course on the prophet Isaiah. We both took a weeklong course there with Barbara Brown Taylor studying new religions in the old South. Exploring different faiths was enlightening. We went to Friday evening prayers at the mosque in Atlanta and also went to Sikhs and Hindu services. While taking a course on theologian Howard Thurman, I learned that he believed there was more than one way to interpret scriptures. When asked whether a certain biblical scripture was true, Thurman had replied that he "didn't know; he wasn't there." I appreciated that. It didn't feel like a cop-out to me. It felt like it allowed room for philosophical thought and questioning, for seeking on one's own.

Paul McCartney of the Beatles had a reputation for taking his wife everywhere he went. He explained that he didn't get married to be away from his wife. I feel the same way about Elo—I did not get married to be away from her! I try to include her in everything I can. I always wanted her to know that I am only away from her because I have to be. If it is not necessary, I will not be away. Early on, she went along when I refereed high school basketball games, taking her books to study for classes. She has attended almost every home game I have ever coached and many on the road. I loved having her along because we were together on the ride over and back—wherever it was. And, she always seemed glad that I asked her to go. When I was asked to coach a USA team and take them to the Soviet Union, I said that I was honored, and I would accept, with one condition. That condition was that they needed to get one more visa, as I wasn't going to go if Elo couldn't. She became the pool photographer and journalist for that trip.

Eleanor is my partner in all that I do or consider. We have this independent interdependence that has been a part of our grace. It just feels like our journey has been richer the way we've done it. I did not marry her to change her. She remains an intelligent and capable woman, and I need all of that. She provides me leverage in the world. I respect that no matter how long I was away from home, I knew that she cared for our home life. I desperately needed her to take care of us, and even better that she would want to do it as much as I wanted it done by her. I always wanted to be the man that she perceived. Some men will jokingly say they "married up," in terms of class, education, and character. That comment is sometimes their attempt at being self-deprecating and complimentary to their spouse, whether they sincerely mean it or not. When I say that same thing, it is no joke for me. I believe and know it because that is what I have experienced.

A FATHER

Our son Michael was born in January 1962, four years after we married. After our first year as parents to Michael, we added to our family with a second son, Mark, in January 1963. Both of our sons were brought home to the Transylvania University Men's dormitory, where I had become the men's resident director after graduation. During this time,

I was beyond happy as an assistant basketball coach. Elo was still an undergraduate, majoring in English, so she was busy with her classes at Transy. We were happy together, but at some point, all of us in that dorm room became too much, so we moved into a small house.

I am like most parents in that I probably have quiet reflections on whether I could have done more. I will probably always wonder just how much wear and tear my family endured while I was out there trying to conquer the world, while I may have missed creating special memories in our family life. Each coach reaches a series of forks in the road where he has to make decisions about his biological family versus the children of his choosing—his players. This was particularly challenging for me, especially as a young coach without any flexibility in my schedule. I was working my way in and up, so I was left with having a lot of bosses that told me where and when to be. The list of chores handed to a young coach varies depending on circumstances, but it includes hard work wherever you are. When you are young, and sometimes when you are old, you have to travel to scout and recruit players, work young players out before and after practice, edit game footage, run for this, race for that. All of this and more is just part of the process of career development.

I recall an incident with my children that cut so deeply that I hold it in my emotions as though it happened this morning. Eleanor and the boys came to the airport to say hey and bring me fresh clothes as I prepared to complete the final leg of a road trip. The boys were toddlers at the time. We visited within the brief time allowed by my layover. As they were about to return home, with me en route to wherever I was headed, Michael asked his mother, "Is that my daddy?" It broke my heart. Had I had been away so much that my little boys did not recognize me? Had I left them unsure of my role in their life?

Granted, it may have been simply the meandering of a very young child's imagination, or maybe I really had unintentionally missed a growth spurt, but what does a father do with that? As a very young coach, charged with bringing home the bacon, you are sometimes unable to be around long enough to fry it up in the pan. I understood that the deal I made would include my being away for stretches of time, but it remained troubling for me that at times, I may have been away for too long.

As an assistant coach, I spent a lot of time on the road, flying all over the country, scouting games and talent. Why would I choose to do that when I had these two young sons? Well, I was doing my job. I was doing what I could do and needed to do in order to put food on the table and keep a roof over our heads. But that incident made me really think about whether I wanted to stay in that position as the assistant coach. I knew what my priorities were as I tried in earnest to develop my career but remained troubled at being away from my family too much. My deep desire to be a certain kind of father is amplified since I have no memory of my father being home with me. As sincere as I remain in my intentions, I am like many parents—I have occasions to ask myself if I did everything possible. Intellectually, I am sure, but the uncertain emotional answer to the question will sometimes linger.

During the college coaching years, in particular, I did not always get to see the boys in the evening during the season as I didn't get home until after eight at night. When I could get away a little early, I always called to let Elo know that I was on my way, and she would delay their bedtime. Typical of split-level houses of the 1960s, our bedrooms were up six stairs, just off the kitchen. Mike and Mark would hear me come in through the garage door and get ready to jump from the top into my arms as I passed. Of course, I was supposed to be completely surprised by this act of daring, yet again. In reality, I had to get set for these two to come flying at me, as sometimes they forgot that they were supposed to come at me one at a time! Another major part of our nighttime routine was storytelling; they pushed me for details as I winged my way through made-up stories that, to this day, they remember as being quite wonderful.

Since both boys had January birthdays, which was the height of the basketball season, we had birthday cake and candles at breakfast time. Depending on our schedule, those celebrations might not even be on the exact date, which may have been okay for the boys. What was most important was that there was a recognition of their special days.

The hardest adjustment for Elo and me was the lack of family time with all of us together. On those nights when the boys might be asleep, she and I caught up on the events of our days as I built elaborate forts and structures out of wooden building blocks for the boys as a surprise for the next morning.

A coach and his children can be a peculiar matter. It is as though everything I espouse around citizenship, personal responsibility, and integrity are qualified by whether my children reflect those attributes. I am keenly aware that time and again, famous people and coaches have flourished in the public arena while their families floundered. I did not want that for my family and me. Providing proper attention to a family can be especially challenging when a man is giving leadership to other people's children and potentially neglecting his own. There are some people out there conquering the world but losing the soul of their household. Somewhere in there, I put it upon myself to answer the age-old question of "Does this cobbler's children have shoes?" I decided that it would make me a failure if, for all of my strict discipline and chants about character in the public square, at the same time, my own sons had no discipline or signs of character.

To My Sons—Harvest
In life tis said, we reap what we sow
Believe in this, for experience will show
The sum total of your life will definitely reflect
The values you accepted, and those you reject

The seeds that we planted are put in your mind
Some buried, forgotten—others surface, growing fine

A PERFECT GIRL

Take a moment to analyze them, as you live day to day
Do the best that you can, there's no other way

Let's look at four virtues encountered in life
Both wisdom and justice bring struggle and strife
Then fortitude, of course, deals with the heart
And moderation seems a good place for a start

Life's values that count don't come in a car
Or living high on a mountain or playing golf under par
But relating to others in a genuine way
Makes for a "quality life" where God has his say

A life lived in "quality" meets the measure of man
A few characteristics make it easy to understand
Love what you do and proudly proclaim
Each day a new challenge, to be conquered and gained

Develop your creative skills, for in the unconquered mind
Life's treasures are buried which only you can unwind
Seek freedom of choice to work as you will
Regardless of circumstance—be strong, be fulfilled

Religion is a choice you encounter and choose
For spiritually to avoid means assuredly you lose
So plant your rows for harvest, fertilize them with care
Nurture and protect them, so others may share

For you, my two sons—plant seeds that grow strong
Where love, truth, and self-discipline will forever belong
Be positive of this as you map out your crop
We will always be there—your Mom and your Pop

–Lee Rose

Sometimes, I felt that there may have been an inequity in our parenting arrangement, in that all I had to do was coach a group of young men, who were more likely to do what I told them to do while Elo, like all coach's wives, spent twenty-four hours, seven days a week on parental and family responsibilities. She was occupied by two little boys, who gave the phrase "a handful" total meaning. My boys have never given us any real trouble, but they did try us from time to time. They were really good boys (or maybe we lowered our strict expectations so success was attainable). I feel that for most parents, they never really view their children as "bad" or "unruly"—they will leave that for others to judge silently. When the child in question is your own, you tend to view them as a handful, or a pistol, or even mischievous, but never truly bad.

As a parent, I saw my boys as some combination of Leave It to Beaver and little Opie Taylor from Mayberry. They were just this rambunctious pair that remain the light of our life. In some ways, to accept any other perspective might reflect poorly on the parents. Besides, what harm were my children really causing beyond their self-imposed nicks, scrapes, and occasional bruises? I recall a neighbor (a medical professional) seeing Elo at a game with the boys and reflecting how lovely it was to see her away from the emergency room with Michael or Mark, stitching or repairing something.

Our sons were both in constant motion, and were always together. There was always something with Michael and Mark when they were little boys. Sometimes, it might be as simple as observing them playing football with each other. They had seen instant replays on television and decided to add the replays to the plays they were particularly fond of in their own scrimmages. They would make a play, then repeat the play like a dramatization to create their own instant replay because that was how they remembered it from television. Always full of surprises. One day, in the middle of one of my basketball practices, all of a sudden, someone began to beat the cover off the drums in the bandstand. Just as I was about to give the trespasser the what for, everyone's attention revealed that it was Michael who had discovered there were drums that needed beating. There was this one game early in my career, when they may have been only four and five years old, and they disappeared into the stadium. Just before the lost child alarm was sent out, someone recognized two pint-sized additions to my team bench. They were just quietly and calmly sitting at the end. Looking back, I am comforted that my sons felt they belonged where I was enough to join me.

As they got older, I tried to include them where I could. Mike and Mark loved going to the gym with me, loved working at the summer basketball camp. When they helped Elo and me with the many chores we inherited while running the basketball camp, I paid them for their effort. I always wanted to create a deeper understanding for my children around work and reward. In some way, perhaps I was concerned that they not feel entitled, which can happen when children receive too much early on.

While I was coaching at Transy in 1973, I was asked to work with and give clinics with the Ecuadorian Junior National basketball team. We went as a family and spent eighteen days in Quito. It was the first international travel for Mike and Mark, who were ten and eleven years old. I was thirty-seven and Elo thirty-three. We stayed in a casita on the grounds of a lovely hotel not far from the center of Quito. The pool at our hotel was very large and beautiful, and to the delight of the boys, especially, there was an equally large and beautiful noon buffet—a pig roasting, empanadas, and fruit of all kinds were served. Quito has a high elevation and is very close to the equator, so we truly had four seasons each day. Cool in the morning, hot at noon, autumn-like in the early evening, and very cold at night. Our two-bedroom casita was behind the hotel and had about a five-foot wall behind a little patio seating area. We had taken our tennis racquets along on the trip; Mike and Mark made up their own game using that wall as a backstop and played for hours.

As a family, we all played doubles on our first ever clay courts at a beautiful club where someone had made arrangements for us. Transportation was always provided—though it was often a pickup truck. I sat in the front seat with the driver, who was also a basketball contact. Mike, Mark, and Elo saw lots of Quito from the back of an open truck.

My clinics were all on outdoor courts at different places around the city. Upon reflection, it was unbelievable, and I remain grateful that this association for the Junior National team would do all of this for us.

In my conscious thoughts and intentions, I am hopeful that I have been and continue to be an attentive father to Michael and Mark and a compassionate husband to Eleanor. This is especially the case when I measure it by my intentions for it to be so. My sons have lived an excitement-filled life, always one event and then the next. I doubt that they have very much to complain about with respect to their quality of life coming up in the family culture that we all created. We were not perfect parents, but I feel really good about what we achieved. Even during the lean years for our family, we often were able to shelter Mike and Mark from hard times—that's what parents do. Parenting is this perilous activity whereby when you are hanging on by a thread, you convince your children that the threads are vines and try to persuade them of the joy in swinging from one vine to the other.

COACHING

Oh, the places you'll go! There is fun to be done! There are points to be scored. There are games to be won. And the magical things you can do with that ball will make you the winning-est winner of all. Fame? You'll be famous, as famous as can be, with everyone watching you win on TV, except when they don't, because sometimes they won't.
—**Seuss**

SOMEWHERE ALONG MY way, I was given a copy of the very popular *Oh! The Places You Will Go* by Dr. Seuss. This whimsical, yet philosophical book by the great storyteller muses on the ups, downs, backs, and forths of a career well-lived. After writing two technical books exclusively about basketball fundamentals and game strategy, I now want to move beyond just the *X*s (defense) and *O*s (offense) as we often refer to the technical detail of the game. While basketball remains my backdrop, this time around, I want to speak more to the humanity attached to the sport.

On each turn, when someone says "coach" to one who is a coach, it feels like a salute of deference and regard. There are times when I feel that only a coach can fully understand another coach. So much of who we are and what we are made of is difficult to explain to the next person. We coaches are an odd lot in the world.

Most coaches enter the profession in little league, the Amateur Athletic Union (AAU), or sometimes just helping out with their child's sporting event. The higher up you go, the fewer positions are available because the glory lives in the higher ranks of college and professionals. Some will drop out of this competition for the few spots that exist as time goes by, while others may choose to stay in the hunt for that one day when their opportunity presents itself.

It was clear to me that the end of college also meant the end of playing basketball. But how does one suddenly walk away from this thing that has almost always been present in your life? I could not, and it seemed that pursuing a coaching career would be the natural progression for me. Many other athletes face this dilemma. After a player's eligibility to play in college or even the professional ranks is exhausted, the most logical, natural, and obvious path for many of us is to somehow carve out another niche in sports. The desire to remain in the sports industry might give way to being a coach, athletic director, general manager, or some other position that will allow participation on this great stage.

Coaching allows me something, if incrementally, of a sacred time gone by. I thrived on the smells, the rhythms, the emotion of sports as a player, and all of that is recreated in a different way as a coach. For me, coaching can be the best of times right alongside the rest of my life's greatest challenges. I have spent my entire professional career in the coaching profession. My coaching career had me work with college teams—Transylvania University, the University of Cincinnati, the University of North Carolina at Charlotte, Purdue University, and the University of South Florida; and NBA teams—the San Antonio Spurs, New Jersey Nets, Milwaukee Bucks, Charlotte Hornets, and Charlotte Bobcats. I organized and supervised NBA Summer Draft Camps for fifteen years. For six years, I also organized and supervised the eight founding NBA-Development League Teams.

Come what may, I have always chosen to move forward into this thing that has always had a hold on me: sports. While the city, team, or level of play varied, I never considered any other work culture for my family and me.

I am part of a unique group of men and women, a fraternity even, bound together in our shared experience and passion for the culture of sports. I am proud to be what I refer to as a basketball "Lifer." By definition, a sixty-year career in basketball classifies any coach as a Lifer. Lifers are those who have worked the basketball camps, refereed, spoken at too many sports clinics to recall the number, and traveled long days and late nights scouting players. We have gone through recruiting battles and can vividly remember each outstanding recruit we may have lost on the last day at the last moment. Every coach experiences the nervousness of signing a player that they couldn't be sure of until the ink was dry on the paper. Even then, you remain a little anxious as you wait for your freshman recruit to show up on campus. That anxiety is followed by the question of whether they will stay for the full term of their eligibility or leave early for a number of potential reasons. Furthermore, will they fulfill the promise of their potential? The questions never rest because there are no guarantees in basketball or anywhere, for that matter. No subject is ever settled until it is final, or in the old sports adage—it's never over until it's over.

It is as though we are born to be coaches, but we do not necessarily become coaches simply out of desire—it is a bit more complicated than that. I believe every coach is born with this thing within us that we can develop, but if that gift is not there, it cannot be created. Some might hear that and assume that being a coach is natural, that coaching is destined to come easy to some and not to others. While there are a variety of coaches and coaching styles, each coach is guided by their own unique mixture of what is born within them and all the very hard, and at-times, unattractive, grinding work required for our outcomes.

Often, coaches move from one coaching situation to another. We journey from place to place, literally and figuratively, with ambition and emotion as our currency. Always in pursuit of the notion that this time will be better, if not perfect. In so many ways, we are insatiable. For all of the chatter about player loyalty, when it comes to college players transferring from one institution to the other, or professional players leaving their old team in free agency for a bigger, higher deal, coaches and players are quite similar. Coaches and players alike are constantly reaching for something more. The motivating factor for our serial commitments and eternal reaching is both a real and imagined quest for resources, administrative support, a larger contract, family, personal details, and on and on.

There is a famous bit of coach sarcasm that suggests that it is easier for the twelve players to adjust to the one coach, than for the one coach to adjust to the twelve. The meaning is that it is perhaps more reasonable for a team to adjust to a coach's demands than it may be for a coach to try to satisfy each of their twelve players. Coaches normally distance themselves from the arrogance of this sentiment, but it is probably the way they feel deep down.

With whistle firmly in hand, a coach can control the destiny of a player for good or bad. I tried to be sensitive to some of these at-times harsh realities. There is a tension that is likely to exist between a coach and their players. Try as we may, emotion and subjectivity creeps into our frame. Coaches sometimes have a peculiar relationship with their players. If the coach likes a player, you cannot change their mind. Likewise, if the coach dislikes a player, you cannot change their mind.

Conversely, players may often have a love-hate relationship with their coach. Strange that a player can feel a certain antagonism toward their coach but still desire deeply to please them. No matter how this pupil feels about his teacher, he is ever conscious that his coach stands between him and touching that basketball during a game.

It is evident that coaches have power and control. The greater issue is what do we do with this sacred responsibility that we hold over these often-young people's lives. Coaches are human, so they are destined to be flawed in some way, large or small. Since perfection is impossible, I determined that my quest was to keep trying to get it right, until I did. I am not sure how successful I was, but I was sincere.

TRANSYLVANIA

My search for a coaching job began in 1958 when I was about to graduate from Transylvania College with a Bachelor of Arts degree. Even with a newly minted degree, I discovered that having that paper doesn't guarantee employment. It gives you certain credibility, but you must make contact with someone who is in the position of hiring in order to get a job. So often, it's whom you know that provides the connections vital to finding employment. And, often, "experience" is a requirement as well. When you are a brand-new graduate, you are unlikely to have experience unless you have done internships with programs in their fields. These types of internships were not common back in 1958.

I had run into a number of dead ends and found myself discussing this with Coach Newton. He contacted the Woodford County Superintendent and arranged a meeting for me to discuss a teaching and coaching job at Versailles High School, twelve miles from Lexington in Versailles, Kentucky. The most attractive feature of this job was that it was the only job offer I had. As such, it was a perfect fit for me, and I accepted.

The position included teaching six classes of seventh-grade social studies a day, being an assistant coach in football and basketball, and being the head baseball coach. It was also my responsibility to drive the school's athletic bus to all away games. This first job challenged me to use my time wisely, as I also had lesson plans to prepare for the classes I taught. The consistent pattern I discovered with my early career was that much was driven by what the institution needed. If they needed a bus driver, the last person hired became the bus driver. If the coaching position had required I be a beekeeper, I suppose that I would have had to do that. The job description was born out of need, not necessarily driven by experience. Being involved with all three major sports, I was always getting ready for either a practice or a game—all for the whopping salary of $3,200 a year, which equated to $10.25 a day. We are not talking big bucks here.

Just as I was finishing that first year of high school coaching, a unique opportunity presented itself to me. Coach Newton's assistant Jack Wise changed jobs, and Coach Newton immediately offered me the position as Transylvania's Assistant Basketball Coach. Being offered a position with my alma mater was especially attractive. Coaching positions were hard to come by, and I was well aware of how fortunate I was to have the opportunity to be an assistant at the college level. I was offered the position because Coach Newton knew me. He told me that he knew I would work hard and that he could trust me.

In my role as an assistant coach, I was there to do the head coach's bidding. My purpose was simply to provide facts and set the head coach's table. When I was an assistant coach, I embraced my subordinate role, biding my time until I was no longer the assistant coach. When the change occurred that placed me in the number-one chair, then and only then could I make the final decision.

Until then, as an assistant coach, I always tried to stay in my lane. I believe in order and discipline—it was necessary for my progress, and I assume the same for others as well. I never served in the military, but I appreciate the progressive nature of the authority (minus the bombs and blood) especially as that authority aligns itself with responsibility more than the privilege of the position.

Everything that the head coach does is not necessarily what I might decide to do as it relates to the plays we run, the use of players, or general offensive and defensive strategies. It is not what I would do because I am not him. The seat that we occupy often drives our perspectives. I always tried to avoid actively second-guessing my head coach. I thought a better use of my energy and time as an assistant was to play out in my mind what I would do under the same circumstances, but unless asked I always kept that evaluation to myself until I was in a position to utilize it. As an assistant, I lived by the old adage that if my opinion was requested, only then would I offer it. It is very tempting to second guess the boss and want to change some things around, to interject your ideas into the practices and games. While it is a natural inclination to think you know better than the boss, don't do it.

There are many reasons to stay in your place, but chief among the reasons for an assistant coach not to undermine the head coach is that it may lead to your never seeing the light of day as a head coach yourself. The boss is not always right, but the boss is always the boss. Most head coaches' egos do not respond well when they sense that their staff or assistants are not completely on board with their plans. Additionally, it is counterproductive. I found it better to try to understand what the people around me were thinking instead of rejecting an idea out of hand because it was not mine. If you are paying attention, you will learn from every coach you work under. You have this great opportunity for exposure to different philosophies, strategies, drills, methods for how to relate to your players, and a multitude of offensive and defensive techniques. I discovered that some of my lessons came in the form of what I would emulate, as well as what I would choose not to do when it was my turn to make decisions. What we choose not to do is sometimes as helpful as lessons on what we should do.

When you are a boss, you are entitled to your process. If you are an assistant coach or a player, you will have your moment to shine—just not until that time arrives. Know your role and the time to play it. As a player, be the best player you can be within the system that you are in; if you are an assistant, be the best assistant. We all have our roles to play. Especially since most people don't really want the responsibility of the big boss, they just want the privileges that the big boss appears to have. Until you are actually in charge of the logistics for a game, you cannot imagine how many details and decisions are involved in being a head coach, including things as seemingly small as towel assignments for ball boys. However, the harsh reality is that the buck really does stop with the head coach. Heavy is the head that wears the crown. There are just so many moving parts—practices, shoot-a-rounds, pre-game team meals, pre-game chalkboard talks, game time, halftime, the media following the game, and packing up and moving on to the next. It brings to my mind the Scott Turow quote: "They never saw the flame, never felt the heat, still tried to tell everyone else about the flame."

I would go so far as to encourage young coaches to choose carefully when committing to a head coach and their program. Sometimes, you have to take a job to feed your family, but all money is not good money. Perhaps it is better to hold out than to take a position that you cannot fully support or one for an organization that you can't believe in.

I was very fortunate to work with some outstanding head coaches in my early years, as a player and as an assistant coach: Baldy Gilb, Harry Stephenson, C. M. Newton, and Tay Baker. I always admired their level of professionalism and how they organized every detail of their basketball programs. They never left anything to chance. Every day and in every way, they were prepared. I felt so fortunate to have these men be my early examples of how coaching should be done. I also admired how they related to the players and the players' families who had entrusted these young people to their respective programs. There was always something that felt moral and ethical about how they dealt with people.

In the fall of 1959 Elo and I had been married about five months and were living in a small apartment above the garage of my high school basketball coach's home. Elo was busy with her classes at Transylvania, and I was underpaid but beyond happy to be coaching and working with the team. The preseason practices were just about over, and everything was going well. Our first two games of the season were road games against Rio Grande and Wittenberg, both in Ohio. Two weeks before that trip, I got a call from Coach Newton, saying he had been diagnosed with the mumps and was confined to his home. He would definitely not be available for any more practices or to travel to the two Ohio games.

As Coach Newton's only assistant, this threw me into the position of acting head coach. He and I began immediately discussing practice schedules and game plans. Overseeing all the details involved in preparing practices, travel, and game plans was a great learning experience, especially seeing all of this as a rookie. At small colleges during the fifties, there just wasn't money in the budget for additional staffing, so every detail fell on my shoulders as the only assistant. Coach Newton would eventually return to the bench as our head coach for the remainder of that season.

In addition to being the assistant basketball coach, I became the head baseball coach and director of the intramural programs and taught a full load of classes in the Physical Education Department. With my salary of $4,000, I believe they got a bargain. One of the things I learned early on was that coaches' base salaries are usually in line with the compensation for teachers, which is peculiarly on the low end. This usually means that we have a very high profile, but our compensation is disproportionate to our popularity—the famous but not so rich at all. A coach can be the centerpiece of campus life on gameday, but none of that necessarily adds up to more money in your bank account. In this modern time, most coaches receive compensation in a way that they can be coaches full-time. In the old days, I would have extra jobs to help make ends meet. During this time at Transy I refereed high school basketball games in order to help with our finances. Throughout my career, I always seemed to have something entrepreneurial in my life—almost anything that might fit, from an ice cream vendor to running basketball camps.

The challenge for coaches and other high-profile individuals is that there is all of this expectation and assumption that because coaches are courtside and on television weekly for the hottest ticket in town, therefore, they are wealthy—not so. The early years are tough for most young families. There you are, young, inexperienced, and on the entry-level of the pay scale, regardless of your profession. It is just that way. As a coach, sometimes you are so eager to do the work that you probably settle for less than you are due in contracts, instead of fighting and jeopardizing what could be more at a future time. In the early days I wore what looked like a fine suit from a distance. Having only one car drove our decision to be in neighborhoods where Elo could walk to the grocery store and library.

Coaching at Transy helped me realize it was mandatory to have a post-graduate degree to coach at the college level, so I applied and was accepted at the University of Kentucky. I immediately began working toward getting my master's degree in their Educational Administration program.

One of the greatest impacts on my career occurred during the 1964-65 season. Coach Newton took a yearlong sabbatical to work on a post-graduate degree, and once again, I was asked to act as head coach. I accepted and asked Bob Pace, my former college roommate and teammate, to be my assistant. Neither of us had any college head coaching experience beyond my two games a few years earlier, but we were eager. Perhaps our greatest advantage as we struck out on our new adventure was that we were naive and ambitious. We didn't know what we didn't know, so we were not particularly fearful of trying anything.

In one of my last years at Transylvania as a coach, we were playing our closest rival, Georgetown College, at home to see who would advance in our conference tournament. Transylvania was ahead in the closing minutes, and point guard, Ron Whitson was standing at mid-court, dribbling out the last seconds of the game when a Georgetown player just walked up and slugged him in the face with his fist. The player was ejected, and Ron hit his two free throws as we won the game. This incident caused a mild uproar that the officials had to resolve.

The very next morning when I got to campus, the first thing I heard was that we had severed relations with Georgetown. President Lunger had sent a letter to the Georgetown president, announcing that all athletic activities between the two colleges would be terminated. I do not know who he consulted with to make this decision, but he made it quickly and decisively. As I reflect on this action, I admire him for taking a stand to do what he, as president of the college, had the authority to do, and for taking action without hesitation. This was a decision based on an ethical premise. Dr. Lunger was a leader who was not fearful of taking what he understood to be the right action for our athletes and for the values of which our college tried to adhere.

THE PLACES YOU GO

During that time, we made it to the National Association of Intercollegiate Athletics (NAIA) Tournament Finals in 1965. This was the first national tournament Transy had ever made.

When we arrived in Kansas City, Missouri for the finals, I called the Harry S. Truman Library with the farfetched notion of meeting with the former president. I believe that we owe it to ourselves to try things, and sometimes, the stars might just line up. I still cannot know for sure why they said yes, but I am glad they did.

The entire team was excited, and it truly was a special experience. Following a short introduction and a ten-minute talk, President Truman opened up our visit for a question-and-answer session. I was so proud of how our players interacted with him and he with them. As if on cue, one of the players asked the president, "Isn't it awfully hard to be the president of the United States?" His response was his trademark saying, "If you can't stand the heat—get out of the kitchen." He then shook hands with each player and coach and wished us well. This was a special moment in my life and career, to not only be in the company of this thirty-third and celebrated president, but also to hear these very famous words come out of his mouth in our presence. It was even better that I was able to share it with our team.

When I think back on my wonderful meeting with President Truman, it gives me pause in the midst of my struggles in this modern time with our current national state of affairs. I know that I should be more mature and realistic as I age, less naive and hopeful, but I cannot help myself. I continue to want the office of the President of the United States to mean something. I should know by now that the world is imperfect, with many imperfect people in it, yet I remain hopeful. Regardless of anyone's political affiliation, you are bound to feel a bit discouraged by what comes out of our leadership from time to time. Lyndon Johnson and his unjust war, Richard Nixon and his tapes, Bill Clinton and the unmentionable, George Bush and the missing "weapons of mass destruction," and now Number 45. I can barely say his name, so I retreat to referring to him as being the forty-fifth president of this great country. In mountain culture, we say "bless his heart," as we weaponize ourselves to talk about someone. So, I will say that here—God, bless his heart, but Donald Trump is taking America to some unfortunate places. It is like each day I have to widen my notion of what is wrongdoing. Just when I think he has hit bottom, he starts digging for yet a new low. My hope now lies in how America has survived and even thrived through it all, come what may.

I spent a great deal of time as a coach and advisor for the U.S.A. competition on the international stage. Those were proud moments for me to stand with my hand over my heart in allegiance to the United States of America, at home and in places like Kobe, Japan; Vilnius, Lithuania; and Geneva, Switzerland. I remain emotional when I see that flag presented and hear our national anthem played in all these places. I remain faithful to America's potential as a great nation and a world leader.

My time at Transylvania was interrupted by a three-year stint as an assistant coach at the University of Cincinnati. Three years into that position, I received a call from Transylvania asking me to come back, this time as head coach. Coach Newton was leaving Transylvania to be the head coach at the University of Alabama. Almost simultaneously, Coach Newton called and asked me to join him as an assistant on his staff at Alabama. Had it not been for my three years at the University of Cincinnati, I would have jumped at the chance to rejoin Coach Newton as his assistant. Here, again, I knew what this was all about—it would include recruiting, scouting, and facing the same dilemma of being on the road and away from home that I was currently encountering at Cincinnati. Alabama was a great university, and the offer to work there was tempting, but I felt my young family was the higher priority, so I declined. I also felt that I was ready to give a go at being a head coach.

By far, the greatest benefit to my position at the small college of Transylvania was the opportunity to be much more involved with our sons. Mike and Mark loved sports and played whatever sport was in season. On weekends, they would invite some of their neighborhood buddies to pile into our station wagon and spend hours playing in Transylvania's McAlister Gymnasium while I worked in my office. They loved going to the gym and playing games, and I really enjoyed having them near me. Depending on where we were in the basketball schedule, they would play dodgeball, basketball, and tag, and occasionally jump on the trampoline—that is, until Mark broke his arm and that activity was discontinued.

We also played on a small-scale basketball court in our backyard and had great baseball and football games on the field across the creek that ran through our backyard. A small home-made bridge provided access to that field, which we converted to baseball in the spring and football in the fall. For the next seven years, we lived in the only home we ever built. Our backyard backed up to the Tate's Creek School complex, which had grades one through twelve in three main buildings. When the blackberries on the nearby hill ripened each summer, the boys and I would pick berries, and Elo would make wonderful cobblers. These were experiences that would have never happened had we stayed in Cincinnati. They were wonderful family experiences that we enjoyed then and cherish now. They were our halcyon days.

Small-school programs like Transylvania can be a wonderful experience. The culture is often intimate and welcoming. What small-school programs lack in resources, they make up for in enthusiasm, especially if a coach is successful—which I was. Yet after my time at Transylvania, I wanted to move up to a successful Division I program.

MOVING UP

Wherever I go and whatever I may be doing, I assume that someone is observing me. Not necessarily because of who I am, but because it's just natural that we all observe each other for one reason or another. I am mindful that I may never get another chance to make a first impression. You just never know who is looking at the details of your work performance. When the legendary Coach Adolf Rupp came into my life and career, I thought that there must be an angel looking out for me. Coach Rupp was a four-time NCAA champion at the University of Kentucky and the most powerful coach in the country at that time. Even after his passing, Adolf Rupp remains a giant of a coach, with 876 wins over his forty-one years of coaching.

Coach Rupp had been in charge of the National Association of Basketball Coaches (NABC) Clinics. The NABC always had its annual meetings and clinics for coaches during the NCAA Final Four Tournament. In 1971 Coach Rupp invited me to present "The Imperative Free Throw." Beyond us both being in Lexington for a period, I am not certain exactly what he had observed in me, but he saw something, and I am grateful for that. Even with an excellent win-loss record at Transy, to say I was surprised by the evolution of this relationship would be putting it mildly. At Transylvania, we were just a small NAIA college, and here Coach Rupp was asking me to present to coaches with more experience, from much larger programs. That was hard to wrap my mind around. I believed I was qualified, but was puzzled as to just how he knew whether I was suited to this assignment. I was always a teaching coach, and to this day, I keep stats on NCAA tournament games about free throws made and missed and the percentage of games that are lost from the free-throw line.

I wanted Coach Rupp to feel that his confidence in me was justified, so I spent hours preparing for that presentation. I wanted to show how vital this unguarded shot, fifteen feet from the basket, could be in determining the outcome of so many games. It seems that the free-throw shot should be renamed because it is anything but free and can be the bane of many otherwise-talented players. As a coach, I always wanted my best free-throw shooter in the position to be fouled at the end of a close game—that is the person you want on the line. As important as I knew the free throw was, I remained floored when I realized the number of big-time coaches from major conferences who came to hear my presentation.

Coach Rupp and I would go on to have an excellent relationship over the years. He twice offered me a position on his University of Kentucky staff. For the first offer, he called and asked to meet with me for lunch. He wanted me to take the job as his first assistant, replacing a departing Joe Hall. He had even shown me where my office and parking space would be and said he would get back with me about the details of the contract. I had worked out in my mind an exit strategy with my job at Transylvania as head coach and athletic director. However, two days later, Coach Rupp called to say that Hall had changed his mind and was coming back. He said he simply had no choice but to "un-offer" me the job. I understood and thanked him for his consideration. We spoke cordially on the phone, and that was the end of that saga. It was interesting that neither of us had to say anything to the other about not making a big deal about this. Neither of us wanted to embarrass either of our universities in any way.

At a later point, Coach Rupp asked me to be the freshman coach at UK. This was back in the day that freshmen were ineligible to play their first year, so they had their own separate team and coach. I told him that I would not feel comfortable leaving Transylvania for a freshman coach's position after putting in so much time building my program. I felt it was one thing to go to UK as his first assistant, but to leave Transylvania to be the freshman coach seemed to be the wrong move. I was happy being the head coach and athletic director at Transy.

Even though none of those positions with Coach Rupp came to fruition, I believe those exchanges set the groundwork for a trusting, respectful professional relationship. I suppose that I was also flattered that such a successful coach wanted me to be part of his operation. Years later, however, I was interviewed again for UK's head job when Eddie Sutton was chosen.

THEOLOGY

I AM OFTEN asked, "How did you do that?" By "that," the person is usually asking me how I made it to both the Final Four and the NIT Finals twice with two different college teams. The first time was with the University of North Carolina at Charlotte, and then I did it again with Purdue University. This could be considered especially impressive in that I did it with the players I inherited when I first accepted the job. I basically inherited the talent without the benefit of forming a unit of my choosing.

The short answer can be found in what I *didn't* do. I did not try to make something into something it was not. If there is any magic at all in my sauce, it is in knowing my limitations, or more affirmatively stated, making the best out of what I have. In some ways, this is a metaphor for our lives. Any of us will rarely have a perfect setting to do great things.

I cannot testify to what went wrong in these places before I arrived beyond the fact they had not been in post-season play. My most immediate task when I came in was to determine what I had to work with. One day in the future, everything would be as I would have it, but initially, I was needed to maximize what I had. At UNC Charlotte, I allowed Cedric Maxwell to be Cedric. I could always rely on him to make free throws and work the low post against all comers at the most critical moments. I set up Cedric where he could shine when I was the coach at UNCC. When I arrived at Purdue, I let Joe Barry Carroll be Joe. At Purdue, Joe gave us at least twenty points a night in the low post, along with ten rebounds and blocked shots aplenty so that was what I worked around. Why focus on what a player or any person does not have? I prefer to set my players and the team up in the best possible way to give me all of their best parts. I suppose that there will always be areas for improvement, but core talents should not be sacrificed for wish lists. No player is perfect.

There are times when I have to be creative because the hard facts of the matter are just not in my favor. That holds true whether I am in basketball or making decisions in the larger world outside. When a team is faster than my team, no matter how much I wish, we will not be able to be as fast as they are. I just have to accept that I cannot create speed. I need to attack some other aspect of their game where they are vulnerable. If we are not as fast as they are, perhaps we should seek not to outrun them but to slow down the pace of the game. Perhaps we can force them into errors and then capitalize on turnovers.

Managing the facts is not new to me. When I couldn't afford the best house in the neighborhood that I wanted to live in, maybe I would have to buy a less expensive house in the same neighborhood. If I could not afford to send my children to private school, I could move to the neighborhood that had the best public schools. Or, looking further back at my initiative to add popcorn to the cokes I sold at the stadium as a kid hawking concession products, it's the same idea. No matter how hard I pushed cokes, I could only sell so many in the time allowed. However, if I added popcorn to the menu, I doubled my opportunity. Maybe I was learning even back then that there is power in being flexible and exploring the options of what one can do with what you have on hand.

A coach must recruit the best players possible and then build a team around that talent. The system has to accommodate the talent within it, meaning that my first option was to recruit players who fit perfectly to my preferred system. When that brand of player was not

THEOLOGY

available, I would seek the best athlete and explore if I could build around what his talent brought. Basically, this means that players sometimes had to play out of position—a good two guard sometimes had to play the small forward, or a forward would become the center, in order for the team to be a cohesive unit.

Here's a small sidebar on point guards. People often would say "guards are a dime a dozen," which may be so, but let me make this very clear—*good* guards are not. When constructing a team, regardless of the level, much attention is given to the point guard position. Call him the straw that stirs the drink or the high-octane gas that makes the vehicle run. You must have a leader, and the point guard can be the spear that leads the attack. Teams cannot win without leadership, regardless of the level of competition. I suppose some of a guard's leverage on the game is that he is in possession of the ball most of the time.

I always stayed open to what I may not know. I could never know where the solution to my puzzle might come from. I would constantly expose myself to new drills and offensive and defensive strategies. When you have an open mind, it might lead to a few subtle modifications or a complete overhaul. I attended clinics, read materials about coaching, and never, ever resisted experimenting. My core discipline remained the same in many ways, but that was not because I was not open to new ideas. I was open to most ideas, but what I found was that many ideas, once I explored them, encouraged me to keep doing what I was doing. Another benefit to leading from an open mind was that it prevented me from trying to fit a square peg in a round hole. Some things just don't work, and some things fit well in some places but not others. Failure to recognize these simple truths will make you crazy and is highly unproductive.

Players change from year to year, and this affects the leadership and chemistry of a team. This constant changing of the guard is why coaches must be flexible, especially when part of that change is a new coach coming to a team. There's always going to be matchmaking of coaches, players, and the system that is best suited given the details. This constant change is why coaches cannot always duplicate the same game plan from year to year. There are simply too many variables at play for this to happen.

This is a culture that truly illustrates that you only know what you have after you have it. A player with the most potential can end up just being a good person but never reach any of the hopes that you had for him athletically. Then there are some that blossom like a flower without notice, grand and glorious, into the most spectacular athletes that you could have ever hoped for. Athletes are much like fingerprints—there are no two that are the same.

A coach can't sit around, pining over a player who left or was injured. I can't build a team or a game plan around someone who's not in the game. We have to work with who we have at the time, and hopefully find a way to win with who we have, not who we wish we had. It also doesn't pay to wait around for a better team next year because doing that is a great way to have a losing season, and eventually, lose your job. The notion of "start where you are, work with what you have, do what you can," has long been a philosophy and discipline of mine, one that I discovered to be invaluable. It seems compatible with my practical nature. I am disinclined to daydreaming about what the world may be one day, in a perfect place when all the stars line up just right. So much is lost while we wait, hoping for a better day. There will never be a perfect time to do what needs doing. Why not make something out of what you have at the present moment? Acting on what is present has been helpful and advantageous for me.

RACE

I grew up in a space where everyone was white, and most seemed very poor. I am aware that white privilege exists but also that it doesn't mean all white people have an easy row to hoe. Having grown up in the very poor clay of Appalachia, I am not totally persuaded about how great my white privilege was.

As bad as things might have been for us and those around us, I recognize that it might be worse for some folks who are black simply because they are black. I try to maintain compassion for my neighbor as I move through my own details of a world that I may never fully understand.

From our move to Lexington in 1945 until I graduated from college in 1958, there was never any racial integration at any school I attended, and I never remember any discussion about the subject. We knew that the world was full of a variety of people, but because we did not see them in our daily lives, they were not a particular focus for us. I would see people that did not look like me in pictures, but they always seemed far away and not specifically relevant to my moment-to-moment life. I saw the image, then moved on to the next thing without much consideration of something or someone so far away. Besides, I was a child, and that is what children do. I am guessing that it might have been different for me if I had seen different folks in my school, at the county store, or at my church. I did not, so I would only begin to really explore my feelings about race and diversity as I got older.

When I was in high school, there were two public schools that white students attended—Henry Clay and Lafayette Public School. Dunbar was the only public school for black people in Lexington. Things remained that way until 1967 when the federal government forced integration.

The only integrated activity that I recall during my teenage years occurred following our high school football season. Football players from the different high schools would show up on Sunday afternoon, and there was a pick-up game between the black and white players. We played on a big field past the old railroad tracks just off Main Street. It was rough ground, and some of the field wasn't even covered in grass.

Only a few players had any equipment. One or two had helmets, a couple had football cleats, and both teams wore sweatshirts—that was about it. There were no officials, and the games always started with a coin toss. Seldom was there ever a dispute. Never was there a fight. There was always a handshake once the game ended. I sometimes wonder if the adults could have taken counsel from how well we got along. It's interesting to reflect that here we were, in the mid-1950s, when almost everything was segregated, but a bunch of us young teenage boys all just came together and played. We all loved to play football, and for that afternoon, the only thing that mattered was the game. The thing about sports competition is that for that moment during the contest, everything outside fades into the background. It feels like the only important thing is the bliss of the game. When you play, your teammate is your brother, and the opponent is just the opponent. You want to "beat them," but that is all. Perhaps some of the world's problems could be solved if we accepted what is good in sports as part of leadership to help right the world.

Lou Johnson was a star player for Dunbar High School and a great athlete. Lou was our age, but it felt like he was a man among boys. His body looked like he had stepped out of a picture of what a football player should look like. Lou went on to play professional baseball for the Dodgers. Another Dunbar player named Othorp was about my size: small, maybe five-foot-nine, and lightweight. He and I played hard and always shook hands when the game ended.

After my senior year at Transy, when our basketball season ended, someone put together an integrated, all-star team that played other similarly organized all-star teams throughout central Kentucky. Our team was composed of players from the University of Kentucky, Eastern Kentucky State University, Kentucky State, and Transy. Not all of the teams were integrated, but since every player was talented, it suggested to me that the teams' composition was more a function of player ability than race. While we were on tour, this one guy named

THEOLOGY

Jack always seemed to play hard from the word go. I asked him where that energy came from, and he told me, "Man, I got three wives! I want to stay out here and play. If I lose and have to go home, I have to face them." I don't know if that really has anything to do with anything, but I laugh out loud each time I think of Jack's troubles.

My immediate focus has always been sports. I am not suggesting to anyone that my passion for basketball made me oblivious to the fact that I am immersed in a race-sensitive society. I am not naïve; I am clear that racial division and racism do exist. Sports have been imperfect yet effective as a method of bringing groups together. While in the throes of heated competition, race issues are still out there, but not near.

In many instances, I was the only one on the team bus that looked like me. Basketball took me deep into black culture. I say black culture, but I remain a bit confused about determining whether the reference should be black culture or African American culture, let alone trying to determine when to say "people of color" or "black." I never want to say anything disrespectful. I want to think that we are all just Americans, but I remain ever sensitive to saying the wrong thing, however well-intended I may have been.

When I moved over to the University of Kentucky in 1959 to study for my master's degree, my classes were integrated with black and white students for the first time. We were all polite enough with each other on the surface. There seemed to be no issues about this racial coming together, although I certainly could not have been the only one at that time coming out of a racially segregated environment in one way or the other. Mostly, we were all concerned about our schoolwork and the papers we had to present. On the subject of race and culture I found myself always qualifying my opinions with "as far as I know" and "it appeared" because that was all I could speak to with confidence. It would likely seem that way to me anyway because I held my head down as I immersed myself in basketball, class, and studying, in that order.

I recall one of my recruiting trips as a young coach, which took me deep into the center of a black community in Memphis. I got turned around and decided to go into a restaurant for directions. I asked the friendly woman who greeted me about where I was and sought her direction on getting to where I needed to be. She said, "Let me get the manager."

This big, burly guy gave me a look of concern and puzzlement as he offered, "You really don't want to be wandering around in this area." I have never had any nervousness about entering what was essentially a black neighborhood. The only true anxiety I felt in my situation was being lost, and that maybe I was going to be late for my appointment. His sensitivity to my (obvious-to-him) vulnerability touched me. The man got me turned around and on my way. Looking back, it was probably lost on me how vulnerable I was on a number of fronts. However, in this instance, I think I had entered what was the bad neighborhood, not necessarily the black neighborhood. The two were not the same to me. I suppose it is true that God takes care of fools and children because on that day, I am grateful that God and the restaurant guy were looking out for me.

There was an instance when Elo taught piano lessons to two sisters who lived four houses down the street. The boys went with her to the girls' home once a week after school for the lessons because we didn't own a piano yet. One of the girls would help out with the boys while the other sister had her lesson. This was a good deal all around and had gone on for over a year. One day, the mother called to say that the girls couldn't have lessons that day; the next week, she called again to say the same. Both times, the call was not as easygoing and "neighborly," as was normal, and she gave no specific reason. Elo said something about this to a dear friend, who lived directly next door to the girls and asked if she was aware of any illness with the sisters. Elo's friend said that the mother told her that she couldn't allow her girls to be taught by someone who would actually have a black family in her home. And indeed, we had. We had invited a player and his parents to have breakfast with us one Sunday morning. We shared the hospitality of our table with them and had a wonderful visit.

Mike and Mark were four and five; how could we look at these little boys and tell them they were no longer welcomed in the girls' home? It is hard to explain prejudice, and quite frankly, we couldn't understand it much better than they could. I have discovered that often, if a person isn't reasoned into something, they cannot be reasoned out of it. We all see race and the variety of ethnic groups that exist in the world in which we live. The question is not necessarily *if* we see race—of course, we do; it is a function of sight. The larger question for each of us to consider is whether we bring negative reactions to someone whose skin isn't the same color as our own. How do we unpack what gets wrapped and tied up about color?

BROKEN HEARTS

In October of 1962, while I was coaching at Transylvania, Eleanor and I were at President Lunger and his wife's home, having dinner with a group of faculty members. That night, the Cuban Missile Crisis showdown was coming to a head. America and The Soviet Union came closer to Armageddon than our history had ever known. This cold war had escalated to the point where a nuclear attack seemed very possible. The nation was full of fear of such an attack. It had grown to the point of constant discussion of what survival supplies each of us should have on hand. The nation was terrified that a nuclear exchange would leave millions of people dead in its wake. Fortunately for us all, President John F. Kennedy and the Soviets' Khrushchev were able to come to a non-violent resolution.

Having the faculty together gave everyone a certain comfort as we could discuss this global event in a civil way with people who came from diverse backgrounds. This was a particularly vulnerable time for Elo and me as a young couple as we were pregnant with Michael, who was due in three months. Being in this college culture was a support system for us as we had these calming voices of reason and context. This was in an era before the competitive landscape of the internet and the twenty-four-hour news cycle. There was also a certain comfort and trust we gained from the nightly news team of Charles Huntley, David Brinkley, and Charles Kuralt. They came into our homes each night in a manner that felt earnest and honest. Somehow, that settled us.

The sixties were a turbulent time in America. President Kennedy was assassinated in Dallas, followed by Dr. Martin Luther King Jr. in Memphis, and then young Robert Kennedy as he campaigned for the presidency of the United States. I joined many others in this deep emotion of sadness regarding what was going on in the country during that time. Whatever innocence we had was wiped away. Those scenes of murder and mayhem can never really leave you. It left me feeling numb. It just felt like the world I knew was falling apart. The Yeats poem "The Second Coming" was quoted often during those times:

> *Things fall apart; the center cannot hold:*
> *The blood-dimmed tide is loosed, and everywhere*
> *The ceremony of innocence is drowned;*
> *The best lack all conviction, while the worst*
> *Are full of passionate intensity.*
> **—Yeats**

Everyone old enough to remember the assassination of President John F. Kennedy remembers where they were and what they were doing on November 22, 1963. That weekend in November was one of the most focused and emotional of my life at that point. Like most of the nation, we watched every replay of the scene. Jacqueline Kennedy crawling to the back of the limo in desperation, trying to reverse the horror of an assassin's bullet to her husband and our fallen president.

That scene was followed by the swearing-in of Lyndon Johnson on a plane.

I can never forget every somber moment of the horse-drawn coffin carrying President Kennedy's body to Arlington National Cemetery. All of our family could hardly bear to see another moment, but we could not tear ourselves away from the little television (with rabbit ears) in our kitchen. It remains incredible to me how the entire world was bound together in a very peculiar way at the death of our nation's leader. This is the kind of moment when a fast-moving world slows down, and all seem to be reading from the same page. We came home from church on Sunday of that very sad time and sat our little boys on stools at the kitchen counter to have something to eat before their naps. We watched in further disbelief as someone that none of us had heard of named Jack Ruby stepped out of the crowd and shot the alleged assassin, Lee Harvey Oswald, before Oswald could stand trial for the murder. All of these many years later, we continue to have more questions asked than answered surrounding the John Fitzgerald Kennedy assassination and the many events that followed, but what I do know is that we witnessed it all.

There are historical events that occur along the way that you look back on with the recognition of how unimportant basketball can become. Getting the best players, getting the best out of players, beating rivals, and winning championships remain very important for a coach, but they pale in the larger scheme of things. No matter how important those things were to me, the threat of war and presidential assassinations make you realize what's really important.

WHOLE PERSON, WHOLE EDUCATION

The student part of "student-athlete" has always meant something to me. I was ambitious for my players to develop into whole people. I really do not believe they had to choose between athleticism at the highest level or good citizenship—they could embody both. During one of our visits to Chautauqua Elo and I sat in on a lecture by Dr. Robert Franklin, President Emeritus, Morehouse College. He discussed their students, known as Morehouse Men, saying, "We wanted our students to graduate while being well-read, well-spoken, well-traveled, well-balanced, and well-dressed." I always tried to emulate the same expectations reflected in his presentation.

On the college level, I had a practice of having weekly meetings with my players, which I found helpful for communication and staying in touch. Things go by quickly during the basketball season, and if I am not careful, there are things that need tending to that may go unnoticed. It is true that one stitch in time can save having to add nine stitches later. If I am able to detect a minor thing before it grows into a full-blown problem, that is a good thing, especially when dealing with young people prone to behaving in line with Romans 7:19, which approximately says: that I do, I should not, that I should, I do not. They are, at times, unable to resist their urges.

The primary reason for player meetings was to check on classes and grades and to ask if there were any personal or home issues that we needed to discuss. There are issues that arise when young people are away from home for the first time, and they need to have a mature person listen and perhaps offer advice that will be helpful. When face to face with an athlete, all sorts of issues reveal themselves that will not be apparent when he is running up and down the floor with a basketball. I am astounded when I hear a coach be surprised that he has an athlete that is at risk of being academically ineligible and beyond astounded when coaches say they are unaware of what their players are doing on or off the basketball floor.

I recall a conversation that I had with one of my players when we were discussing challenges he was having keeping up with his classwork. He was always on time for study table and put in the hours, but he just couldn't seem to make the mark. Something moved me to have him tested. The simple test revealed he had a learning disability.

THEOLOGY

The short of this story is that he received help and special tutors to improve his situation. He never played a day in the NBA, but he did graduate with a college degree and returned to his community for a career as a public servant. I want him to take full credit for the work he put in. I am grateful that by communicating off the court, we were able to get to the root of his difficulty.

So often, these young men can make it through the athletic system without any diagnosis of larger life issues that need attention. That's completely ridiculous! I really believe that a coach may choose to ignore what is happening, but he most likely has an inkling. As the saying goes, they knew or should have known. The same can be said when these young people are out in the village getting into trouble. Friends and strangers will frequently approach other coaches and me with an inside tip on what one of our players is doing. Sometimes, it is their intention to help; other times, it may be just to gossip or to have me believe they are a well-connected big shot. I say all of that to be clear that as coaches, we most likely know what our young men are doing. The choice we make is whether we will act on it or not.

The accountability for my players is the deal that was made between my young men and me when their families agreed to trust me with their child. That is a part of the job description of a college coach. There was plenty of time to talk about basketball issues, before, during, or after practice. My greater emphasis for student-athletes was to be sure to make the student part of the term mean something.

I am simply old school enough that I believe firmly that the end result of going to college is not solely to be able to get a job. Whether a player is fresh out of college or ending a celebrated professional basketball career, included in the process should be education, learning, and developing a worldview. I try desperately to be a student of the world outside of basketball, and I have always encouraged that in my players as well. I know that there will come a day for every player when they can no longer play basketball, and I want them to be as equipped as possible to navigate the world that does not include a basketball. Though I cannot require it, I do encourage them to interact with other students and professors on campus. I want them exposed to the diversity of ideas that come in the classroom or at a play, musical program, or lecture at the university by some scholar.

All too often, we see young men enter the professional world of sports and not be prepared in any way to interact with the world beyond the basketball court and their hotel room. I suppose that is okay in some way, but it seems such a waste of opportunity at having more. There are games played in great cities all over our country, and I believe it is part of the student's education when they venture into that city and its cultural scene, especially if they can do that without getting into trouble. Certainly, this is not a path suited for every player—or coach, for that matter—but when it happens, it is inspiring.

I was always impressed by Cedric Maxwell and his enthusiasm for chess. I was impressed that this talented athlete moved beyond checkers and backgammon to this elegant game that rose out of the Gupta Empire in the sixth century A.D. I attribute his calm and intelligent style of basketball play as being somehow informed by the complex nature of chess. I felt a certain pride whenever someone would report back to me that they saw this player or the next at a play or lecture on campus or some cultural event in the city. I would sometimes think to myself, "Good, that may come in handy for them one day."

I often wish for my players and others around me to remain curious about themselves, others, and the core of whatever activity they are doing. The honest answers to the questions that you pose to yourself and others will give way to you working on the right things, and proper focus of your energy. One wise writer suggested that many people want to be thought of as being interesting, but he encouraged that instead of seeking to be interesting to other people, each of us should seek to remain interested in the people around us and the world in which we live.

THEOLOGY

DISCIPLINE

Things move fast, so rules are necessary. Rules are helpful in creating order. Maintaining discipline is an even greater challenge on the professional level because there you are dealing with adults. Unlike high school and college, coaching professional athletes has a particular wrinkle. You have to tell grown men what to do and not do. You need order and are constantly trying to get fifteen adults to embrace the same meaning of a particular word. I had to strike a balance between what is preferred and what is necessary.

All teams have rules regarding being on time for meetings and practices, behavior on buses, dress codes, injury rehabilitation, doctor appointments, and community involvement. When disciplining a player for failure to abide by the rules, I was committed to being careful to have the penalty fit the crime. This was particularly difficult when the trespasser was not easy to get along with, and even worse for the rare player who might just rub me the wrong way—I am human, after all. But once the penalty has been fulfilled, I forget it and move on. Getting caught up in personalities and grudges distracts from your ultimate objective—getting the most out of your players and winning.

Adults are guided by rules the world over, but there is perhaps a greater challenge with celebrity alpha males. Much of their journey allows passes, winks, and nods in a world that is otherwise very strict for other adults. I try to keep in mind that the penalty is not the objective; modifying the behavior is. In my later career with the NBA, this whole discipline thing became even more complicated. Playing time and yanking a scholarship goes a long way in making a coach's point when dealing with some misguided nineteen-year-old, but when the young men in question are professionals with millions of dollars on a guaranteed contract, it becomes a different matter. What impact is a hundred-dollar fine going to have on a player who collects a million-dollar check monthly? You really are only left with hopes that they will want to do the right thing, which can remain only a hope.

They are constantly testing boundaries. My disadvantage is that when they bump their heads, I have to try to make it all better for their sake and the sake of the team.

Whether the playing field is little league or Madison Square Garden, we may be expecting too much of these young people to be perfect. While sports are often thought to create character and ability where there may have been none, I am not fully convinced that the game creates character. I think the game and its continuous test of fire can *reveal* if a player or coach has character or ability, but it does not put it in place. The person has it, or they do not. The circumstance that players and coaches find themselves in, day in and day out is the stage on which their truth reveals itself. You can build on existing character, but I doubt that character can be created where there was none.

There are those instances of controversy that can pop up when young men do what they should not. Every team I have been a part of had at least one bad egg, maybe two, that needed to be watched carefully. A very unexpected situation raised its ugly head when I was coaching with the San Antonio Spurs. We were in Montana, playing a pre-season game. Following our morning shoot-around, some of us were walking through the lobby, when suddenly, all of the people in the lobby came to a complete stop. The in-house security camera captured all of our attention as we witnessed two men who appeared to be fighting in an upstairs corridor, one of whom had a knife. Normally, my response would be to turn to the safety of my players and coaching staff. There was a wrinkle to my response to this situation, though, because a close-up shot revealed the two men were our players, Alvin Robertson and Frank Brickowski. And, their weapons of choice were butter knives. I'm not sure if I registered just how dangerous the butter knife wailing would be, but I became upset two-fold at how completely unprofessional and childish these men had become. The hotel's security arrived immediately and broke up the fight. This incident was an embarrassment to them individually, their family, their teammates, and the San Antonio Spurs organization. The NBA can be a rough and tumble world, especially given that we do not live in a vacuum. Most of what we do is likely to be broadcasted in living color to the larger society with all of its grime and details. Not only is there the embarrassment of the trespass, but there could also be actual physical harm.

Both players were starters, and their penalty, determined by the general manager, was that they had to sit out the first half of the next game. That was a meaningless penalty that had no impact on the team or either one of the players in terms of establishing the importance of standards for behavior. In some ways, I suppose this was the raw exchange that I had made when choosing the NBA over the NCAA. It is difficult, if not impossible, to prevent grown men from running with sharp objects, and they may hurt themselves and others. This was an adjustment for me. I suppose that the general manager felt no moral requirement to shape these men into finer men. Because of my history in working with younger men and boys, I always maintained a self-imposed moral responsibility to them and their families who had entrusted me with their treasure and to myself. Additionally, I've always believed that the more I can maintain order and discipline, the more we can get done on the basketball floor.

PREPARATION

It really is true that you never know where you are going until you get there. Jack McKinney was hired in 1979 to be the head coach of the Lakers. The team was off to a good start with a 10-4 record. One day, McKinney took off on his bike to meet his assistant coach, Paul Westhead, for a game of tennis. Along the way, he flipped over the handlebars, striking his head on the pavement, sustaining a serious head injury. Westhead was named interim coach and ushered McKinney's Laker team to their 1980 World Championship.

The Laker tale got even richer when Laker broadcasting guy, Pat Riley, replaced a fired Paul Westhead on the heels of a bit of internal controversy. This high-stakes musical chairs of coaches gave us the now-famous Los Angeles Lakers Showtime at The Forum. No one can plan exactly when an opportunity will reveal itself. What we do control is our preparation and state of readiness. In the Lakers' case, the assistant coach and the broadcaster were both elevated to positions that were unimaginable until the opportunities appeared.

No one knows when an opportunity is going to come along; it often doesn't seem that opportunity gives a lot of advanced notice. When you agree with that premise, it follows that being organized and prepared might give you an advantage. At a minimum, prior preparation allows you an opportunity to succeed. That works for students, ballplayers, coaches, and people of any profession.

The only way forward for me is to get ready and stay ready because there is no substitute for being organized and prepared. At a minimum, being prepared allows me an advantage over those who are not. If the third-string quarterback isn't paying attention to play calls, he will be in a heap of trouble if the starter gets injured and the primary backup becomes academically ineligible. Being up to date with what is going on in the classroom or the boardroom can be your blessing.

I learned early the critical importance of getting prepared and remaining prepared. When Coach Newton became ill, I was ready to sit in the first chair as head coach, driven by all of the preparation I had done early on. Substituting for Coach Newton was an incredibly challenging experience, but it went pretty much without incident. As I learned along the way, situations like this are not always seamless. I give credit to Coach Newton who directed my early learning experiences and guided me throughout my career. He provided the basis for my foundational development in the coaching profession. Things were made less difficult because Coach Newton and I knew each other well and were comfortable together. I had played three years for him as an undergraduate at Transylvania and had been the captain of the team my senior year. I understood his system and style of play, which made it easier to work with the players.

THEOLOGY

I received a tip early in my career while attending a coaching clinic and hearing an older coach talk about what would ultimately become a career lesson for me. He recommended that we act like sponges and soak up as much information as possible on what we, as coaches, were experiencing and observing each day. He went on to explain that these experiences might be helpful as they relate to future events.

I think it is necessary to maintain a continuous notebook and keep logs on topics such as effective planning, personnel, strategy, and just about every subject that occurs in a coach's day. Throughout my coaching career, I kept a daily notebook on players, practices, and every other detail, which I viewed as a potential resource. It provided me a tool to reference and eliminated the need to begin again when the subject matter returned. These notebooks helped determine what might be most effective. I kept them close at hand so that I could refer to it quickly as I planned for games. Circumstances would arise that might not necessarily be the same but would rhyme with a past circumstance. It might be something as simple as how individual players had performed within our strategy as well as how opponents had fared against that strategy. I began this note-taking discipline long before personal computers existed. You will simply have to imagine the volume of notes by hand, writing game plans, typing them out (or hopefully having a secretary to type them), and putting them in large, red, three-ring notebooks, which I kept in my office. Developing these notebooks and maintaining journals during my career prepared me for most events that followed. This practice certainly came in handy when I had to step up and step in.

GAME DAY

Basketball contests are like snowflakes falling through the sky—they appear the same, but each has its own unique detail. I sometimes wonder if that is why players and coaches alike go through long and sometimes excruciating detail when they are describing a game gone by, a war they fought so many years ago. Through each detail, they are telling you why this game was not like the last as they roll the video in their mind. We often move through our storytelling, wanting the listener to have the clarity and purpose that we hold.

Philosophically and practically, practice belonged to me, and the games were for the players. I am among that class of coaches who believe that practice is the tool to get my team where I need them. I have this trade-off with my teams, whereby if practice can be mine, I can pull back (loosely speaking) during the game and allow that be the time for my players to shine. I explained to the team that I considered the practices to be my classroom. This concept was paramount in my coaching philosophy. Teaching would be done on the practice court and in the film sessions. Corrections that needed to be made and mistakes that needed to be pointed out would be done at those times. It was my responsibility as the coach to come to practice prepared to teach. It was their responsibility to come to practice prepared to learn. When it was game time, it was also their responsibility to execute.

I loved being in the gym. It was my laboratory. Whether home or away, I was always comfortable when I walked into a basketball gymnasium. I especially looked forward to game day. It was the exam to see how well everyone had learned their lessons from the classroom of my practice floor. I felt that the game was like a chess match, and I looked forward to working out a strategy and having players execute it all the way down to checkmate. There are routines and rhythms that come with game-day that are the same whether you are in a small gym in Pikeville, Kentucky, the mecca of Madison Square Garden, a Big Ten arena, or an outdoor, makeshift court in Vilnius, Lithuania.

I intentionally went out of my way to never do anything to embarrass anyone in front of a sold-out arena. I knew deep down that I would have plenty of private opportunities during practice to fix what was wrong within my team.

CONDITIONING

Fatigue can make an otherwise intelligent and reasonable person confused and exhibit poor judgment. When a person is weary, they can't really think straight. A certain level of conditioning eliminates pulled muscles and other injuries, in addition to building stamina. I have always insisted on conditioning for my team and me.

As an assistant coach at the University of Cincinnati, I took the opportunity to take a summer course in kinesiology, which includes the study of fast-twitch muscles and how to go about building speed. I knew that our fast-twitch muscle fibers are responsible for initiating the explosive speed and power movements required in athletics. In comparison to slow-twitch muscles that control endurance, fast-twitch muscles are designed to fire and fatigue quickly. Through the kinesiology course, I began to develop a system that would build speed and stamina when conditioning basketball players in preparation for the beginning of practice.

Before I put the program in place, I first experimented with it on myself. Basically, I ran a mile in eight segments. The idea was to speed run for part of one minute, then rest for two minutes, then run for another minute, et cetera, until the full mile was completed. This conditioning also reflected the stop-and-go pattern of a basketball contest. That was in contrast to the old days when you might put a player on a track and have them run a couple of miles to no avail. Players would have to start over getting themselves into shape when they reached the gym floor because long-distance running is not the best preparation for basketball.

I chuckle with tongue in cheek that no leader should require their troops to do what they are not prepared to do themselves. Although, fortunately for me, I only needed to participate in the design phase. Eight segments in succession seem simple enough until you actually have to do it. The devil is in the details, or in this case, the devil is in making the time. By running these eights myself, I had a good feel for the best time allowance and how it would vary for guards, forwards, and centers. Over the years, I studied this conditioning regimen and maintained extensive records. There were also rules on the turnaround such as that hand and toe must go across the end line, and if you missed your time, you ran an extra eighth with five seconds added after the team completed theirs. I gave the big men more time because they were often slower than the guards and small forwards.

A preseason of this form of conditioning was really difficult for my players after they had spent a summer limited to the relaxed nature of pick-up games around their hometowns, along with summer foolishness and late nights. However, once they got through the deep chill of my preseason conditioning ritual, they were prepared to concentrate on basketball, not getting in shape. The scrimmages could be more competitive because everyone was just playing basketball and not trying to get their sea legs.

Everett Bass told me many years after he'd graduated that this conditioning regimen made him give serious thought about returning to Transy to play basketball. Fortunately he stayed and became one of Transylvania's all-time great players.

ON FAIRNESS

I have always been concerned with fairness and justice in playing time. Coaches are confronted daily with the call of Solomon as they decide who is best suited for each chore. Who should get the playing time, and why? That decision is like most decisions we make—a mixture of instinct and objective measure. I sought long ago to make my decisions less subjectively and more objectively. Some players are clearly superior to others, depending on the category and topic. I needed to develop a systematic approach when the call was close as to just what would be the tiebreaker.

I developed a metric system to judge all players by their personal performance. We referred to it as PR—Performance Rating. I assigned a number to the quality of performance in categories around physical fitness and athleticism. While not perfect, this PR system was helpful in reducing the appearance of favoritism as a factor in playing time. I am sure that there are arguments for and against this system, yet it remained helpful.

I posted the results and detail weekly, so the facts were always there in front of the players in plain sight for all to see. Consequently, there was never a question about favoritism. What really made the system work was that the players bought into the approach of grading all of the different aspects of basketball and execution and the relative value of each. Fortunately for coaches and players alike, the scoring reflected the talent that should be on the floor at a given time.

For a long time, I wondered just how I would respond if a player defied my perfectly flawed system. Then came my day of reckoning. Steve Walker tested higher, but Arnette Hallman was clearly the more athletic of the two. Although Steve had earned his place in the starting lineup and priority in playing time, he bailed me out of my controversy. He gave his blessings, which could have only come from him, to play Arnette instead. I am always going to admire those young men for their demonstrated maturity in agreeing to do what was best for our team in the end. I was prepared to honor the commitment that the PR system conjured, which may or may not have given us a better outcome. I walked away from that experience motivated to reinsert my coach's judgment to help the science along.

HUMILITY

Sometimes, it is good just to beat another team and feel good about it—no spiking the ball, swinging on the rim, or wagging fingers. Some of that philosophy, for me, comes from my upbringing, where showing off was discouraged. It smacks of kicking someone when they are down, even when we chalk it up to the nature of competition. Additionally, I wonder if you really want to give the other side additional inspiration to beat you. I advise my players and staff not to give opponents any extra motivation.

CHEATING

As members of the National College Athletics Association, we all agreed to conduct ourselves a certain way, guided by certain rules and regulations. This set of rules and behavior is an attempt at leveling the field, so no team has an advantage over the other beyond our natural talents. They are very clear about not paying players and their families money, not playing academically ineligible players, and other crimes and misdemeanors that might persuade players to join your team. To do so is cheating. Even after the student is on campus, it is further considered cheating if the athletic department decides to provide grades for eligibility and other special accommodation around eligibility and premiums that non-athletic students do not receive.

There is this place that I reached with some recruits, where I knew I had lost them or them me. When they alluded to wanting cars, cash, and fixed grades—or asked for them outright—I knew that we had reached a place that could slide into one of no return. I felt at a severe disadvantage when they reached beyond my offer of a quality education at a world-class institution and the opportunity to become a better athlete and person. There was a bright line of separation for me between right and wrong, and that was never negotiable.

I was clear in my heart and mind that not only were those things against the rules, but they were also a disservice to this young person later in life. The great John Wooten said that it is criminal for us to do for these young people what they should do for themselves. Much of this falls within that space of learning and development referred to in The *Prophet*—the breaking of the shell that encloses your

THEOLOGY

understanding. I wonder if, by seeking to do everything for our young people, we deny them the process that strengthens them in preparation for future challenges.

Certainly, there is an argument that student-athletes are not regular students, so they should be treated specially, but that may be an argument for another day. However, it certainly should not go unnoticed that these young men and women who compete in front of packed stadiums are bringing in major revenue and marketing for their university. Perhaps the NCAA should seek a middle ground on compensation for these young people or else enforce the rules everywhere. Presently, they present themselves as highly contradictory and hypocritical as a governing body of these colleges and university athletic programs. I suggest that at least, we all follow the stated rules, rather than having the rules apply to some but not to others.

I have deep and eternal resentment toward cheaters, and maybe even more so toward those who get away with cheating. I struggle with this and have had many philosophical discussions with too many people on what defines cheating. The simple answer could be what Supreme Court Justice Kennedy offered on another topic: "You know it when you see it." In that instance, Kennedy was answering the question of what pornography is, and it's a great analogy. There are many suggestions and discussions on changing the rules or even easing eligibility requirements. It is difficult to be certain where the line is. What I feel strongly and deeply about is that whatever we all agree on should be strictly followed. What is the value of rules if the rules are only randomly and inconsistently followed and enforced?

I have worked so hard for so long with all of the tedium and grinding that comes with honest competition that I just feel contempt for anyone who would take a shortcut. We all enter into an agreement on what the rules will be, and I deeply feel that everyone should abide by that covenant. Our word should be our bond. When others cheat, it feels like we are all runners in a marathon, but when I show up at the finish line, some have already arrived because they caught a taxi along the way instead of being stronger and faster. To add insult to this, I had to bear witness to them reaping the rewards after cheating. Me in second place, despite all of the work I put in, as I witness them on the medal stand accepting their undue reward. This is how it feels to me when another coach cheats in the competition.

Larry Brown coached two teams in NCAA tournaments where the NCAA vacated their wins. On the occasions when the NCAA decided to enforce their rules, they would strip a team of its titles or accomplishments if cheating were discovered. It is a bit peculiar to think that everybody has to pretend now that all of that excitement and glory of a team's success could actually be wiped away in the present time. Though, I suppose some punishment is better than none at all. The first was that '79-80 UCLA team that beat our team when I was coaching Purdue. Brown also coached at the University of Kansas, and they had to vacate their wins in 1988-89, following his departure for the NBA. His tradition continued when the NCAA banned the SMU men's basketball team from postseason play and suspended Brown for nine games after concluding that he had lied to an investigator and turned his back on a case of academic fraud involving one of his players. The controversy at UCLA had a direct bearing on our Purdue team. Nothing can compensate the players, their coaches, and the university for losing in the Final Four to a team who then had their second-place finish vacated.

I am not naive; I always knew the problem was bad, but I was astounded to discover the frequency and volume of games that schools had to vacate historically as punishment for violating NCAA rules. College cheating in the NCAA is nothing new—violating rules happens in many fields. Far too many coaches have had multiple offenses, been caught, and then moved on to another prestigious university. It's a joke that has long been whispered in private: "Cheat up and move up." What I have never understood is why the administration of a university would hire a coach who has previously violated the rules and had games vacated. For those who really would like to understand the propensity for cheating in college, I'd suggest you check out those who've had to vacate games in the past. I was astounded at the total number of coaches and especially the number of those who were repeat offenders.

For as great as that number is, the absolute number may even be greater of those who cheat and get away with it. Some of this may flow from the intense arms race that schools engage in as they turn up the heat to get the next great player. They do what they know they should not do because of their lust for winning at any cost, in any way. Some schools and their coaching staffs are much like criminals who got caught but have no contrition for their violations. Their true quest is finding a way to get away with it the next time. As with our situation in the Final Four. The really sad feature of this dilemma is that the players—and the teams that lose to cheaters—have no recourse.

How hard is it for the NCAA guardians to understand that "True Winners Don't Cheat?"

Where are the NCAA ethics and integrity? Who are the guardians of the game? I realize I might be old school, but it seems inappropriate to have coaches recognized with Hall of Fame honors when they are two- and three-peat offenders of rules. Rules can only be effective if there are consequences for violations.

I lived as a person and a coach with this code of ethics and have never been shy about voicing any part of this philosophy. While coaching at Purdue I attended one of our Big Ten fall coaches' meetings in Chicago, and there I made my move. When all the Big Ten business issues had been completed, the president asked for recommendations from the floor. Everyone remained silent; I raised my hand and proposed the following: 1) Any coach caught cheating should be automatically fired. 2) The offending school would be fined $100,000. 3) The team would automatically be on probation for two years. 4) Recruiting restrictions would be determined by the NCAA.

The complete silence in this room filled with coaches spoke volumes. Due to the lack of response of any kind following my proposal, you can correctly assume that the motion died. I am certain they wondered where on earth this coach who had just entered the Big Ten was coming from.

I also recall a later conversation with a former player of mine. This young man was well educated, a successful professional, and a pillar in his community. When I mentioned some of the violations of his state university, he responded that he didn't want to know about those details. He said he simply wanted to go to the games, enjoy them, and ignore the particulars about any infractions. This was both shocking and disappointing. It is this mentality that not only permits violations to continue unreported and uninvestigated but undermines any chance of reform. Perhaps it is unrealistic, but I wish that he and other fans would care, would want to know about what is going on in the program of a major state university, would want to know about the violation of rules, and perhaps even want to speak out against them.

The impression I am left with is that people go to basketball games for many reasons but mostly to see their team win. It appears that many administrators, gatekeepers, fans, and players are not interested in moralizing over recruiting violations or in hearing about the academic progress of athletes. They are only interested in the game and the win. If a team can do that nicely and neatly within the bounds of some random rules, so be it. Otherwise, they prefer not to know the grimy details of how the sausage was made—pass the mustard, please.

COACH-PLAYER RELATIONSHIPS

Players look to coaches for direction, leadership, and, most important to the player, playing time—a platform to perform. Few players come to the game ready-formed and prepared for the show. They all need something. I have coached players along the spectrum from the true greats like Michael Jordan to the twelfth man on the bench. Quite frankly, with someone like a Jordan, mostly a coach needs to recognize that he is special and provide him a platform to demonstrate his promise. Sometimes, a coach has to be wise enough to know that what a player needs is for the coach to get out the way. Both players and coaches need to determine just when that sometimes arrives.

Fundamental to the working partnership is trust. Some players will run through brick walls for a coach they trust who has their best interest at heart, and some coaches will stay up nights in search of a solution to what is best for the player.

HELPING

I consider myself a teacher, and I've tried to be a leader.

Telling a player to get better or work harder is never going to be enough for most players. As a coach, you need to establish a set of tools that you can utilize to engage these young people. Every coach needs to adopt a set of tools that can be used to communicate and measure outcomes. I favor categories of statistical data that will allow me to not only challenge my players but equip us to measure success, even if only incrementally.

As much as possible, I utilize competitive drills and visual examples. When I coached with the Charlotte Hornets, I worked with Glen Rice, who was already an All-Star player and outstanding scorer. When Glen and I came together, he had already made quite a career for himself has a catch-and-shoot player. He did well receiving a pass in an open area, shooting the ball, and making the basket. However, I felt, and Glen agreed, that he could also improve his numbers by mixing it up and taking a couple of dribbles to get closer to the basket, which could increase his field goal percentage. Generally, the closer you are to the basket, the higher your percentage of completion. For all of our discussions of technical detail and strategy behind our shared ambition for him, the most critical component was his desire to do what was necessary to get better. It was like the old saying that everyone wants to be great, but not everyone wants to do the preparation required. We coupled his desire with film sessions. After a couple of game film sessions, Glen began to understand the value of attacking the basket with one or two dribbles. Not only did he increase his field goal percentage over time, but he also ended up at the free-throw line for an extra point regularly because he was fouled as a result of advancing toward the basket. For Glen, my instrument was films, films, and more films. His scoring increased, and so did his confidence.

TRAGEDY

As exciting as pedal-to-the-metal thrilling competition at high levels can be, there are events that will occur in a coach's life that will bring you to a full stop. Several of these occurred when I was coaching at Transy.

One came in the instance of a phone call from the mother of one of our freshman players, Chris Heylmann. Mrs. Heylmann called our home phone one morning; she spoke very quietly and said that she just wanted Eleanor to tell me that Chris would not be returning to school that day. Elo made the normal assumption that he was sick or was having car trouble and asked if he was okay. Mrs. Heylmann said, "Chris was found dead this morning." It had been a cold fall evening, and Chris and his girlfriend had parked but left the car running. They didn't know the tailpipe had a hole in it, and fumes seeped through the floorboard, asphyxiating them both. That funeral for that fine young athlete and his girlfriend was the first of too many over the course of my career.

Another very serious situation occurred one morning when my phone woke me at 4:30 a.m. with a call from the hospital. I was told that one of our players had been in a car wreck. I got to the hospital quickly, and as I entered the emergency area, I met the young man's mother—she was in total shock. The basketball player, Lynn Stewart, had been in the backseat of a car when it crashed. He reflexively threw up his arm to protect his face, and a piece of the bumper tore his arm off. It is in moments like this that the saying "basketball is just a game" takes on a deeper meaning. My whole world was reduced to answering the question of how I could help this young man and his family.

Oh God Forgive Me When I Whine
It was early one morning about half-past four,
The telephone rang, and I leaped to the floor.
I was a coach now with a team of my own,
That's when you become concerned with the ring of the phone.
I arrived at the hospital at a quarter of five,
Met the mother of the boy and he appeared barely alive.
The young athlete had met with a terrible fate,
He was out driving a little too late.
He threw up his arm to protect his face,
When a piece of the bumper ripped an arm from its place.
His career ended, he awoke in the bed,
With crying and screaming, he wished he were dead!
Oh God, forgive me when I whine,
With legs to take me where I want to go
With healthy arms that go to and fro
With eyes to see what I want to see
Oh God, forgive me when I whine.
—**Lee Rose**

COMMUNICATION

I try to keep things simple on the social side of the road within my relationships with the players I coach. The little that I understand about some aspects of these young men is to the extent that there is overlap with my own upbringing in mountain culture. Many of them are from the South, just as I am. Southern culture is consistent, regardless of what side of town you live. We are all observing and experiencing similar things, though who we are and where we experience it, sometimes dictates perspective. What I try to do is meet them in the clearing. I imagine and hope that they appreciate that I never invade their personal space by trying to be "cool" or being too familiar with them by speaking to them the way they speak to each other. On most days, I see them as young men moving around the world, as young men the world over do. Most overestimate just how much they know about a variety of subject matters, including basketball, life management, and girls. I remain amused that young athletes the world over can have a single purpose and focus on basketball for forty-eight, game-clock minutes, but when off that clock, their attention turns with equal zeal to the primordial call of the young.

Some things are just bad communication. As an assistant coach, one of my chores was to officiate the scrimmages that conclude most practice sessions. Our routine of discussion and planning was followed by a scrimmage to work out the details in real-time. There came a day when our star player Mason disagreed with my refereeing. What started as a little side-eye moved to eye rolls and slid ultimately into an announcement that he was no longer talking to me. This pouty, childish reaction was what every parent is bound to witness when their children are going through the terrible twos, but Mason was no two-year-old. He was a six-foot, seven-inch, two-hundred-seventy-pound, thirty-year-old man. Being embedded in this "titer tatt" was yet another wonder of my universe at the time. His announcement was not particularly troubling for me because we were not close enough for me to miss him. From that moment forward, we had little if any interaction beyond the practical details of me as the assistant coach and him as the star player. When I came home that day, I told Eleanor, "I have a very important thing to tell you—Mason is not speaking to me. He got very upset at practice. That just makes it perfect, doesn't it?" She gave me a puzzled look of

THEOLOGY

inquiry, followed by my explanation. I can only imagine what went through her head, hearing that this all-star, millionaire, basketball player, and her husband, this otherwise reasonable and refined man, had fallen out with each other during playtime at recess. There we stayed for several weeks of Mason ignoring me as he placed me in my very own timeout. He was never aggressive, just always looking the other way when he encountered me. Then one day, just as suddenly as I had been placed on timeout, I was removed from it, and everything returned to as it was before. As I have heard the young people say, "We was cool" again.

Getting off to a slow start in a very long basketball season can happen for a multitude of reasons: lack of talent, lack of depth, and injuries can all factor into losing. In one situation, it was due to all of the above. The players were struggling with the losses when the recently named head coach addressed the team. He said he knew some players were particularly stressed out, and he wanted to extend an invitation to anyone who felt a need to discuss the situation to do so. He emphasized that his door was open to them, and anything and everything discussed would be confidential between him and the player. That promise sounded sensitive and inviting, but the player who took Paul Silas up on his invitation discovered something quite different. After their private "confidential" meeting, Paul entered the locker room and immediately began an emotional tirade, calling out the player by name who had come into his office. Everything went further downhill from there. He accused the player of making up excuses about playing hurt and told the team that the player had blamed his teammates for not playing better.

This breach of confidentiality had a permanent impact on team morale. Each member of the team was aware of what had just happened, and at that very moment, the coach completely lost their trust and confidence for the rest of the season. If you give your word to a player that you will hold a conversation or comment in confidence, you must honor that word. The next day, following a film session, as we entered the gym to practice, the accused player, our team captain, passed me in the hall singing in a low voice, "I hear you knocking, but you can't come in!" Once that faith is breached, no apology or contrition will repair what has been broken.

While coaching at the University of Cincinnati, I had occasion to walk over to the Black Student Union, where some of our players hung out, to deliver a message to one of them. Try to imagine how this was the time before cell phones (or answering machines for that matter). Catching players in the recreation room just before the evening meal was a normal pattern. On one such assignment, I was sent to remind Johnny Howard that Coach Baker needed to see him after dinner. Johnny was playing pool with a group of guys when I entered the room. When he finished his shot I gave Johnny the message and, without any warning, he blew smoke in my face. I was taken aback a bit; more by the fact that he was smoking than the fact of the smoke in my face. Johnny was a star player, and I respected him; there had never been an unpleasant word between us. Since Johnny and I had never had a problem, I read no more into it—I gave him the benefit of any doubt I would have had. I conveyed Coach Baker's request and turned my focus immediately to the fact that I had to coach the freshman game that night and needed to get back to the arena. I turned and walked out, wiping what had happened with Johnny from my mind.

The next morning, prior to our coaches meeting, Coach Baker called me into his office. He asked, "Why didn't you tell me about the Johnny Howard incident?"

I said, "Coach, I completely forgot about it because of our freshmen game last night." Coach Baker said Johnny had told him about the incident and said that he regretted it. I told Coach Baker that there was no problem; it was forgotten as far as I was concerned, and that athletes can have bad moments and bad days, too. I truly didn't feel it was a significant incident. At most, Johnny was a young man exercising poor

THEOLOGY

judgment in front of his peers—more misplaced ego than any animus. We went on with our season and had a good year.

Many years later, I was in my hotel room, preparing to go down and board the team bus to head to the arena when I got a call from the front desk. The young woman on the line said that she had a Mr. John Howard at the front desk, and he wanted to speak with me. Until that moment, I had no idea where John had landed since our time together at Cincinnati. So much time and distance had passed since the cigarette smoke incident, and we had never spoken about that event. I told the front desk to send him up. Johnny knocked on the door, and I let him in. We chatted nervously as people do when they first see an old acquaintance, talking about how we were doing and what he was up to. He had since graduated, completed law school, and was now a college professor. We continued talking for a little while, as Johnny told me that he just wanted me to see him and know that he was alright. Then, he said that he'd made a mistake all those years ago when he blew smoke in my face, and he wanted to apologize. I accepted his apology, and we shook hands. We talked for a few more minutes, and then Johnny Howard was gone. His coming to me as he did was a class-act, and I'll always respect him for it. As I made my way to the bus and took my seat for the ride to a basketball arena like I had so many times before, I felt sorry that he'd had that on his mind all those years but was grateful that he'd looked me up and could complete the circle of that incident for himself. I wish I had the picture that I hold in my memory of us shaking hands, followed by a heartfelt hug.

This whole matter had so little to do with basketball, but this is really the stuff that makes up great coaching. I encourage coaches to be as patient as they can be with young players and their sometimes-unacceptable conduct. I want us as coaches to disengage our egos and lead these young men to a better place. So much time and human potential can be lost forever when people will not meet each other halfway.

EVERYBODY IN

I felt it was my responsibility to find a way to involve everyone in my team process. Everyone has to have an investment in the process and any success flows from it. The trainer, the manager, the daily stat keepers, and the ball boy must feel there is an opportunity for them to make a contribution that makes a difference in how far we go as a team. At a minimum, they must understand the role they have and the contribution they make to our success. The greatest challenge for most leaders is determining early and often if everyone is embracing their roles. Even more so, they must determine if their ambition matches up with their talent. We have all heard someone say, "I can do that." My response has always been, "Yes, you can, but will you?"

In later life, one of my players became an entrepreneur and captain of enterprise. He and his wife invited Eleanor and me to one of those fine places where pupils host the teacher to impress him with how well the pupil has done in the world. We were making our way down memory lane and talking about the good old days when our attention turned to the topic of the elements of success. He explained to me that he would not ever consider discussing a business deal with anyone unless his intended business partners were all seated equally in the deal by terms and cash. In other words, he wanted everybody to have skin in the game. Whatever the subject, when a person has skin in the game, it means they have something to lose, something at risk. Sometimes, it is a function of the shared attachment to some higher commitment or purpose. He went on to share with me that such an arrangement did not guarantee his success in the deal, but it did guarantee everyone's sincere intention. It made me a little proud to hear this former player tell me that he felt some of his discipline was a result of my introducing him to the notion of skin in the game.

THEOLOGY

NETWORKING AND RELATIONSHIP BUILDING

I feel sorry for a person who has decided that they have done everything in their life by themselves. I do not see how that is possible. I am certain that everybody needs somebody sometimes and that no one does anything worthwhile alone. As a poor boy growing up in Appalachia, I hustled hard to earn a dollar here and a nickel there. When I was in the middle of my hustle then, and my more elegant hustle later as a coach, I was keenly aware that others had helped me along the way. Success can never be a solitary experience. No one succeeds in a vacuum.

All along the way, I've been keenly aware of the contribution that my mother and grandmother made to my life when I was a child. That was followed by my teachers and coaches as a young man, and then there are those relationships that I developed as a coach on the college and professional levels. Everybody will need somebody sometime, regardless of your strength and ability. On the way up, you will need relationships to open doors for opportunity; on the way down, you will need a friend and a warm place of comfort in the cold world. In the midst of it all, you will need allies as you pursue your ambition, no matter how modest or grand. It is necessary to maintain relationships that act as a voice for you, advocating for you out there in the world.

Success is not a solitary experience, and I don't really trust anyone who suggests they did it all by themselves. I challenge anyone to show me differently. As a young boy I received help from the man who gave me a job hawking cokes and popcorn at the stadium, as well as people like Harry Stephenson who was generous when he stepped forward and recommended me for a job, that in the end, had an enormous impact on my coaching career. I recognize that even back then, I was receiving support and encouragement. There will always be someone who will say, "Let me know if I can help you." Many of them will actually mean it, whether they are able to do anything or not. However, it is entirely another thing for someone to actually step forward and do something.

Relationships are important. Early on, I learned that cultivating and developing positive relationships with those you share core values is an important part of your overall success. In a very practical way, it can be beneficial to career development. From a quality-of-life perspective, it also can make you more attractive to be around. People are glad to see you come and sad to see you go. I also learned that this positive relationship can lead to someone "putting you on the stump," which means helping you get the job.

This term, "stumping," is known by some to be what politicians do when they go out campaigning to get elected. I believe that stumping/campaigning is even more impactful if someone else is singing your praises. In order for someone to effectively stump for you, they have to know something about you. The more they know that is positive, the better. Otherwise, how can they have confidence in your character and your abilities enough to speak on your behalf? Throughout a coach's career, they will need someone to advocate in a way similar to the way C.M. Newton, Tay Baker, Adolf Rupp, and others did for me when I was trying to make something happen for myself. Sometimes, your conduct can be observed by others, unbeknownst to you. Perhaps I carried myself in some way, even back then, that captured the attention of important figures in a way that motivated them to want to help me help myself. It can be so much harder when you go it alone.

The one wrinkle to this promotion and advocacy is that after the word has been passed and the endorsement made, the work has to be done. As the one being advocated for, I have always felt my part of this whole collaboration is that I have to show up and make my advocate proud. In some instances, the person who sent me is putting their reputation and own character on the line when they swear by me. I am committed to making good on those declarations. I felt complimented whenever someone was generous enough to support me with an endorsement. The endorsement alone could never be enough.

THEOLOGY

I always felt committed to proving to myself and to them that I was worthy of the trust they had in me.

In my early coaching career, my mentor and friend, Coach Newton, put me on the stump. He recommended me for various coaching jobs and continued to help me throughout my professional career. I am forever grateful for his support throughout my college career. It was also through his contacts that I got involved in the USA Olympic process, when I took three different USA teams into international competition in Japan, Russia, and Europe. This also led to me serving on two Gold-Winning Olympic selection committees.

Networking can even extend to how I manage my relationship with the media. We can all fairly represent ourselves, but what is helpful is to have others represent us when we are not present. The best part of your story can never have more impact than when it is being told by others.

They say that you should never get into a disagreement with people (writers) who buy ink by the barrels. While I have always felt I had to maintain boundaries with the press, I try to be ever mindful that their words carry weight in the world and that they can stump for me and my team. I can typically speak to one or maybe ten people at a time, while journalists have an audience of thousands. While I have rarely been a media darling, I am very aware of the benefits of being within their graces. As a coach, I felt that I just needed to be myself. Coaches need to live within their skin and do whatever got them there. Aside from feeling that I might be perceived as putting on, I knew the press corps had an instinct about who is genuine or not. Whether I wanted it or not, they may have walked away, feeling that I was serious and intense—which I may have been. I still believe it is important to do what you are comfortable with. Even now, I find it a bit awkward to talk about myself. However, I realize there were many times when not playing to the press did not always turn out the best for me or our team's publicity. The press is simply a microcosm of all folks; they do their job of telling a narrative a bit more easily if you spend time giving them backstories. They really aren't the opposition; it just feels that way sometimes.

There are coaches who are media superstars with their quips and one-liners. Coaches Al McGuire and Jerry Tarkanian both had teams in Atlanta in 1977, and both qualified as masters of quotable quotes. I didn't try to compete with that because I just didn't see it as part of the game. It was my feeling that the competition was between the teams, not the coaches' verbiage. I could have possibly become one of those media darlings if that was important to me, but it just did not fit me. I was impatient with that part of the process and felt that my job was to be working on game strategies or conducting practices. For me, the reality was the game, and that was always my focus.

Before I learned better, I thought that merit, knowledge, character, and an energetic work ethic were the primary requirements necessary for obtaining a coaching job. Certainly, there is a place for those qualities, and without them, you are behind and perhaps out of the process. However, another equally relevant complement to that important skillset is *who* you know. Those personal contacts I made—the friends, coaches, acquaintances, university professors, and professional relationships—became great allies throughout my career.

Each major league sport, in its own way, has had a series of efforts to promote fair hiring practices. I am not sure of how effective any of these programs are, but in some way, the effort may be needed to help fairness along. In the management level of basketball, as in other businesses, most hires have connections and know someone on the inside. It makes sense to me that if no one knows who you are, how will they be able to present you with an opportunity?

As the director of the NBA Development League for seven years, I encouraged those young men to network with co-workers and stay current with what was going on in their environment and culture. I advised these young coaches when they were starting out to find someone to be their champion, someone who would put them on the stump. I have tried to help put young coaches on the stump, especially as I got older and my network broadened. I counseled that they need someone to vouch for them, to put in a good word. Some people view relationship building and networking as sucking up or something that is unflattering. As talented as you may be, you should never underestimate the value of having people know who you are and for you to know where you can find the people you may need when the time arrives. There will come a time that you will need to make a call or ask for a meeting in order to get something done. In the words of the old Dean Martin song, "Everybody [needs] somebody, sometime." Well, he actually said love instead of need, but hopefully, you get my point.

One of my first coaching jobs came on the heels of a happenstance meeting with my former coach, Harry Stephenson, and the University of Cincinnati Associate Athletic Director, Bill Schwarber. Harry discovered that the new head basketball coach at the University of Cincinnati, Tay Baker, was looking for a second assistant coach to complete his staff. Harry recommended me for the job, and a day later, I got a call to interview for the job with Coach Baker and the AD George Smith. At that point, I didn't know any of these men, but Harry did, and his advocacy put me in the position to interview and then be offered the job. This was a practical example of the importance of having someone in your corner when it comes to getting a job recommendation and, ultimately, the position. During my time in the NBA, folks such as Bob Bass, Willis Reed, Del Harris, Senator Herb Kohl, Sam Vincent, and Stu Jackson, were all very supportive of me. My knowing and having worked with them over the years was the foundation for many of the opportunities I have had.

THE RIGHT ASSISTANT

One of the reasons some people have success as head coaches is because they have the right assistant coaches supporting them. I had the great benefit of working as an assistant to great coaches, and once I became a head coach, I relied on the assistants that I hired to assist me over many years. Everett Bass was one of those talented individuals. When I took the UNCC job, the first person I contacted was Everett. Our relationship went back to Transy, where he was my first recruit. He had shared his interest in getting involved with coaching with me over the years. Everett was extremely competitive and an outstanding player for us at Transylvania during my first go-around. Following his graduation, he continued his education at Kentucky State in Frankfort, where he earned a master's degree. Later, as an assistant coach, he was our major recruiter as well as a player evaluator and defensive strategist.

Recruiting is the lifeline of successful college coaches, and Everett Bass was one of the best. When you are recruiting young players, you have to be in constant contact with them. You want them to know that you have a sincere interest in them and their families. Someone from your organization has to represent your interests. As an assistant, you spend a great deal of time building a rapport with the players you are trying to recruit to your school. You want the player to feel some sense of relationship with this place that you are trying to persuade him to come to for four years. Everett and I had history, so he knew what I wanted and expected from a player. He also knew the temperament and culture of these young players. He conveyed to the recruits and their parents that the athlete would have to work hard and that much would be expected of him in terms of conditioning and team play. Recruits and their families mostly want to be assured that they will be treated fairly. The families of players we were recruiting felt a certain acceptance and confidence in this tall, handsome, talented man, who, in many instances, looked like them and had been where they were.

When Everett wasn't on the road, his specialty was working with defensive fundamentals and assisting in defensive matchups. He was knowledgeable about our offensive and defensive style of play and was an outstanding communicator. There was a counseling function in Everett's role. He was able to listen to what I wanted and communicate that to different players when teaching our complex system. All people do not process information the same way, and Everett had an innate ability to communicate and help our process. I guess, from that standpoint, he was multi-lingual. As the makeups of teams are constantly changing, our players came from a multitude of cultural, economic, and racial backgrounds. Everett always appeared comfortable wherever he found himself at the time.

Sometimes it might be something as simple as passing his hair clippers to one of the players so that player could remove facial hair. It is hard to imagine in this modern time that back in the 1970s, players were not allowed facial hair, let alone tattoos. Maintaining a clean-shaven face was not a major problem unless you suffered from something called Pseudofolliculitis barbae. It causes razor bumps and massive skin irritation for some black men because of the nature of their hair growth. The short of what could be a long tale on black hair and skincare is that some black men cannot shave with a razor. The solution could have been for the player to wear a beard, but that was against our rules. I cannot recall if this rule was stated in NCAA regulation, but I always preferred our young men to be clean-shaven. The solution was for them to use barber clippers. The clippers cut the hair in a manner that prevented it from curling back into the skin, and causing in irritation, discomfort, and bumps. I am telling you what seems to be much about nothing, but it matters if it is you and your face becomes inflamed and irritated each time you shave.

Everett's gesture to one player was to lend him clippers on a trip and encourage the young man to get his own when we returned home. This was a benefit of having a man like Everett on our team. There is just no place I would have learned that. It's out of my cultural area, so to speak. In addition to helping players with matters of grooming and hygiene, he was always a huge asset to me, players, and other staff members in many ways.

ALWAYS LEARNING

I have learned many lessons over the years. Some by experience, others by instruction, but always learning in a variety of circumstances. When I was young, most things for me were sports, so I attached most of my lessons learned to a particular sports activity. Along the way, I discovered that what looks like a basketball lesson can easily apply to so many other places in the world that have very little to do with the bouncing or tossing of a ball. The politics and science of basketball are very similar to those of every other arena in the world. My friends from different disciplines (higher education, business, and society in general) marvel at how basketball's lessons apply to what everybody else does in their lives and careers. The fundamental principles of basketball can be found everywhere if you just look.

Dr. Jim Broadus, Dean of Education, Transylvania, was a consummate educator, intellectual, and gentlemen. Dr. Broadus had been a national negotiator for President John F. Kennedy during the civil rights movement when Governor George Wallace stood in the doorway at the University of Alabama, attempting to block desegregation efforts. For me, and many others, Broadus was a wise soul. One of the end results of our conversations was that as a young man, I became even more encouraged to always be inquisitive and to take advantage of others' wisdom. His office was just off of our practice floor.

On most days, he would watch different parts of our practice with interest. As the players finished and left the floor, he and I would sit on the edge of the stage next to my practice floor in the gym, looking out at the court and exchanging ideas. Dr. Broadus was eager to analyze why something was done or not done. If there can be academic discussions about basketball, we had them. He wanted to know why I made the players pick up a teammate when he fell; why players are required to say out loud it was their fault when a turnover occurred. Both were done because basketball is a team game, and everyone

THEOLOGY

involved makes up the one unit. When an error was made, my players were encouraged to acknowledge the mistake and perhaps generate team building around a commitment to getting it right the next time. I tried to help him understand that picking up a player after a fall is a subtle gesture of affirmation. When I help my teammate up off the floor, it is a brief yet effective way to let them know I am there for them. And if I am there for you, perhaps you will be there for me.

Dr. Broadus wanted to know why, when we practiced our full-court press attack, I used eight men on defense instead of five—that was done because it presented a greater challenge for the offense and emphasized how our cuts and passes had to be more precise when attacking the pressure of eight defenders. At the same time, we might draw parallels to where these principles might appear out in the larger world, mostly around concepts like team building, leadership, preparation, and consistency. Good team comradery and great relationships can lead to individual and group success. His questioning helped me verbalize and examine the reasons for my actions. He made me think through the drills I organized for our practices, and perhaps I offered him a new way to look at the same thing all over again. Many of our exchanges revealed just how related basketball culture was to so many other non-basketball places.

I recommend always making yourself available to advice and seeking discussions with people other than those in your particular field. And if you are fortunate to find such a wise soul, engage in dialogue with them and encourage them to fire away. I would add that I try to be careful in my selection of the people I choose to listen to. Just like a great mentor tests his pupil on occasion, I believe the same can be said for the mentee checking in with the mentor. This is perhaps especially so when you have a mentor who is very eloquent in speech but lacking in content. Being mentored is an active process for both parties. The quest is to determine just what their contribution is to your life or career. More precisely, do they make you better?

CINCINNATI

MOST OF MY early coaching career had me at Transylvania, with the exception of the three years I spent at the University of Cincinnati. I was truly excited about going to UC to coach Division I, the highest competition on the college level sanctioned by the NCAA. Expectations naturally run high when changing jobs of any kind, and this is especially so when making what is perceived to be an upward move. The resources, the budgets, the facilities, and the stiff competition night in and night out had everyone believing that it did not get better or higher than Division I. The university had an enrollment of over twenty thousand, and the Armory Field House only seated eight thousand. Sellouts were the rule. The standard had been set when Ed Jucker coached the Bearcats in back-to-back NCAA Basketball Championships in 1961 and 1962. It almost became three in a row, but they lost in the final game in 1963 by two points. The expectation at UC was to win and win big.

Cincinnati was a much larger, fast-paced, metropolitan city with both a professional baseball and basketball team. The Cincinnati Reds baseball team was always a draw for that region, and the NBA Cincinnati Royals had Oscar Robertson—the Big O—as their star at that time. Robertson was an enormous star of that generation of basketball players. One of his claims to fame was that he averaged a triple-double for an entire season—double digits in scoring, rebounding, and assists. This was a heady time for Cincinnati, and I was a part of it.

COACH LEE ROSE

Tay Baker was the head coach at Cincinnati when I arrived. He became my boss and mentor. A young coach starting out could ask for better than Coach Baker but would be unlikely to find it. The head coach for any team sets the culture for that team. He was a no-nonsense man of few words and an outstanding basketball strategist. My time at Cincinnati would prove to be an excellent complement to the earlier training I had received from Coach Newton and Coach Stephenson at Transylvania. It was fertile ground for me as a young and ambitious coach who was eager to learn how to do things the right way.

The difference in coaching in my earlier position at small-college Transylvania compared with the University of Cincinnati was like running a 100-meter sprint at Cincinnati compared to a slow jog at Transylvania. There were all of these moving parts that needed to be gotten just right. Moving from the assistant at a small school to an assistant on the big stage meant I was the low man on this totem pole, but it made sense to me. I fully expected to move up that pole as my experience and understanding increased. Hard work had always been my ally, and this place would be no different. If my hard work paid well or had a purpose, it was fine by me.

Having moved up to Division I also had its benefits. The staff at UC all went to The Cloisters in Georgia in the summer for a retreat and planning session. The Cloisters was a very fancy resort area that I'd read existed but had never seen in person. I was in high cotton, or high tobacco, pick your crop. I felt like I had moved up to the first-class cabin. This was the first luxurious trip of the many I would ultimately experience over my long career.

There were plenty of golf outings with boosters and alums, as well as golf games just with staff. Any golf for me is probably more golf than I need in my life. I just never caught the inspiration. However, I discovered that golf was more than just golf—it was political. Coach Baker detected my reticence around the sport. He summoned me to his office for a conversation on the fine benefits of golf. It seemed that a lot was going to happen during a golf outing that he did not want me to miss. Between holes, there were conversations and exchanges about important stuff like job openings and strategies. Sometimes, there was just old-fashioned gossip exchanged about who was doing what and who they may be doing it with or to.

Coach Baker directed me to a fellow to buy a set of golf clubs that ended up costing me a hundred dollars. I went as "suggested," but all these years later, I still want my hundred dollars back. Better yet, I suppose that if I had just passed that hundred dollars to my golf partners, I would have been in better stead with them, instead of them having to drag me from hole to hole.

The coach was full of lessons. One day, when I was sent to scout the University of Louisville, we had a terrible snowstorm; transportation in and around the city was almost paralyzed. Something about the geography and climate of the Ohio Valley created some of the most serious snowstorms that I would see in my lifetime. Traffic was at a crawl, and I got to the office around 11:00 a.m. I called about road conditions to Louisville and was told that no cars should be on the roads. Coach Baker called a noon meeting, at which time, I told him I could not drive on the highway and would not be able to scout the University of Louisville that night. Coach Baker asked if I had the bus schedule, and I said no. Had I checked the train schedule? I answered no again. How about the airport? No. Leaving from nearby Dayton? Again, of course, no. With each response, I sank deeper into disappointment at myself and for the team.

It might seem like a simple matter, but I learned a great lesson: when trying to solve a problem, make sure you exhaust every possible solution. Don't be so easy to give up just because the first option does not work. Moreover, don't give in just because you have a reason to. I walked away from that meeting feeling awful, all because I wasn't prepared for what, in hindsight, would have been simple enough to do. I said I would get right on it, and I did. I would go on to use this as an example time and again with all my assistant coaches. I eventually made my way to Louisville to scout the game. Unfortunately for me, there was no magic solution to my problem. I was left with driving what felt like inch-by-inch to Louisville. I suppose my takeaway lesson was that sometimes you just have to do what has to be done—even when it is the most difficult option.

Following three straight very successful seasons at the University of Cincinnati with NCAA tournament appearances and top-ten rankings, I decided to see if there were any openings outside of Division I programs. During the course of my career, I wanted different things at different times. I doubt that any coach is 100 percent sure about what they will do next—we just know we are going to do something. It was like I was responding to the different seasons of the year. I learned a lot about basketball at Cincinnati, and it was great working with Coach Baker. He would become a lifelong friend, for whom I still hold the utmost respect and unforgettable memories of our three years together. He was kind and ethical as a person and as a coach. I am glad he was a part of my journey.

It's interesting how things play out. It appeared that I would have to decide between seeking a position that would improve my family life with my young boys or continue to be absent from home life. There was just no question that I wanted to be in a program where I could spend more time with my family. I had discovered first-hand how consuming a Division I job could be. I simply didn't want to spend so much of my time away from Elo and our two sons while they were so young.

As I've mentioned, I was raised without my father. It was important to me to be in a more settled, family-friendly environment, such as what I knew existed at Transylvania. For that reason, as the 1967-1968 season came to a close, I was looking at available college opportunities that would demand less time away from home. The University of Louisville called and offered me a position on their staff, but I declined. My feeling was that being an assistant at Louisville would be a carbon copy of my University of Cincinnati experience, just more of the same. I accepted the head coaching position at Transy, which lasted six years.

UNIVERSITY OF NORTH CAROLINA, CHARLOTTE

IN THE SPRING of 1975, while at Transy, I was contacted by the University of North Carolina at Charlotte to discuss an opening for head coach and athletic director. I went to Charlotte for an interview and met with a large panel consisting of alumni, current students, professors, administrators, and community business leaders who were supporters of the university. The UNCC interview process was an indication of the enthusiasm and involvement to come. I had this opportunity to interact with students, faculty, athletic officials, and others across the spectrum of supporters and fans. They left me feeling that this was their program also. That was the beginning of an unforgettable three-year journey. I would truly look back on this time as the good old days.

From the beginning, everyone at UNCC appeared and performed like they had skin in the game. The relationships and support I had as Athletic Director and Head Basketball Coach were what any basketball person longs for. It felt like our basketball team was part of a larger team, all pulling in the same direction with the administration, faculty, athletic staff, students, fans, city, and volunteers, who helped make the program what it was. The support of the community manifested in so many ways. It just worked better when the people that I worked for and with had shared intentions and spirit. For me, it wasn't a matter that I had to be right; it was simply that I worked better as a coach when I felt that we were all on the same page values-wise. Given the differences that can exist within a group, finding a group like this is always a challenge.

Almost from the moment the university hired me, Dr. Dickey gave me the most welcome advice I ever received from an administrator: "When you encounter problems, and there will be problems, bring them to me, and let's solve them together." Now that was music to my young, ambitious ears. The longer I continued my coaching journey, the more I realized just how rare that kind of cooperative spirit and support was.

The indomitable Ms. Bonnie Cone, founder and matriarch of the university, had willed the university to existence with her passion for education and her business acumen. She mixed all of that with the perfect balance of charm and friendly persuasion. We lived in the same neighborhood, and she always bestowed her affection on me by calling me "her coach." I liked that.

Charlotte was an easy city to get used to and like. The people were at the ready with warmth and hospitality. The energy surrounding the very young university was palpable. UNCC was this small school just a twenty-five-minute drive from the heart of Charlotte. They had only played basketball at the Division 1 level for five years.

In addition to a group of very capable team leaders, there were also some talented basketball players eager to prove themselves. At UNCC, I wore many hats in addition to those of coach and athletic director. I was responsible for raising the necessary funds to grow the athletic programs as well as to oversee the operations of the athletic foundation for funding the sports. When I arrived, there were only five full-time staff members in the athletic department. This number was increased to seventeen over the next three years, with many part-time and volunteer coaches helping to maintain the athletic programs.

UNIVERSITY OF NORTH CAROLINA, CHARLOTTE

While UNCC was much larger in size and resources when compared to Transylvania, it remained a small school relatively speaking. Coaching at smaller schools, I came to doubt the popular notion that small necessarily meant less. While it's true that the limited resources and smaller scales of these institutions quite often make the circumstances stacked against the smaller program, it is important not to give up or give in. The larger schools that compete in places like the Big Ten, for example, have larger budgets, the first shot at player talent, and greater facilities. Small programs take what is left. It is often a David versus Goliath matter. Those who have the choice are likely to follow the resources in the major conferences. Even for players who are unlikely to play at the next level as a professional, they still prefer the benefits of the big programs because that may be as big as it ever gets for them.

Our on-campus gym, the Mineshaft, held 3,200 bleacher seats. The name Mineshaft referred to the gold, which had been mined in the area back in the old days. Given its dark interior, the name was very appropriate. Every home game was packed with as many standing as the fire marshal would allow.

The centerpiece to this Charlotte basketball team was Cedric "Cornbread" Maxwell. I cannot be certain if the nickname cornbread came from a love of cornbread or some writer's suggestion that Cedric reminded him of the character in the movie *Cornbread, Earl and Me*. That was a small-budget film from the mid-seventies that coincidently starred another future Hall of Famer, Jamaal Wilkes. At any rate, the nickname stuck for Cedric for a long time. Cedric had averaged 12.2 points and 8.8 rebounds per game as a sophomore prior to my arrival. After a year of us working together, he was scoring 20.0 pts and averaging 12.1 rebounds. He was a classic free-throw shooter. Every shooting clinic worth their salt encourages a shooter to put plenty of arc on the ball and finish the lift with the middle finger, directing the ball to its destination. Each time, as Cedric paused and began the setup dribble at the free-throw line, he followed it with a shooter's pose before releasing the basketball from the fingertips of his elegant hands.

My initial task was going to be setting a more respectable schedule of competition. I was eventually able to schedule schools like Tennessee, Maryland, and other major sports programs. Our small gym had its charm and benefits, but I was intentional in my scheduling of as many major programs as possible. I wanted to attack the myth about small programs head-on. When we went on the road and played in twelve-thousand-seat coliseums, I was hoping the experience would help our team adjust to large, hostile crowds in preparation for moving up. I encouraged everyone's involvement in our little program. I was constantly trying to get university administration, the student body, and the city itself to elevate our requirements and expectations of ourselves.

BITE OF THE BIG APPLE

At the end of our first year, it was ambitious of me to want us in postseason play, and the National Invitational Tournament (NIT) in particular. This postseason tournament was held in New York City at the famed Madison Square Garden. You would think there would be an exact science to the selection process and development of the competition bracket, but it's actually a case of the application of rough justice—the kind of rough justice that says the system works, but it isn't necessarily tidy.

I had never before stepped foot in the famed Madison Square Garden (which by the way, is more round than square). Yet, with the help of kind words by Adolf Rupp and our respectable team record, there I was. I went in through the massive front gates and took the escalators up to the playing level. It was just our staff guy Kilgo and me as we arrived with our information in hand to pitch the tournament committee on why we should get an invitation to their dance. A gentleman introduced himself and escorted us back through dark

UNIVERSITY OF NORTH CAROLINA, CHARLOTTE

tunnels to a room where the seven-member NIT committee convened. It was a classic, smoke-filled backroom.

The cigar smoke hung heavy as Kilgo, and I stood out like two mules in the Kentucky Derby. I had watched scenes like this in the movies, but there I was living it. When I finished presenting my case for why UNCC should be entered into the NIT competition, Pete Carlesimo said, "That's it," as more of a statement than a question. The whole process had taken about ten minutes, and nothing about our exchange gave me any feeling of optimism. There were no questions, no "thanks for coming," no "have a safe trip home"—just "that's it." We turned and walked out with a feeling of complete despair and emptiness. There was nothing to do but head back to Charlotte and wait.

What seemed like forever as we waited for the news was actually just until the next day. At about 1:30 p.m., I got word that I had received a call from New York and was to return the call immediately. I ran back to the office. I called Pete Carlesimo, and he issued the invitation to UNCC to participate in the NIT along with the statement, "Be sure you don't let us down." We were the sixteenth team invited (in a sixteen-team field), and the pressure was on!

In 1975, the NIT played all its games there at the Garden, where it was "win or go home." Part of the great attraction of the tournament was the very fact of being in "The Big Apple" for the entire tournament. Eleanor and our two sons, Mike and Mark, were thrilled. We were all excited to be invited. Again, I reminded the team that we needed to make a good showing because the committee had gone out on a limb to select three teams from North Carolina to the tournament, and we'd been the last one selected. Our showing here could be the beginning of something special. If we did really well, we could create a good reputation for ourselves and our program. Our euphoria about being invited soon evaporated when we realized our first opponent was the University of San Francisco, a team that had been ranked as high as sixth in the national rankings that year. We could do this—it would not be easy, but we had our work cut out for us.

COACH LEE ROSE

We beat San Francisco and continued to advance in the tournament. Each tournament win felt even more fantastic for our program than the win before. All this winning brought with it a very unique problem—making provisions for what was becoming an extended stay in New York City. We had left Charlotte with just enough hotel and meal money to get us through one game. We wired back, requesting more money. In fact, we wired back on four occasions because we always received just enough money for one more game.

Our time in New York City was an incredibly rich yet challenging experience. All the needs of the team had to be taken care of while operating out of an incredibly small hotel room. Again, cell phones were not around at this time. Phone interviews with media from all over the country took place on our hotel phone. There were personal calls relating to our two junior-high-school-aged sons, friends calling with congratulations, and requests for tickets. Eleanor would yet again flower in her unofficial position of handling what needed to be handled. She often conducted our phone business by sitting inside the small closet in our room in an attempt to give each other a little privacy.

We had to find practice sites and then find the subways to get there. Roaming through the crowded streets of Manhattan with a basketball team, coaches, a trainer, and a manager was surely a sight to behold. Mike Stikeleather was our team manager, who worked out the logistics of getting the team laundry done, scheduling team meals, and many other things. Dave Taylor, of the Sports Information Department, had his hands full setting up media interviews for the team. Only later did Dave share with me how fragile his health was at the time, but he'd decided that this was too big to be missed. He decided to be sick later. Like everyone involved in our program, he did his job—period.

The support of the community manifested in many ways. Following one of our practice sessions, a reporter asked me a question about our school song. I told him we didn't have one. This got back to Charlotte, and within two days, Loonis McGlohon, Charlotte's resident composer, solved this issue in fine style by composing a team song. Having anyone who actually knew the words was another matter.

We attended several Broadway plays, and seeing the original casts of *The Wiz* and *Pippen* was an exciting experience. On one of those nights, we had what shall remain one of our great highlights. Walking back to the hotel as we returned from seeing the famed production of *42nd Street* on Broadway, the marquee at "the garden" read, "Welcome Coach Lee Rose and the UNCC 49ers." We were even invited as a team to march in the St. Patrick's Day parade down 5th Avenue. Suddenly, Charlotte's team was the talk of the city and much of the sporting world.

Every year, there is some storyline that attaches itself to a team in postseason play. One year, it was something silly as a series of events leading to a player losing his shoe while in play. The great storyteller and sports commentator Al McGuire named the player "Shoeless," and it stuck. Shoeless was a player of modest talents but became famous throughout the entire run of that postseason tournament simply because his shoe fell off. In our case, in the NIT, our UNCC team was known as "The Mean Green Machine." In addition to the obvious being that our team color was green, I suppose that mean rhymed with green. I would like to think that it stuck because we played in a focused and determined manner. Not sure how mean we were, but our team came to work for the full forty minutes. We were aggressive and fearless. Our Cinderella story would swell with each win, with each moment that our team hustled and executed, and with each free-throw that Cedric Maxwell hit and followed through with that drop of his hand.

Everybody loves a winner. Not only do they love a winner, but sometimes winning games also wins you the favor of the money people. There are all these backstories to glory—in some cases, I did not know about some of them until years later. That is not because the story wasn't known to others, but because I was 100 percent focused on the games. During the time the NIT was going on, the University was focusing hard on a campaign for higher-education bond money. UNCC had only $4,000 in total campaign contributions to use for publicity and no money from state funds. The university desperately needed TV exposure for the bond campaign but had almost no money to buy ad time. I was told later that the Charlotte camera crew who was televising our games from New York was told to pan on the cheerleaders at timeouts and half-time breaks. The cheerleaders were parading a handmade banner (made from a sheet quickly donated by one of our administrators) that said, "GO 49ERS! VOTE FOR BONDS!" The cheerleaders navigated around the floor, the team played beautifully, and UNCC carried the rest of the state of North Carolina in higher-education bond votes. This could have been straight out of one of those movies on the barnstorming days of the old American Basketball Association (ABA).

The next team we faced was North Carolina State, an Atlantic Coast Conference (ACC) team. Playing an ACC school is one thing, but beating them is something else, especially in postseason, tournament play. Playing North Carolina State in the semifinals of the NIT Tournament was a big test for us. They had only beaten us by three points at their place earlier in the year, so getting them on a neutral court in the tournament made us feel we might have an advantage. After the dust had settled on our long, hard battle with the Wolfpack, UNCC had defeated an ACC team for the first time in its young history. Even better news, we had advanced to the NIT finals—the devil in that detail was that we would be playing against the powerful University of Kentucky.

I had coached against the University of Kentucky several times in my career, and it was never an easy assignment. Aside from the pure strength and athletic talent of the Kentucky program, I had strong emotional ties to both the city and state. It was in Lexington, home of the Wildcats, that I'd learned to play and grown to love the game of basketball. I had gone to bed for years listening to radio broadcasts of UK's games. I received almost all of my education in that city, all the way through earning a master's degree from the University of Kentucky.

UNIVERSITY OF NORTH CAROLINA, CHARLOTTE

As was the norm, Kentucky was a powerful team and had rolled to the NIT finals on the backs of their All-American recruits, Rick Roby and Mike Phillips. We had gotten there, but we'd paid the price. Our starting point guard, Bob Ball, had re-injured his back and could not bend over; his backup, Skip Shipman, had sprained his ankle in the last minutes of the win over NC State and was unable to play. Junior Melvin Watkins, a 6'4" small forward, was introduced to a new position "Point Guard" that night. He did a great job and followed up by later becoming our point guard of the future. Cedric performed well and each successful loft of that basketball, sending it on its way through that net, edged him closer to the final vote as the Most Valuable Player of the NIT. That was a highly unusual accomplishment because we did not win that game. That night belonged to Kentucky.

The city of Charlotte had a parade for the team when we returned home—and what a parade it was. Kids were let out of school, there were speeches in the middle of Tryon Street, and people lined up three and four deep along the way. The streets were packed, and the townspeople were in love with the team. We accomplished a goal that we had set for the season before it began: to play in a major postseason tournament and to beat an ACC team. After only five years of Division I participation, UNCC exceeded the NIT committee's expectations (and perhaps our own) and created community and state-wide interest in this small institution and its programs. I was named the Sporting News National Coach of the Year in 1976 and also was awarded the Citizen of the Year in Charlotte.

GETTING BETTER

Excitement, enthusiasm, and expectations were running high as we began our second year at UNCC. Mike and Mark sat on the end of the bench at all games—they loved everything that was going on. The schedule was stronger, there were more home games planned for the downtown coliseum, and season tickets and athletic foundation membership were on the rise.

We also added a solid player with the addition of Chad Kinch, a 6'4" guard from Perth Amboy, New Jersey. Chad called us three weeks before school was to start, asking if we still had a scholarship available because he had decided that he would like to come to UNCC. This young man was a fierce competitor. For a long time, his was the name I used when I wanted to illustrate how something should be done. Much like parents that use one child as a standard for the other children, I would invoke the name of Chad Kinch to the many players who would come after him. Adding Chad to our returning starters of Watkins, Maxwell, King, and Lew Massey gave us a very potent starting five. We encountered three losses on our way to a 24-3 season. Then we defeated the University of New Orleans 71-70 in the finals of the first Sun Belt Conference Tournament Championship and received an NCAA bid.

The super highlight for Chad and all of the faithful came in the Midwest regionals in 1977 against the University of Michigan. I can still feel the thunder of his dunk over the much larger All-American, Phil Hubbard, that set the table for our victory. "The Dunk" remains legendary among 49er fans all these years later. It is that type of play in basketball that other plays must measure up to if they are to be considered worthy of mention.

As if playing in the finals of the NIT was not enough, our second season (1976-77) was a dream year. The team was winning, and most of the games were moved downtown to a larger arena. Enthusiasm built, and by the time we got a bid for a play-in in the opening round of the NCAA tournament, the city was buzzing. The UNCC 49ers were the talk of not only the ACC-dominated city but also of the state. The pairings put us in the Mid-East Regions, in Lexington, Kentucky. I felt like the local Lexington kid who had done well, bringing his team back home to play in the hallowed Rupp Arena. I can only write words about this because I will never be able to explain fully the wonderful emotions I experienced. Talk about heady times.

UNIVERSITY OF NORTH CAROLINA, CHARLOTTE

I had a unique coach's experience during one of our practices, when two of the greatest basketball coaches of all time, Coach John Wooden and Coach Adolph Rupp, observed our entire practice. It was a rare and welcomed moment for me as I visited with these two renowned legends after our practice session. I had a history with Coach Rupp but only knew Coach Wooden as this larger-than-life coach from a distance. He and Coach Rupp were peers and had attended my team's big tournament games like the one against number-one-ranked Michigan that year.

Coach Wooden was the guest analyst for our game. He and I chatted about his observations of our next opponent, but much of that was lost on me. I was trying to have it sink in that I was actually in conversation with "the" John Wooden. Coach Wooden had completed his term at UCLA after winning an unprecedented ten NCAA Championships. He was now doing television analysis for the networks. He was departing the active coaching scene as I was entering the national scene. What I do recall is how incredibly gracious he was to me. In many ways, it is that way with the giants of most industries. The truly great ones are mostly gracious. It is as if they know who they are, and now they want to get to know you.

Coach Rupp came over to me after the game and said he had been yelling for me to open up the court and drive, which we eventually did, and that won the game for us. I did not hear him during this friendly offering of coaching, but I appreciated that the great Adolf Rupp had enthusiasm for anything I was doing. Our win over Syracuse put us in the Final Four in Atlanta against Marquette, along with Las Vegas versus the University of North Carolina. The winner of those games would face off for the national championship. What an incredible fairy tale for us. After just six years of Division I competition, we were one of four teams still in play in the nation in 1977.

Attending any Final Four tournament is a unique experience. It is a whirlwind of non-stop noise and faces that swirl together into a blur of longtime friends and associates and of those newly met, whose names and university affiliations I struggled to remember. For the fan who may mortgage his home to buy tickets for the games, it is mostly about the games. But for the coaches and administrators of the hundreds of colleges and universities aligned with the NCAA, it is additionally filled with many committee meetings and clinics, along with lectures given by the hot coaches of the moment.

I was keenly aware when we started that Final Four journey that I was on new ground. I always felt myself a coach who was comfortable at practice and at ease during games but not overly excited about publicity and my press clippings. After the experience of the NIT in New York City the year before, I was not a stranger to the national press. But the Final Four obviously condenses the coaches to four and increases the number of media many-fold. Coaches need to be themselves and do whatever got them there. Or perhaps it is important to do what you are comfortable with. For me, the reality was the game, and that was always my focus.

I imagine if the older version of me could counsel the younger version, I would encourage myself to reach out to the press more often. I did work with them the best I could; I just wonder if our communication could have been better. Perhaps it would have even greased my skids if I had opened up to them just a little more. In some ways, I sense that they liked their conversations with me well enough. Members of the press corps seemed to stand at attention when I spoke and often brought their best preparation. Not because they were intimidated by me, but they seemed hopeful to gain some angle, edge, or insight into the game that had been played or that was to come.

I have heard sports described as the great human drama, and perhaps that is so. But, as the baseball great and satirist Yogi Berra said, "It ain't over until it's over." You prepare as best you can, and then you take your chances. There is a part of the game that leaves you knowing nothing for sure—you just do not know what you have until you have it locked away. As tense and challenging as competition is, we continue to put ourselves through this cycle. It seems part of our condition as humans, players, and fans alike that we put ourselves through this process that acts like a roller coaster for our mind and emotions. We create this enormous, self-imposed tension, followed by release. We are drawn to this thing as a moth to the flame.

I replay the semifinal game with Marquette over and again in my head, all the way down to three seconds left in the game. Marquette had the ball on the end line, ninety-four feet from their basket. This was just time enough for a basketball pass the length of the floor toward their goal. I assigned Maxwell from behind and Phil Scott in front to guard their center, Jerome Whitehead. Somehow, they completed the pass to Whitehead, who turned and made the field goal from the dotted line, just below their free-throw line. Marquette won the game 51-49. They went on to become the NCAA National Champs in 1977.

As we left the court, the University of North Carolina coach, Dean Smith, was standing in the corridor, waiting to take his team to the floor for the second game. He said to me, "Your kid Maxwell got fouled," in reference to a close call made by the referee, going down the stretch. While I appreciated the intention of this great basketball man, it was of little aid and comfort in my agony of defeat. I learned later that for years, basketball referees used this last-second play in clinics to demonstrate what could have been called in those last three seconds.

The great run by the 49ers came to an end. It was a mountaintop experience with a fine group of young men.

The disappointment of our Final Four loss left us feeling that we had let down the city, until our plane landed back home. When we stepped off the plane, we were surprised by ten thousand people waiting to welcome us back. Once again, the students and the city gave incredible support to the program. The scene at the airport upon our return was loving pandemonium. Our airplane had to be diverted to one side of the tarmac to accommodate the thousands of faithful there to meet and greet the team. It was overwhelming in the very best way.

I took pride in the fact that thirteen of the fifteen players involved in those first two years graduated from UNCC. Maxwell was drafted eleventh overall in the NBA by Boston, was voted MVP of the 1981 NBA playoffs, and became a world champion. How could a player who had only been offered a partial scholarship until UNCC gave him a full ride accomplish all this? After his graduation, Cedric came to our home for dinner. He added a simple yet gracious touch to a great relationship by presenting Eleanor with a single rose.

Chad Kinch was also drafted into the NBA, but life for most basketball players is an unpredictable matter. So much can go wrong in the face of what could be right. For all of his New Jersey confidence, Chad was really a vulnerable soul in need of direction and positive influence. Basketball came undone for him later in his career. After less than a year in the NBA, Chad lost his way and is said to have fallen into the drug culture, and died from AIDS in 1994.

Our third season was full of promise. We had a full conference schedule with all the Sun Belt games being played in the downtown coliseum. We ended the season 20-7, hoping for an NCAA bid and thinking we'd get solid consideration for the NIT. Neither happened.

The tradition in NCAA tournament selection is that major college programs have a slot reserved for their top finishers. For smaller programs like UNCC, even though we had demonstrated our eligibility throughout the season, it felt that the selection committee pulled names out of a hat to determine our fate. In addition to requiring a near-perfect, regular-season record, small programs must have a bit of luck and charm to get invited to the coveted big dance known as the NCAA Tournament, or sometimes even the less coveted, but still desirable NIT.

After two years of a high-level postseason performance that few teams ever achieve, it was unconscionable that the selection committee would overlook us. We had gone to the final game of the NIT and lost by 4 to powerhouse Kentucky. We had lost by 2 to the eventual NCAA champs the following year. I asked the Sun Belt conference to support us in our NIT effort and have no way of knowing how much of a priority they made this.

For me, the players, and the overall basketball program, it was devastating. The disappointment of losing is equal to the amount of energy expended in trying to win. We had invested all of our energy in trying to win and develop a successful program, and now we felt defeated in equal portion.

The old saying goes that even a good song ends, and so it was at UNCC. This was one hell of a ride, but I just could not resist the pull to compete on a larger stage. As wonderful as all of the soft and sentimental moments were with this place that had become home and an administration that had performed at a world-beater level, I needed to know for myself what it would be like for me to coach in a major conference. Furthermore, I wanted not to have to fight and claw for a lottery slot allowed for small programs in the postseason.

THE BOILERMAKERS OF PURDUE

PURDUE CAME CALLING at the end of my 1978 season with UNCC. From a career-move standpoint, that call seemed like nothing but positive. I just wanted the chance to coach against the best coaches in the country, night after night. And that was what Purdue offered.

I was finishing my third year of a three-year contract with UNCC and was in the process of discussing a new contract that we had not yet agreed upon. Everyone has to deal with fork-in-the-road decisions at some point in their life and career. Do you continue your journey with what you know or strike out on another adventure? Purdue presented me with what I could not turn down. The Big Ten was one of the premier conferences in the country for basketball, then and now. The selection tradition for the NCAA and the NIT for postseason play always went through the major divisions first. Teams in the Big Ten and other major conferences who finish high are assured a bracket position. They could count on that. That was far more attractive than trying to persuade the selection committee to allow you admission to a tournament in which you had earned the right to compete.

Leaving UNCC to go to Purdue was still a difficult decision. My Kentucky mountain boy came out in me as I was flooded with the uncertainty of whether the grass was truly greener on the other side. I had to spend some time considering if this really was the moment that I had longed for professionally or not. I didn't know what to expect exactly in the Big Ten competition, but I expected it would really be tough.

Purdue offered me the position as head coach, and I accepted. I felt that I was hired because I had a fine coaching record. I had experienced winning every place I had been. I had taken Transylvania to five NCAA Division II tournaments (and one Division III), then UNCC to the final game of the NIT and the next year to the Final Four. I felt that Purdue and I would be a perfect match. I knew going in that much was expected from me, and I felt up to the challenge.

At a minimum, Purdue was going to be a grand stop along the way; at its best, this could be a long-term proposition, where my career could perhaps approach the likes of Rupp and Wooden. My mind began to race over just how I would deliver us to top conference play and consistently get our ticket punched for postseason tournament competition. I was absolutely confident that I could and would meet the standards and intended to well exceed them. I expected the enthusiasm in Mackey Arena would be unequaled, especially around a strong program. Boilermaker fans love their team under average circumstances. I could only imagine what it would be like when we were perennial winners, especially if we could add a championship to that.

From my perspective, as this institution's next head basketball coach, Purdue had stability, tradition, a strong alumni base, and fantastic support from the faculty, students, and community. Purdue had all the support systems and resources in place: health services, academic counseling, dormitory facilities, meals and diet supervision, and an excellent indoor track for conditioning.

The contract negotiations were between Fred Schaus and me, the former head basketball coach and now associate athletic director.

Fred and I discussed a standard list of basic items, such as length of the contract, assistant coaches, a television program that I would be part of, and summer basketball camp responsibilities. Normally, the athletic director, George King, handled contracts and conditions, but he was recovering from surgery and could not or *chose* not to be involved. I did not meet King before I agreed to accept the job, which in hindsight, may have been a mistake on my part. I naturally assumed that we were all on board with our potential. I should have spent more time with him and the details that I inherited, but I did not.

Some coaches love to play golf and speak to and socialize with alumni, which is important and good politics for the program, but I was a conscientious objector in this matter. I knew it was perhaps necessary for a head coach, but I felt it sometimes got in the way. I've done plenty of speaking to such groups, but as the new coach at Purdue, my goals were first to learn the lay of the land as it related to basketball. My focus was to take care of all team and player issues, such as academic scheduling, conditioning, individual player conferences, and assigning assistants their responsibilities. It was important that these issues were in place and moving in the right direction. Everything else was just something else.

SOMETHING TO CONSIDER

I met former Purdue football coach, Alex Agase, during my first year at Purdue. He and I were seated next to each other while attending a pre-game luncheon before a Purdue football game. We discussed a number of Big Ten, sports-related issues. Here was a man who had survived while working at four Big Ten institutions and was well-equipped to provide an earned opinion on coaching in the conference. I asked Coach Agase what advice he would give to a first-year coach starting out in the Big Ten. Without hesitation, he replied, "There are two kinds of people in the world—the informed and the uninformed—and you'd better know the difference." I would have preferred that he had expanded on the meaning of the words he said with a little bit more detail. However, I took him to be suggesting that I identify those who shared my values because there would be no persuading those who didn't. I understood his comment further to mean that I would have to ferret that group out for myself. There would be no major acts of persuasion—they would either be in or out or as they say back home, for or against.

THE OTHER

Coaches, players, and fans alike love sports rivalries. Rivalries can promote outstanding competition and can also create year-round animosities, whether it's high schools, colleges, or pro teams. Technically, a win against a rival still counts as a single win on your record, but it feels like so much more. It feels weighted compared to other victories or losses. There is always extra interest and emphasis on the rivalries of sports programs everywhere, on every level. When there is no rivalry, some are manufactured, while others may result organically from some event, perceived slight, or insult. Every team needs the heightened tension that rivalries bring. Some rivalries are so deeply delicious and embedded that no one can even recall how they originated. Rivalries can be like the mythical feud between the Hatfields and McCoys that had gone on for so long, all that anyone knew was if you were a Hatfield, you must do damage to a McCoy, and if you were a McCoy, you should return the favor to the Hatfields.

I grew up in the hills of Kentucky, where basketball was king, and in Lexington, where the University of Kentucky was usually the king of the SEC conference. I knew about rivalries because I had witnessed the UK and Tennessee rivalry when I worked as a teenager selling cokes at basketball games when Tennessee and UK played. I will also never forget the excitement the night West Virginia, with the great Jerry West, came to town. The whole state was buzzing with anticipation of this rivalry game, and the coliseum was electric. Cars and UK fans were decked out in blue and white, full of enthusiasm (understatement) before the game was played.

When taking the head coaching position at Purdue, I inherited the Purdue-Indiana University rivalry. Purdue and Indiana University both lay within the cornfields of the state of Indiana. Perhaps Purdue might be thought of as a campus full of engineers and slide rules—it is considered this very serious and disciplined place. IU, on the other hand, was this more laid-back school of liberal arts. I was new to all of this, so I was never quite sure what the historical rub Purdue had with IU was—I am not really sure if either truly even needed a rub. I suppose that I enjoy mixing it up as well as the next competitor, but the competition is not really that personal for me.

After I signed my contract at Purdue, I was presented a newspaper article describing a name-calling conflict between a former member of the Purdue coaching staff and the Indiana University programs. At that moment, I made up my mind that I would not get into a name-calling conflict with anyone. Before my stay at Purdue, I had a very cordial relationship with IU Coach, Bobby Knight, when I worked as a coach on the USA Olympic evaluation tryouts at Indiana. At the Big Ten fall coaches meeting in Chicago, I made it a point to speak directly to him, explaining he would not have to worry about my saying anything negative about his program because I did not operate that way. I was much more interested in how my team played than random opinions or hysterics between the opposing coach and me.

Coach Knight and I had six contests during my two years at Purdue. We each won three. We would also go on to meet in the old NIT Finals at Madison Square Garden in 1979. We met a season later in the NCAA Eastern Finals. During those two years, there was never a negative comment between us. We were two seasoned coaches who were fierce competitors. Although, I was a bit annoyed when he hugged one of my players around his shoulders as we all walked off Mackey Arena floor after a game. As an afterthought, I imagined that he probably gauged that if he were that near a Purdue player, none of the Boilermaker faithful would throw anything at him as he exited the floor.

As is often the case, people can maintain a public and private image that may be different. The rivalry to me was something for fun, not something serious. What was serious was what happened one morning when Elo was driving me to the airport as I was going to catch a flight to the coaches' meetings. As Elo was making a left-hand turn onto the main highway, the driver of an oncoming car ran a red light and hit us broadside on the driver's side. Elo was taken to the hospital, where they determined she had suffered three broken ribs. Of course, this made the news. Coincidently, when we had played IU at Bloomington earlier that year, Elo had looked up Nancy Knight and introduced herself. She said they had a nice chat at that time. Once Elo's accident was noted in the paper, she got a phone call from Nancy Knight checking in on her. Rivalries are what you make them.

THE SEVEN-FOOTER

Following the press conference announcing my hiring, I flew to Lexington, Kentucky, where Joe Barry Carroll, Purdue's seven-foot, then-sophomore center, was playing in a postseason, USA competition, All-Star game. I knew very little about Purdue's returning roster other than that Joe was a very talented, low-post player. I went to the hotel where he was staying and visited him in his room. Talking to him was my first priority—every team builds around their best player, and he was that player. Joe was unknown to me, and I had to know what he was thinking and exactly where basketball fit into his life. I realized that I was also an unknown to him, so there was a bit of an introduction on both parts.

As our discussion progressed, I asked Joe what he wanted in terms of basketball—specifically if he wanted to play pro ball. Most players look forward to making the big time, so I felt safe that that would be a good basis for conversation. He answered, yes. At first glance, Joe appeared guarded and very difficult to read, but he seemed open to our conversation. I told him that I was aware of what was needed to play in the NBA as I had coached Cedric Maxwell, who was already making a good showing with the Celtics. I told him that it was of the utmost importance that the two of us be on the same page. From there, we discussed how hard it would be and the importance of his taking on the role as leader before and after things got rough.

I explained my basketball philosophy was inside-out—we would focus on getting the ball inside to him, and it would be important for him to continue to improve his skill set. Many teams had a culture whereby they focused on getting the ball inside to post players first, and if that became impossible, they would take their chances on whatever options came after. Then there were teams that required their post players and big men to survive offensively from what they could get in rebounds. As a coach, it was my responsibility to pick the weapon that we would commit to. If I was going to go inside to Joe, I also emphasized that if he didn't step forward and accept the responsibility of being a strong leader, the rest would not matter.

I left feeling comfortable that we would have a great relationship.

Through our exchanges before the 78-79 season started, I discovered Joe to be a very sensitive and serious young man. He said he had asked Coach Schaus directly if he would be there for four years to coach him, that Fred had said yes, and then Fred had resigned after two years and moved upstairs to administration. I could not fully explain to this young man that situations change, and people and coaches are likely to change with them.

Joe also had challenges with the media. There had been a couple of articles written about him early on that he felt were inaccurate portrayals. Over time, I was sure that he would move on to a deeper understanding of the politics of media, but for now, I had to manage who he was at that time before he matured to that reality. I tried to encourage Joe to create a rapport with media representatives. Keep in mind there was just a little media to spread all around during the seventies, pre-internet and social media. A little media, good or bad, went a long way and could be picked up all over the globe. Back then, media coverage was precious and needed to be managed carefully. I discussed with Joe how important it was for him to talk to someone in the media and asked if he would agree to an interview if I could find someone he felt we could trust. I was confident that if he could have a good experience with the media, they could have a special relationship because he was much of what they wanted—smart, funny, and different.

We ended up doing something with *Sports Illustrated* and *The Chicago Tribune* that was successful enough. Joe was mature and articulate but did not budge very much from his original position of little publicly, so I turned my attention to basketball. I assumed that that would take care of itself over time. Joe admitted to me in later years that he was probably wound way too tightly. He reminded me of one day before practice, when I was passing him in the hallway, and I said something like, "Joe, you look like you are ready to go." To which he took off on a riff about the relative nature of ready, and that if a person is ready, what does that really mean? Joe said that I looked at him calmly and said, "I was just saying, hey." All these years later, we still have a big laugh about that.

He did get on board with what I was teaching and the strategy I drew up to take advantage of his skills. Joe wasn't just the focal point of our offense down low, but on the other end of the court, he was the main factor of our defense with his rebounding, blocked shots, and shutting down the middle of the floor. The spirit of starting where I am and working with what I have served Joe and me well.

In his memoir, *Growing Up*, Joe wrote: "I gradually began to climb aboard with Coach, and I was better for it. He had a way of loosening me up, and more importantly, making me focus on what was really important—playing the best basketball I could—no excuses. He taught all of his players the value of discipline and process, cause and effect, choices and outcomes. Coach Rose insisted on the necessity of preparation and study before any event in the classroom or on the basketball floor. Even now, as an adult and businessman, it never occurs to me that I will be able to just show up for any meeting or negotiation, large or small, without some preparation. Coach was not easy, but over time I feel the other players understood his concern was for their wellbeing, and they accepted his efforts to help. Most players need leadership, but so few accept it. There were times when we understood we needed what he was selling, and the proof is in the pudding because he provided me a foundation for a eleven-year professional basketball career and I becoming an all-star player."

That 1979 team included two outstanding point guards in Jerry Sichting at 6'1", a senior veteran guard who went on to play twelve years in the NBA, and Brian Walker at 6'2", who along with his brother, Steve "Bow-Legged" Walker, a 6'5" power forward, was transferring from NC State. Drake "The Snake" Morris, a young, athletic 6'6" swingman, and Roosevelt "Billie Dee" Barnes, a 6'2" hard-nosed guard, were returning veterans. Additionally, we had new recruits: junior college graduate, Arnette Hallman, who was a 6'7", physically talented, multi-faceted defensive standout; and three promising freshman in Michael "Scooby-Doo" Scearce, a 6'7" power forward, Keith "Ice Man" Edmonson, a 6'5" versatile guard/forward, and Jon "Country" Kitchel a 6'5" guard prospect; along with the other returning squad members to give us a good nucleus.

LEFT AND RIGHT

Ask most coaches about their journey through coaching, and they'll tell you stories about the players they worked with along the way.

Roosevelt Barnes was one of those memorable experiences. Rosie, as he was known, was popular with his teammates and Purdue fans alike. His teammates nicknamed him Billie Dee, after the very famous actor, Billie Dee Williams, for his charms and good looks. Fans loved his aggressive, go-get-em attitude on the floor. There are great players that often excel in a particular category at the game—scoring, rebounding, defense, et cetera. Then there are some players like Rosie, who aren't great at any one thing but are good enough at many things to be competitive. Mostly, he just loved sports, all of them. He had been a three-sport athlete at his Fort Wayne, Indiana, high school, and even played college baseball after our basketball season. Rosie's dedication and enthusiasm for sports were admirable. He was entering his sophomore year when I arrived at Purdue.

In our player-coach meeting, I told Rosie I needed my point guard to be proficient in handling the basketball with both left and right hands. He bought in straight away. It got back to me that one of our players was dribbling a basketball around campus. Rosie had decided that he would dribble the basketball left-handed throughout his summer class schedule to develop his left-hand skills.

Athletes who demonstrate this type of commitment to getting better always do. Roosevelt went on to have a productive basketball and baseball career while at Purdue. He even took a fifth year of eligibility under the NCAA rule that allows a student to play another sport after his initial eligibility is up. This resulted in Rosie's playing four years of basketball and one of football. This gave way to a five-year career as a Detroit Lions football player in the National Football League. It came as no surprise to me that he has become one of the top sports agents in the world, following his athletic career. I am sure that Rosie has applied himself there as he did when he was with me. Roosevelt was someone for our program and his family to point to with pride.

THE BOILERMAKERS OF PURDUE

FROM DEEP

In 1979, Michigan State came to our campus ranked number one in the nation. They brought with them the All-American sophomore, Earvin "Magic" Johnson, and senior All-American, Gregory Kelser. Mackey Arena provided an electrifying atmosphere even before warmups. The game was close from start to finish, and points were scarce except for our All-American, Joe Barry Carroll, who led the way with 27 points and 11 rebounds. With the score tied at 50-50, our drama was about to reach its conclusion as the game clock was down to 0:04 seconds. Brian passed the ball to Arnette, who took a quick dribble and released a shot that felt like it had come from the parking lot outside when the ball finally banked off the glass backboard into the basket from the left side. Final score: Purdue 52, Michigan State 50.

Mackey was rocking! Once we got into the locker room, the players and coaches alike were all excited, and we could hear the fans still yelling. Somehow, it just felt right to go back to the court for a curtain call. That was as far as my plan went. In each of our lives, we will do things that feel a bit out of the bounds of our normal behavior, and I had met that moment. The Michigan State team had left the floor, and it was just us and most of our supporters still lingering as they soaked in this incredible victory. I took off, and the players followed me onto Mackey Arena floor as we slowly moved around the floor, waving and fist-pumping. Thank goodness the team followed. I probably would have been a sight running around out there all by myself, but that was not the case.

The fans exploded into the moment as they stood and enjoyed it with us until it felt like their enthusiasm had carried us full-circle. It was such a pure pleasure. I am guessing that Purdue had not seen this level of energy and excitement, maybe since Rick Mount and the glory of the early seventies. Now, here we were, blowing the roof off the place. They were hungry for it, and I was thrilled to be the coach of the team that could give it to them. There aren't many times that a team gets to play the top-ranked team in the nation, much less at home, and then to defeat them. We savored every minute of the win. As I passed Michigan State's Coach Jud Heathcote outside the press room, he said, "Now go tell those writers you planned that last-second shot for Hallman!"

We had defeated the number-one-ranked team in the nation. That was the event that set the stage for any success that followed. Having a big win like that was not only great for team confidence and morale, but it also elevated our national profile. Writers and other basketball folk became curious about just who this team was that just beat the top team in the nation. This was in a time that few teams received exposure, recognition, and publicity, so being number one really meant being number one.

The next week, we traveled to Champaign, Illinois, and played number-two-ranked University of Illinois just eight days after defeating Michigan State. We defeated them, too, in a less dramatic but very meaningful victory nonetheless. It was indicative of the strength of the conference and the cohesiveness of our team that we had beat the top-two-ranked teams in the nation in that short period of time. This is the stuff that makes teams believe in themselves and the system they are playing in.

We became co-champions of the Big Ten that season. The NCAA bracket was smaller back then and resulted in them taking Wisconsin as the sole selection from the Big Ten. I had hoped to avoid the politics of the selection committee, but here I was again for a different set of reasons. We were invited to the NIT tournament and accepted on the heels of some disappointment at not being invited to the truly big dance of the NCAA tournament. However, the NIT had changed its policy of having all games played at the Garden. Now, all teams had to play-in to get to New York. The new format brought only the four semifinalists to NYC. The dates were cleared, and since the 1978-79 Boilermakers had established a new home attendance record, we were an ideal team for the NIT to address the business part of the show.

THE BOILERMAKERS OF PURDUE

The new format favored teams that could produce a big gate. True to our expectations, we had a record 39,505 fans attend the three games played at Mackey before heading to semifinals at Madison Square Garden.

Emotional sidebars filled the New York trip. We were paired against a strong Alabama team coached by my mentor, C.M. Newton. Wins against one's former coach are usually bittersweet. However, that is not the case at tournament time when the alternative is that the loser goes home. Besides, in some way, maybe a mentee is paying tribute to his mentor by being victorious—showing him how well he learned all the lessons passed down. The Alabama game probably became Joe's introduction to the nation. He was unstoppable with an outstanding 42-point outburst in Madison Square Garden in front of the New York media. He scored 16 field goals out of 19 attempts, as we defeated Alabama 87-68. Following Alabama, we would then play our in-conference and in-state rival Indiana in the final as they had also won their way to New York.

What a finale to a fun and exciting year for our team, the university, and me. While we did not necessarily come out of nowhere, we were not expected to achieve as much as we did. At best, we were probably expected to do well enough to be encouraging. We ended up winning some big games in some tough places in a year that was probably scheduled by others to be a time for rebuilding, but now we were in the championship game of the National Invitational Tournament.

Everything came down to one final shot to win it all. If they were not triple-teaming Joe, our simple solution would have been to pass the ball to him inside. Given so few seconds to get the shot up, we went with our great jump shooter, Jerry Sichting. Jerry did everything right in catching the ball and setting his feet just right before taking that perfect jump shot of his that he had made so many other times. But this shot was not meant to be. The ball caught the inside of the rim as though it might go in, then circled the drain and came out on the other side. Our hearts were broken. No matter how many times

I say that what is most important is preparation and execution, that you take your best shot and live with the outcome, and a number of similar philosophical perspectives—it still hurts when the shot does not fall.

We had worked hard and surprised a lot of doubters as we made it to the finals, but even a good song ends and sometimes not so well. We are all confronted with the larger matter of how you respond to a loss—because there will be losses. People are drawn to the games and competition because of not knowing the outcome. We provide ourselves a drama with each outing—the ups, the downs, and the finish, which may or not fall in your favor. Since loss is inevitable, everyone has to make their own peace with the outcome. The great boxer Joe Louis suggested to a writer after a loss, "If you step into that ring enough times, you have to figure that one day you gonna get knocked down." We had accomplished a great deal by being co-champions of the Big Ten and getting to the finals of the NIT, but the loss left us with an empty feeling that stayed with us until whatever the next season would bring.

INTERNATIONAL PLAY

Following my first year at Purdue, I was selected as coach for the United States Pre- Olympic Team. It is common during off-Olympic years that teams are pulled together to compete in anticipation of the grand Olympic competition every four years during the summer games. Joe Barry Carroll and Brian Walker from our Purdue team were selected for the USA team along with other players from all levels of college and AAU classifications. We played six games in twelve days, finishing with a 4-2 record. While not the record that we had hoped for, the international games remained a great experience for both coaches and team members.

One of my jobs was to gather and compile logistical information that would help our USA Olympic Team adjust to the various cultural demands of being in the USSR. The Olympic committee wanted me to give them feedback on everything that could be a consideration when we competed there, such as food, climate, and accommodations, as well as media issues, interpreters, and in-country travel. The small, six-foot beds were something that definitely had to be addressed! I still haven't figured out how Joe Barry and Herb Williams got any sleep during our trip.

Our games were originally scheduled to be played in Moscow since that was to be the site of the Olympic Games, but due to construction delays on their Olympic arena, we were sent to Vilnius, Lithuania—seven hundred miles west. Our USA Women's Team also joined us in Vilnius for their games. We were not told of this logistical wrinkle until we landed in Moscow and were on a bus headed into the city for lunch. Immediately following lunch, we were back on a flight to Vilnius. This change in venue explained the urgency of the questions coming from the international media following our luncheon. Most of them would not be able to make the trip to Vilnius.

The Spartakiade Games invited over 2,500 foreign athletes from all over the world to compete in this dress rehearsal for the Olympics. In one of our games, Herbie Williams from Ohio State brought down the house when he broke the backboard with a dunk. At first, the crowd wasn't quite sure whether to cheer or worry, but soon, everyone was cheering and beside themselves. Many of the spectators drew close to the court to get a piece of the backboard as a souvenir.

All of the fact-findings ended up being for naught as the United States boycotted the Moscow Olympics of 1980 in protest of the Russians being in Afghanistan. This was a political decision, and I wasn't on that committee. I'm glad all those players had a chance to play in those pre-Olympic games because they never made it back to Moscow for the Olympics. Thousands of athletes were denied the opportunity to compete and win on that grand stage.

THE FINAL FOUR, AGAIN

No season that I have ever been involved as coach or player went smoothly—there's always been some wall to climb. It is just that way when you have all of those moving parts of fifteen players, coaches, fans, media, and the unknown. The 1980 Purdue season brought with it the usual challenges that a season in big-time, Big Ten competition will bring. Chief among which, in that season, was that our big man in the middle, Joe Barry Carroll, met a slump of enormous portions.

When you're in a slump, it's like you cannot get anything right. As the simplest of things become impossible, you lose confidence and begin to question if you will ever hit your stride again. Confidence builds on confidence, and the same is said for failure. At some point, it seemed that everything that he had worked up to was fading away. Our team's success was closely tied to how well he did, and he was not doing very well for a couple of weeks mid-season—which can feel like a lifetime in the smaller schedule of college basketball. Fortunately for everyone involved, Joe finally found what he had lost just in time. It seemed we all did. Slumps are that way—they come, and they go.

We recovered with just enough time to gain a bid to the NCAA tournament. Being selected for the tournament may have actually been easier than the schedule we drew, which included tough Indiana and Duke squads. Everyone in the tournament is good, but some teams are really good.

Our game with Indiana was typical of most Purdue vs. Indiana contests. There was always a fiercely competitive match between these Big Ten and state rivals. There was a lot of hype and an even bigger game, especially since Indiana had broken our hearts in the NIT Championship Game the prior year. As we were leaving the floor in the first half, Indiana received a technical foul. This meant that we would start the second half with a free throw and the ball. We hit the free throw and scored on our first possession, giving us a 12-point lead. From there, we increased the lead to 20. The final score of Purdue 76, Indiana 69, didn't truly reflect the closeness of the game.

That win was tempered with bad news. The morning we played Indiana, we learned that Arnette's father had died. His father's death cast a cloud over us. Although we were moments before such an important basketball game, each of us, in our own way, spent some time putting death and basketball games into a proper perspective. In the aftermath of our victory over our archrival, our locker room was solemn with compassion and empathy for Arnette's loss.

Our next opponent was nationally ranked Duke University. That game would decide the bracket for the Final Four. Duke had future NBA players Mike Gminski, Gene Banks, and Vince Taylor on their team. Vince Taylor had come a long way from being our neighbor when he was a child in Lexington, playing basketball in my backyard with our sons.

I have always discouraged my teams from talking trash or doing anything that could excite the opponent to beat you. During my interview session with the press, someone mentioned that Duke's Gminski had told them that his parents were planning to meet him in Indianapolis at the Final Four. He was assuming that they could look past us en route to the Final Four Tournament in Indianapolis. I went into our team locker room and shared what I had heard with our team. I told them without edit, and walked out of the locker room in a kind of "I thought you might be interested to hear" manner. It's not like you need very much motivation in postseason play—this is the level of competition and reward you dreamed of all your life. The short version of this tale is, I think it may have further inspired our hungry team into beating Duke and punching their ticket to the Final Four.

I remember *Sports Illustrated* referring to the 1980 Final Four Bracket of Purdue vs. UCLA, and Louisville vs. Iowa as the surprise party in Indianapolis. They weren't the only ones surprised. Players who had exams scheduled on our departure day had to re-schedule them early, compounding an already-demanding time-management problem. No one anticipated this problem because perhaps no one thought we'd beat both Indiana and Duke and be heading to the Final Four, but we did, and we were. I had been to this special place before with UNCC, but it was somehow special all over again.

There is a sad ending to our tale because we lost to UCLA, and they lost to the eventual champion Louisville. Back in the old days, there was consolation play for losers of the semi-finals. Instead of going home, we played Iowa and beat them for a third-place finish, which took a very little bit of the sting away, but not much.

In my first meeting with the legend, John Wooden, at the 1975 Final Four, he had been incredibly gracious and welcoming with me. He would be again the morning after Purdue's loss in the Final Four to UCLA. Elo, Mike, Mark, and I all attended a Fellowship of Christian Athletes breakfast, where Coach Wooden spoke. Our family went to the head table to speak with him. In the middle of all the others wanting to talk to him, he gave my family and me his undivided attention. I can imagine that we were all a bit worn out with the emotions of our loss the day before and did not look like the happiest four folks. He seemed to take in the picture, looking each of us straight in the eye and saying, "Just remember that sometimes winning it all isn't the most important thing." As gracious and welcomed as these words of comfort were from this legend of a coach and man, at that moment, we all wished that we could find out for ourselves whether that was true or not. In retrospect, we all realized that he was fully aware of our sense of loss and was simply saying that we needed to move on.

There are memories at Purdue not tied to basketball. Purdue Convocations hosted Harry Chapin, the great songwriter and singer.

The showstopper, and a moment that remains in my heart, is when we all stood and sang, "All My Life Is A Circle." The words of that song and the energy of those lyrics made everything feel just right. It felt like the whole house was brought to tears, each for their own reasons. I just remember being with Eleanor (my perfect E)—we were in a good place, having a good time, and all was right.

> *It seems I have been here before; I can't remember when,*
> *But I have this funny feeling that we will all be together again,*
> *No straight lines make up my life,*
> *And all my roads have bends,*
> *There are no clear-cut beginnings, and so far no dead ends.*
> **–Chapin**

Wayne Doebling

SO CLOSE

Many sports fans are drawn to the backstories behind the headlines. I suppose that we all are. Forty years later, I still reflect on my Purdue experience, and people still ask, "Why did you leave Purdue after two very successful years?"

My biggest surprise was not the intense competition of the Big Ten Conference but the total indifference and lack of support from those in administrative positions. Purdue always seemed to have the resources to move to the next level but not the will. In some instances, it was bound up in the inability to disengage ego like in the case of athletic director, George King. The nature of some athletic directors is they sometimes have this ivory-tower view of the world. They tend to sit perched high above it all. For whatever hopes they may have for the university, their greater desire is their own self-preservation and dominion over all they see. So it was with King.

Looking back at our first meeting, I should have known what was to follow. After I signed my contract and we began unpacking boxes, I went upstairs to meet King. As I walked into his office, he immediately greeted me with, "You'll never make more money than I do." I stood there befuddled, feeling that I had just been ambushed; hit by a sniper's bullet. Cut off at the knees. I had "come up" to his office so he and I could circle our wagons in preparation for what was next, and that was my greeting? My intention was for the two of us to spend some time celebrating what was good and fixing what was broken. I would like to tell you that his greeting was tongue-in-cheek or just an awkward icebreaker, but it was not. He was brief, to the point, and meant what he said. That is all, now be gone. I didn't know it then and don't know now what precipitated such an antagonistic attitude. When I returned home that day, I remember telling Elo not to bother unpacking the china—we probably would not be here long. I don't know if I really believed that, but saying it out loud provided me a release of tension.

When I agreed to come to Purdue, I took the contract that they offered me with no real extras. Extras, for me, were having Eleanor travel with me on certain trips, such as the preseason trip to Hawaii at the start of my first season there. I always found the administration's rejection of that particular rider as peculiar. I just assumed they would be encouraged that having my wife there was going to provide yet another reason for me to perform at my best, and therefore, would be in the team's best interest. Perhaps they did not share my reference point, so they could not fully appreciate the inclusion of my family values as part of my discipline. They said no as though I were requesting something unreasonable. It left me feeling a certain way because my request seemed so small when other big-time institutions were giving all kinds of large sums of cash to players and inflating salaries and benefits for coaches much less accomplished than I was, even at that time. All I wanted was to have my wife accompany me on the road. I cannot know if that was an issue around budgets or just ego and control. They even seemed petty around noncash items. When the season was over, and details about the basketball banquet were finalized, I was told that wives didn't sit at the head table. My reply was that Eleanor would sit at the head table, or I wouldn't attend. She and the assistant coaches' wives all sat at the head table, but the idea was not universally embraced.

A MYSTERY

For all of Purdue's enormous, intellectual, and financial resources, the athletic administration was, at times, shortsighted. This is the institution that produced astronauts and scholars of all stripes. There are multi-millions of dollars poured into their coffers from far and wide each year, yet the gatekeepers were set to argue me down on very small matters like whether brothers Brian and Steve Walker should be restricted to the two game tickets per family, instead of the two tickets per player rule.

One of the straws breaking the camel's back occurred as we were making preparations to leave for Indianapolis for the 1980 NCAA Final Four Game. Following the last team meeting, an athletic administrator came by, requesting each player sign for their two Final Four Tickets—that was the NCAA allotment. When Steve and Brian Walker went to sign for their tickets, they were told that they were only entitled to a total of two tickets, not the two each that the NCAA designated. To think that this could be an issue for a program headed to the Final Four spoke louder than any action before that time. Eventually, Brian and Steve, each received their two tickets per player, but it took energy, time, and confrontation to cause the right thing to be done.

An earlier incident occurred after we made the finals at the NIT Tournament, I approached our Sports Information Director at the university the next fall, with what I felt was a simple request. I thought it would be exciting and appropriate for the institution, the players, and the student body to introduce and recognize the basketball team at half-time of the home football games. We were in the middle of building a great brand, and being recognized was part of that. However, the director returned with the message that he was told they were already booked by "Thor, The Wonder Dog." He said there was no opportunity to discuss another date or consider that perhaps the Frisbee-catching dog's act could be cut short just long enough to introduce our student-athletes who had done a great job representing the university. This is the kind of roadblock one comes to realize when describing, "You have to know the territory."

The powers that be seemed to maintain a disregard for my contribution to this very major program in a major conference. They seemed to want to treat me more like rank-and-file, instead of the head coach of this major basketball operation. This included things as simple as scheduling my non-team events. When we moved to West Lafayette, our sons, Mike and Mark, were both in high school, and both were excellent athletes involved in activities that most parents like to participate in when they can. That meant they had football, basketball, and baseball games that I wanted to attend. Too often, there were conflicts in doing so for the simple reason that I wasn't in charge of making the schedule for appearances or consulted about what a good time for me might be. I was fully available to do my part; I just wanted to participate in the process. So often, there was no need for it to be an either/or, it could be a let us do this, then that. What I needed was for the making of my schedule to be a more collaborative event with me involved. My coaching record never suffered as a result of prioritizing family. In fact, my contribution as a coach was enriched by not having to totally exclude my family responsibilities. Additionally, I hoped I was setting a proper example for my players and staff around family.

I even came out of the arena one day in the dead of winter, looking for my sons. Our normal routine was for them to come to Mackey Arena after their school day and after school activities and ride home with me. It gave us an opportunity in the middle of schedules to visit and catch up. I was furious to discover my boys standing in the cold after having been told that they could not wait for me inside because the arena and practice were closed. Who does that to the head coach's children?

REGRETS, I HAVE A FEW

Only my immediate family knew that I was going to leave. I didn't make a big mess out of it because I wasn't raised like that. In Appalachia, we take our lumps and keep moving as we prepare for a better day, a better way. You can't take teams to the final game of the NIT and then advance to the Final Four the very next year and not be self-satisfied with the accomplishments. When I resigned, I had no desire to make public all of these specific situations or to name names. When it comes to moral and ethical matters, I am hopeful that my nature is guiding me to do the right thing. Unfortunately for people like me, we lay in the wake of certain events with our righteous indignation while institutions move on like the old song, "Old Man River"—they just keep moving right along. Coaches, and especially players, come and go, but the institutions remain. If there were things that I could have controlled and changed, I would have. But that was not the case.

The heroic thing for a person to say is that they have no regrets. They go on to say that each turn in the road, however good or bad, has led to the place that they are, and that is just fine; change one thing, you change everything. In a very general way, I believe that to be true. However, I will probably always wonder what could have been had things worked out at Purdue University. I had come to Purdue on the heels of great success at every place I had been. While I shall be eternally grateful for the achievements and great relationships that I had at UNCC, Transylvania, and Cincinnati, Purdue was something else. Perhaps I liken it to an unrequited love of some sort or a dysfunctional relationship that I long to fix, but never will. It may have been my shot at the true big time in college basketball as a head coach.

I believed Purdue was going to be my "dream job," perhaps a place where I would stay for many years. Obviously, it didn't turn out that way. I have had a great career in basketball in so many ways over these many years, and Purdue was truly a grand stop along the way. The good always outweighed any bad. Perhaps it is the nature of the administrative beast that a coach is hired, and sometimes the institution that does the hiring will go about trying to change the very nature and thus the personality of the coach that had attracted them to hire him. Or, perhaps, it has so little to do with me in a personal way at all. Some of these events would've been scheduled to happen to whoever occupied the chair in which I sat.

My initial exuberance was based on my hopes and ambition at the potential of me plus Purdue equaling something special. I thought us a perfect match, yet they always seemed to put me in this annoying position of distraction around those simple-minded matters. I prefer to be able to concentrate on how to get the ball down the floor quicker or how to get the ball inside to our All-American, whom everyone was triple-teaming at the time. I imagine that even Purdue might wonder from time to time what would be if they gave their talented players and coaches as much regard as they hold for the institution. At times, it feels like a regime that declares, "Everything for the state!" followed by, "We are the state!"

I originally signed a four-year contract, but after one year, I met with the administration and told them I'd like to negotiate down from four years to two years. My thought was that both Purdue and I would probably want to reset the table after we had spent time getting to know each other. Maybe at the end of year two, we would have gotten settled in enough with each other to make our best deal. The adjustment was made immediately. While I was sincere in my request, I did take notice of their cavalier attitude in making this accommodation for the coach who had just led them to the finals of the NIT with an inherited team. I am unable to explain much of it—I can only report how things happened, not why. Even all this time later, it remains a mystery to me why they approached things the way they did. This was a far cry from the support and relationships I'd enjoyed at UNCC and Transylvania.

I loved coaching at Purdue, loved the players, and absolutely loved the community. My tenure there was short, but I loved the part of the stay that was about basketball and the game itself. Elo and I also made some life-long friends there whom we still spend time with. As for those things I didn't enjoy, I could not change them, and it wasn't my nature to stay and try to convince those who didn't want me otherwise. I am in agreement with scholar Charles Reich, "To be successful, you must love what you do; you must be creative and have the freedom to do so." I discovered that with Purdue, I didn't have the freedom to do what I loved. I did not want to leave, but it felt like I had to.

After retiring from coaching I was invited back to Purdue in November 2011 for the rededication of Purdue's Mackey Arena. Everyone was so warm and receptive. Sometimes you *can* go home again to savor the moments.

UNIVERSITY OF SOUTH FLORIDA

THE UNIVERSITY OF South Florida was a relatively young institution located in Tampa with 23,000 students when I came into their picture in 1980. The USF Basketball Program had just come off of a dismal 6-win, 21-loss season. They had not had a winning season in the previous four years with an overall regular-season record of 42 wins and 67 losses. A losing record and a scheduled new arena created a perfect storm for a coaching change. USF declared themselves ready to dedicate more resources to building a competitive basketball program.

In the spring of 1980, I met the athletic director, Dr. Richard Bowers, and discussed the USF basketball situation. Dick had been the athletic director at USF for fifteen years and knew the territory. He explained that USF had sold a total of just twenty-two season tickets the previous year for their brand-new, 10,000-seat Sun Dome. That detail alone indicated the tremendous amount of work to be done. At our first meeting, I was encouraged that he had a written list of fifty reasons why I should take the job. Certainly, I could think of a list of reasons, but I was encouraged that he had one, too. He guaranteed me 100 percent support and felt that together, we could build an outstanding basketball program. Dick explained the circumstances and details and was upfront about our challenges.

It is common that anytime a college changes its president, its athletic director, or builds a new arena, a coaching change is discussed, if not made. Change in one major area is likely to bring change in what is perceived as affected by the other parts. Maybe it is like how a nice suit deserves a new pair of shiny shoes to complete the outfit. Dr. Bowers and I had a firm understanding that they wanted a *first-class*, competitive basketball program to go along with the new Sun Dome, and he was committed to helping me obtain it.

Dick organized a reception with administrators, athletic supporters, and boosters, known as Green Jacket Club members. Being the huge baseball athlete and fan that I have always been, I was impressed to be introduced to George Steinbrenner of New York Yankee's fame during this time. The Yankees had their spring training facilities in Tampa, and his shipbuilding business was also based there. He was an avid basketball fan and would attend many of our basketball games at South Florida. Most people know George as this hard-hitting, fist-pumping, table-pounding owner. That was part of who he was, but there was also the George Steinbrenner that fancied himself as a coach and my advisor. I cannot tell you just how much of his counsel and conversation I acted on because by this time in my career, I had a pretty good idea of how I wanted to manage my team. However, I did enjoy the back and forth with him, and I am sure that he liked the fact that I seriously engaged him in sports theology. There was this part of him that resembled more a military officer than a coach, as at times it felt everyone on the other side had to be dead at the end of some of his victories. To say that he was intense might be an understatement. This was, however, not the relationship that George and I had. He and I had respect for each other, and for the success we'd had in our respective athletic careers—he as an owner of the New York Yankees and captain of industry, and me as a college basketball coach. We were friends.

My time at USF was less than ideal; there were many things that went wrong. Yet, like the teacher who instructs children to always say something nice first I tend to be guided by the adage of beginning with a compliment before offering criticism. And so it is in my reflections on the journey with USF.

During my six-year tenure as the coach of the University of South Florida, we competed in the NIT three times. We won the Florida Four Tournament by beating rivals Florida and Florida State in back-to-back seasons and were named the nation's Most Improved Team in 1984.

WHAT I LIKED

There is a warm feeling for any coach as he recalls the players he meets along the way. Charlie Bradley was one of the most exciting players to play at USF and maybe even in the country during his time. We were fortunate enough to persuade this local Tampa player to stay in the area. When Charlie signed with the young USF program out of Robinson High, it was a big deal for the local community and us. It turned out, we didn't know how good it would get from this tall, slender leftie. He appeared to do remarkable things with ease. In many instances, he worked so hard but made it look so easy. He went from averaging a modest 5 points per game early on to averaging 22.3 points as a junior and 21.7 as a senior. He led the nation in scoring for 11 weeks at one time with a 28.2 average. He had 24 games of 30 points or more. He once scored double figures in 84 straight games on his way to becoming a member of the inaugural class of the University of South Florida Hall of Fame.

Then there are other wonderful narratives around the rise of potential and promise. Our assistant coach, Everett Bass and I went to the Sabel Palms housing community in Fort Myers, Florida, where Curtis Kitchen lived. I recall sitting in Curtis's home as his mother told me how excited she was to have everyone so interested in her son.

COACH LEE ROSE

This proud and dignified mother went on to share that part of her history was when she lived in Georgia in a house with a dirt floor as a child, contrasting that to now, having all these people interested in her family. As our focus returned to who this young man could be if he just had an opportunity, I was reminded of the weight of the responsibility I was accepting if Curtis chose to accept my invitation to come to the University of South Florida. I wanted to participate in stamping his ticket to the outside world that offered so much more than he had known. Later on, Curtis would share that where he lived was one of the toughest communities in the Fort Myers Dunbar Community. This was a place where shootings and fights were as common as breathing. He thanked Coach Bass and me for being real with him and wanting more for him than he could believe in or imagine at the time. He said that he knew in the back of his mind that I saw him being like Cedric Maxwell as a player. He remained grateful for my including him on the National Team in The World University Games in Kobe, Japan, in 1985.

Curtis worked hard in practice every day. It was as though he could see and feel the opportunity that lay before him. Each workout put him closer to his goal and farther from the place he knew. Curtis played briefly in the NBA before settling into a career as a business owner in Seattle. I would see him occasionally during his brief tour as a professional. The first time we saw each other, I came up behind him on the floor during warmups when I was coaching in the NBA and asked, "Curtis, what are you doing here?" We both found that amusing and reflective since we were so far away from where we had first met. As proud as I am of the time that I share with my players during their basketball career, I feel equally proud when they return to assure me that they indeed found their place in the world and want me to know.

Part of a successful coach's creed is transforming his pupil and himself as well. It does something for me when I am able to participate in a young person's development. With each encounter, I try to leave these young people better in some way than they were when we came together. My great benefit from these relationships is that it is common for me to learn something about myself as well. The list is long of the young men whom I have met at a vulnerable time in their life. To participate in transforming them to their greater selves is rewarding for me. It does something to me to see these boys become men.

THE GOOD AND THE BAD

For all of the success we had at South Florida, the good memories were sometimes soiled by what felt like one controversy after the other. Just as we cleared one hurdle, there appeared another. It just felt like I could never get the momentum required to establish the first-class program that we all agreed we wanted.

When I arrived at USF, the administration made plenty of declarations to the world and me of their desire to move up to the next level and foster a first-class program. As the years passed, I realized the problem was like the old saying: "Everybody wants to go to heaven, but nobody wants to die." For as delightful as heaven may be, it comes with a cost, a cost that they increasingly refused to pay. It was as though they wanted to declare it and have what they wanted just appear miraculously. All indications were that I was running into a situation where expectations were being made without consideration of the heavy lifting required to realize the dreams. Increasingly, I came to expect pushback everywhere because it was everywhere. It was like the old tongue-in-cheek saying, "I'm not paranoid; they really are out to get me!"

The issues that confronted me were bigger than just having a deeper understanding of the matters at hand. I had to move beyond the superficial, into the understanding of the politics of the land. Increasingly, it became important to make a connection between what people were saying and what they were doing. Who can truly know what lies in another person's heart? What we can determine is how we are being treated once the dance and dust have settled. Beyond the politics, there were instances when I would be in yet another meeting, staring into the faces of people who had full authority but lacked a full understanding of the task before them.

Furthermore, there was no humility around their lack of understanding of what needed to be done. They did not know, and they did not know that they did not know, as they sat in their tower of what was more like arrogance than confidence. I have always loved coaching, teaching, and working with young athletes as they work their way through college. But political posturing simply came to be more of my job description than working with the athletes and coaching. The energy and effort required finally sucked the enthusiasm out of me.

I came to that school, fully understanding that the state of Florida was a tremendous football state and would continue to be, but that need not be to the full exclusion of a first-class basketball program. There was room for the two to not only co-exist but thrive. Dick Bowers and I found ourselves "fishing in the desert," while seeking support for what was becoming an elusive first-class basketball program that everyone was declaring they wanted. We learned that the administration's declared enthusiasm did not amount to very much.

One of the bright spots of my tenure at South Florida was the Florida Four Tournament, which we won two years in a row. Even that had a devilish detail. The light at the end of the tunnel is sometimes a train. We had great success with this tournament between four major institutions in the state of Florida. My favorite part of the competition was the subtle, undeclared, yet understood inference to everybody that the winner of the tournament could be considered the best basketball team in the state. That conclusion could be really helpful to a program like USF that was trying to come up. The tournament had been very important for us because it gave us equal footing with those prestigious state schools—the University of Florida and Florida State. It helped in recruiting, scheduling, and alumni support, but when the UF and FSU said it was over, the tournament died. I tried to make a case to the media and our people on campus for continuing the tournament, but without the support of the school president, I was doomed. Should the University of South Florida historians ever lament the lack of respectability for USF basketball, the cancellation of that tournament is a great place to start.

I purposefully sought out competing against major league programs because of the impact that those games would have on our standing and further rise as a first-class program. My perspective has always been that the stronger the teams are that we play, the brighter our opportunity for postseason play. I was never convinced why that was considered controversial, but it was. Controversy number one was on whether I should schedule a small college team instead of a big conference team from the ACC or Big Ten or similar. It filtered back to me in words that felt like a threat, that if we didn't play a specific lower-division team, "they would run my ass out of town." I'm not sure which bothered me more, that sentiment, or that the words were passed to me through Elo, who'd received them from a writer friend. It felt like little children passing ugly words around the schoolyard. One thing's for sure, coaches and their families really need thick skins. The administration finally decided to approve the lower-division game, committing to playing a Division II team, which meant we were taking the program backward.

One of my controversies had very little to do with basketball, with wins and losses, but rather was something that started out fairly benign, just a simple miscommunication. That was until it blew up and into a true storm. Believe it or not, it had to do with a music concert. There was a concert with Crosby, Stills & Nash proposed to be held in the Sun Dome. While I was out of town, a member of my staff told the concert promoters that the concert could not be held at the Sun Dome because we had basketball practice scheduled. Before I got wind of this, the concert had moved on to find another venue. While I am obliged to accept the responsibility of my staff's decision, I knew nothing about it when it was made. The staff member clearly thought his decision was harmless and the right thing to do, yet it resulted in a very negative fallout. From that moment on, I was blasted anytime a basketball article was in the student newspaper. I became the Grinch who stole Crosby, Stills, & Nash. This was one of those situations where no explanation would persuade the listener that it was all just a big old-fashioned misunderstanding.

Once the student newspaper got hold of the news, they were furious that this very popular group was being kept from coming to campus in favor of basketball practice. On the surface, it appeared as a choice of values—a wonderful concert for 10,000 students, or a practice for fifteen basketball players. It appeared to the students and community that a choice was being made for a group of spoiled basketball players to have a practice session over their chance to witness great music. Nothing could be done to smooth over this reaction. I didn't really blame the students for how it appeared to them. At the same time, I just couldn't throw my staff under the bus in an attempt to save my image and reputation. Privately, I wish that my staff or somebody had run this decision past me as the head coach, but I cannot escape the responsibility of leadership. We caught the heat of hell from the student newspaper from that moment on. The sad and tragic overlooked fact of this matter was not only would I have worked it out so that we could practice, and the concert could go on as well, Elo and I would have been right there at that concert, singing along to "Southern Cross" and "Helpless!"

Sometimes, a person will say something that may or not mean anything, but it does cause you to wonder to yourself about the underlying spirit behind those words. USF's President, John Brown, was making his customary opening comments to the five hundred supporters in attendance at our sports banquet. Included in his comments to the assembled was, "I can tell you one thing, I'm sure getting tired of being introduced as 'the man who brought Coach Lee Rose to Tampa.'" I wasn't quite sure what to think of this not-so-lighthearted comment.

UNIVERSITY OF SOUTH FLORIDA

While the audience may have heard nothing behind this statement, it left me feeling like a problem was brewing. I felt like a person in quicksand—the harder I worked, the deeper I fell into the pit. Had my image and reputation become larger than that of the president of the university? Certainly, that was not my intention, of that I am sure. The popularity contest never came to mind for me until his comment. Just by virtue of the separation of our respective duties, I certainly would have more visibility than the president. He was the master of boardrooms and fundraising to take the university to the next level of academic and financial success, while a head coach is on television, in the newspaper, and the talk of the sports world (good and bad). Those just seemed to be by definition and job description different roles, but each was important for its own reasons. I really didn't get caught up in the politics of it all, but it caught up with me.

Dick Bowers was reassigned, and the athletic program continued operating without a full-time athletic director for a long time. Dick and I had worked together even before I had come to USF as their coach. He and I had collaborated in the formation of the Sun Belt Conference, which led to him approaching me to coach USF. I missed him. The basketball program continued to take yearly budget cuts. Student support at the games had been terrific with great enthusiasm early on, but suddenly, the Sun Dome was instructed to move the block of students to a less-desirable section of the stands. This clearly stifled their support of the team and lowered morale. Despite the distraction of being held accountable for the indebtedness of the entire athletic program, we still managed to compete well enough to get two bids to the NIT during those years.

At some point, the rancor reached a place where there was no middle ground for understanding because the trust had disappeared. The scars were deep, and egos had been exposed for all involved—the administration, the students, the media, and me. Things were rough for my staff, too; having to constantly defend yourself every place you go is a tough position to be in. I found myself always in the midst of budget battles and policy and program-direction discussions. Discussions with the president led us nowhere. Given my success with a team where there had been none before, you would think they would have engaged me around some solutions for our many dilemmas. They did not.

My solution was to look for another job. Both sides of this equation were probably ready to put out the campfire. I had four years left on a contract and would be leaving that $400,000 on the table. This was the highest salary that I had earned as a basketball coach and had become the only reason to stay at USF at that point, but that detail had no sway with us. Maybe our situation was like how some people describe a divorce—it was expensive, but oh so necessary.

SEASON OF CHANGE

There were several colleges who'd expressed interest in hiring me, but I truly felt like a boxer who had fought hard and taken all the punches that I could take on this level. I felt a complete change would be the best for everyone—and "everyone" at that point was Elo and me. We had lived with an incredible amount of stress, and that isn't good for anyone. One of my biggest concerns after I made the decision to leave USF was to make sure that my longtime assistant, Everett Bass, would be named as the new head coach. While USF was not an ideal circumstance to launch a career as head coach, fixing what is broken is not only part of a coach's process, it is sometimes their salvation. Everett, as my designated successor, was discussed and written into my resignation settlement. We had agreed that he would replace me, but they did not do what they agreed to do, yet again. I was lied to and have always felt terrible that he did not get the job, but it was consistent with the USF experience, so I suppose that I should be disappointed, but not surprised.

I will leave it to USF officials to represent their positions and perspectives, but from my perspective, I had spent six very difficult seasons trying to pacify an administration that had no clue as to what it would take to build a competitive basketball program from scratch. They had promised me cooperation and a world-class facility, and I received neither. My response was if you cannot keep your promise, let us just not go any further with this masquerade. Once the faith was broken, we were never going to do enough to erase animosity. This became a crossroads for me. The culture of college sports had been one of the richest and most rewarding experiences of my lifetime, but it was time to go. I was clear that I would continue to coach, but I now became curious about a career and life away from the hypocrisy of the NCAA.

Being an assistant coach in the NBA had never entered my mind until this accumulation of disappointing experiences with the University of South Florida. There was something appealing to me about the NBA—it was imperfect yet straightforward and raw about what it was doing. College basketball and NBA basketball are both businesses operating at the highest level of entertainment. In college, many things are cloaked in the emotions of God, flag, and country. The pretention is that the college game is this sweet and pure extension of little boys playing in the backyard against the side of the barn, with just one last game before mamma calls them home for supper. While that may be so in some places, that narrative was generally no longer true once a ticket was required to see players play. Conversely, the NBA was likely to have its foils as well, but that type of hypocrisy would not be one of them.

Several times before, we had thought about the NBA, but it was something that we simply couldn't wrap our minds around doing while the boys were young. When Mike and Mark were younger, they had always been a part of our decision-making process—good schools, child-friendly neighborhoods, and a schedule that would keep my children familiar with me. That was then but now was now. Mike had graduated from Indiana University, where he'd played football, and was working on his master's degree while a graduate assistant at Clemson. Mark had graduated from USF and was playing baseball in the Cape Cod League in anticipation of the Major League Baseball draft.

I contacted some NBA friends and discovered that the San Antonio Spurs had just hired a new coach—Bobby Weiss—and he was looking for an assistant. I met Bob Bass, the Spurs' general manager, in Chicago, and had a great interview. Soon thereafter, he called and offered me the assistant's job. When we got into Elo's VW and drove along I-10 West to San Antonio, both of us knew this was the right job at the right time.

SAN ANTONIO SPURS

OUR MOVE TO San Antonio was one time when there really wasn't anything on the legal pad of pros and cons tugging at us. We made the decision to go to the uncharted waters of the NBA when we were in our forties. Our belongings were loaded onto the moving van, and we took off, driving to San Antonio. By this time, I had been involved in college athletics for twenty-eight years as a player and coach. We shed a few tears and quiet hours of reflection as we drove for two days. At the same time, we were both excited and looking forward to something totally new. I had a one-year contract with the Spurs. I did not know it at the time, but I had also just become the lowest-paid assistant coach in the NBA. At that moment, I doubt that knowing that bit of information would have made a difference in my decision making. My priority was to have an opportunity at a better quality of life, and this would be the price I paid.

The San Antonio Spurs happened to be one of the old-fashioned mom-and-pop professional basketball franchises. They were only two years removed from the old American Basketball Association (ABA) days. At that time, NBA basketball teams lay on a spectrum of wealth and resources. There were deep pockets of prosperity and resources on one end, like the New York Knickerbockers, who were owned by the rich and deep-pocketed Gulf Oil Company. Their team had chartered airlines and stayed at the Four Seasons Hotel. On the other end were a few poor teams like the Spurs and the Golden State Warriors, woefully underfunded and understaffed. These teams were often hopeful that they would make payroll. Every movie that portrayed a sports franchise struggling from payroll to payroll was probably talking about us. Teams' signing of players was driven by who they could afford more than it was based on the best talent available.

Today, everything is so slick and shiny, but fans and players alike would be shocked at just how modest everything was back then. There were these real-life scenes where the team could be playing for a score that rewarded the few fans in attendance with a breakfast sandwich the next day at the local McDonald's. At that point, no one was really interested in winning the game but rather if they were about to win a kibble.

The poor teams were usually owned by small-timers like Angelo Drossos in San Antonio and Franklin Mieuli of the Warriors. The financial barrier to entry was not as great back then as it is in this modern time. Sometimes, the small-timers would form a group of other small-timers that would chip in enough to buy a team and join the league. Their ambition was to fake it until they could make it to better days. Fortunately for the league, most players and staff at that time had little to compare it to, so there was rarely any major revolt about the state of affairs. Most participants were just happy to be a part of the National Basketball Association. It was just the way it was.

In these modern times, with all of the huge television, licensing, and apparel contracts, these same teams have moved on up. The requirement for team owners is even greater. Back in the old days, an owner only needed a down payment to get in. Today, most owners come to the league ownership already prepared with their own barrel of money and resources. It is common for teams to have their own jet planes, accommodations at The Ritz Carlton Hotels, and team training facilities. The NBA today certainly is not your father's NBA.

I remain amused that for as expensive as some of the player contracts appear, I tell my friends to keep in mind the amount of cash the team and owners must have in order to sign a payroll check for that amount.

Bob Weiss was our head coach, and I was his only assistant. You could not have worked for a finer person than Bob. There were only two of us, meaning we were the smallest staff in the NBA. Bob provided the strategies and did the coaching, and I handled the pre-game scouting tapes, the practice walkthrough, and the pre-game board work, and was an all-around general handyman. Bob and I were there for two years and even made the playoffs in 1988.

Eleanor was very helpful to the team and me during this time. She should probably add to her resume that she worked as an NBA assistant along with her other achievements. During our two years there, she would chip in by recording other teams' games on the old VCR tape system, and we would mark and tag those tapes for team film sessions. Today, teams have scouts dispatched throughout the country, providing up-to-the-moment intelligence on other teams. Back then, I would go between Dallas and Houston to scout the teams as they made what was referred to as the Texas swing. The Texas swing was when a team would come into the state of Texas and play all three teams (Dallas, Houston, and San Antonio) within a week. I would scramble back to San Antonio in time to prepare for the morning practice on game day and be prepared to sit next to Bob Weiss as his number-one and only assistant coach.

We had thirty-two wins out of eighty-two games that first year. The silver lining in our unfortunate cloud was we would be in line for a high draft pick. That draft pick would be the very talented seven-footer from the Naval Academy, David Robinson. The bad news for us was he had a two-year commitment to the United States Navy following his graduation from the academy.

Before our dreams could be realized, Angelo Drossos sold the team to local millionaire BJ "Red" McCombs, and everything changed. When a new owner buys a team, it is probably natural that they want to place their brand on this new thing they now own, and dress it up a bit to look more like them. Red hired Larry Brown to be his new coach. The NBA has this ongoing procession of the news going out through the land—out with the old, and in with the new! I would not be totally surprised if some coaches were in the league long enough to cycle back through their former team and be a bit confused about why this new place they were in seemed so familiar.

When Larry Brown was hired as head coach, I shook my head. He continues to pop up in my life like I am in a Batman series, and he is one of those villains that come to deliver bad news and bad things. At UCLA, his team had defeated my Purdue team with ineligible players and team violations. The Final Four win would later be taken away from him and UCLA, but that was of little comfort for me, trying to play by the rules and losing to an alleged cheater. Now, here we went again.

This time would have meant me trying to work with him as he transitioned into his new team. In addition to him not fulfilling his pledge to have me be his assistant, he talked "out of school" with our players about the player evaluations he asked me to prepare by telling others what was supposed to be kept private. Larry took it upon himself to tell Frank Brickowski, of butter knife fame, what I reported to him in confidence and professional courtesy. Frank will probably always hold a grudge against my report to Larry that Frank was not a good influence on team chemistry. I am thinking that is not very controversial given the on-film altercation between him and Alvin Robertson. That just seemed obvious.

Larry's hiring wasn't so bad for Bob Weiss because he had two guaranteed years on his existing contract. When you have a guaranteed contract, a team can still fire you at any time, but they must pay you the guaranteed dollar amount. The team leadership changes (being fired) would probably hurt, but he would have the compensation to comfort him. Not so much for me. I had been given the fabled Texas handshake that I would be taken care of, but that commitment never ripened into a reality. I am always at a disadvantage around a person giving me their word on a matter. I treat others as I would have them treat me. For me, my word is my bond.

Perhaps I should have taken greater counsel from the lesson of my Aunt Blanch on getting what I ask for. When I was in the third grade, my Aunt Blanch, who was a schoolteacher living in Washington, DC, came to visit. During her visit to our home, she talked to me about my schoolwork and asked if there were different reading groups in my class. I told her there were three levels of reading, Sparrows, Robins, and Cardinals, and that the Cardinals were the best readers. I told her that I was in the Robins group. She asked me to read aloud to her, and when I finished, she told me to speak to my teacher and ask to be moved up to the highest group. I did that, and the next day I was moved up without any question. I would not have advanced if I hadn't asked and if my aunt had not insisted that I do so.

That particular lesson that I carry from early childhood was still at odds with being brought up to be modest and unassuming. I grew up assuming that there is some divine justice in the world that always prevails, that good things come to those who wait, etc. However, as the song in *Porgy and Bess* goes—"It ain't necessarily so."

NEW JERSEY NETS

FOR AS ELEGANT and renowned as New York City is in regard to theater, symphonies, operas, and fine restaurants, it remains a challenging place for sports franchises to flourish consistently. This is a place where fans either love or hate their sports teams and celebrities—there seems to be no middle ground. When things are good, they can be great for a team. When things are bad, you will want to be any place but where you are. Additionally, since it has been the center of the media universe, once written, good or bad, the world will know, and it will last forever. There is a great deal of sports enthusiasm for each of the sports franchises on the Eastern seaboard, be it Buffalo, Boston, Philadelphia, or New York. For better or worse, everyone has an opinion on their team. New York is one thing, but New Jersey is another matter altogether.

For all of Jersey's parkways, shorelines, "Garden State," and Princeton University even, the Nets were considered the poor cousin to the spectacular and shiny Madison Square Garden and the New York Knicks. It just seemed that New Jersey had been left out of that party since the old ABA glory days. Players came and went, owners came and went, and marketing campaigns the same. Little materialized over many long seasons for the franchise. In some cases, teams would even create marketing campaigns with a lot of bells, whistles, and door prizes to entertain the fans when a winning record was not there to rally around. None of that seemed to work in New Jersey during this time.

When I arrived in the Meadowlands, the home of the New Jersey Nets, there had been an ongoing plague of antipathy and lack of enthusiasm for the team. Who can know if the lack of enthusiasm by some was an extension of that same challenge with the state of New Jersey?

I first met Willis Reed at the annual coaches' meeting held by the NBA. This is a gathering for coaches throughout the league, an opportunity primarily to socialize and network among each other and also get a little work in. Willis and I shared a table during a break from our many meetings during that weekend. We probably discussed whatever the current topic of interest was in the basketball world, followed by an exchange of contact information. We went our respective ways, not thinking much one way or the other as I entered the next session of the day. So one might imagine how welcomed his call was, asking if I'd like to join his staff in New Jersey. The call came at a time when I really had no place to go. I was about to be squeezed out of San Antonio. I understood that it is necessarily the way those things go in the NBA, but it didn't make me feel any better about being out of work. Players and coaches refer to anyone who does not have a position or contract as being out of the league. It has the tinge of being homeless or like a motherless child. Then there may come a day that you are back in the league, and everything is right again. That's what Willis' offer did for me.

I had this sense of satisfaction at joining Willis in New Jersey on the heels of having been dismissed in the shuffle of new ownership. My satisfaction perhaps grew upon seeing the Spurs lose 61 games under their new structure that did not include me. I want to think that I am better than that, but I may not be. In some matters, I am just not able to reach the high road that I seek. That might include pulling for someone who does me what I view as wrong. I am not seeking to do wrong to them, but should they do poorly without me, I am okay with their lack of success in my wake. Especially since their decline is not at my hands; I am just an observer. Players feel that way when they return to play against their former teams, and coaches probably generally feel that way about teams that they formerly coached. Maybe it is like eating chocolate, a victimless indulgence. The Spurs had gone on to have ten more losses than Bob Weiss and I had the previous year with far fewer resources. The new coach, Larry Brown, had four assistants and a much larger budget, while Bob Weiss had only Eleanor and me. I was okay with that.

I was familiar with Willis Reed, the basketball player long before I met him. He has this long list of basketball accomplishments, including NBA All-Star, Most Valuable Player, and Champion, to name a few. He was also named one of the NBA's Top 50 All-Time Players. When we came together, he was willing to share his knowledge about the political and social side of basketball at this level. Although Willis had some coaching experience with the Knicks and Creighton University, I am sure that he was open to my sharing some perspective on the composition and strategy of coaching basketball from a veteran coach's perspective.

I really enjoyed the time I spent with Reed. He was generous with me from the start. He told me what my salary would be and gave me a bit of advice that I had never heard before. As he laid out the details of how much I would earn under my three-year contract, he insisted that whatever else I wanted, I must have it in writing because "that is the only way you will have it." That bit of very good advice encouraged me to be more active in my contract process. I have never cared for the negotiating process and the tension that it sometimes creates. This had been a recurring point of tension for me on my professional journey that I shied away from.

I know that a contract is necessary to outline the details of an arrangement, but I wish there were some magical standard of fairness that would lead to a fair and reasonable deal and let everyone just get on with it. I have never been a fan of what goes on in the negotiation process. I recognized that I had always been vulnerable to what felt like sincere commitments from others, whether they be personal or professional. I am fully aware of the time-honored reality that a verbal contract is not worth the paper it's written on, but I will, unfortunately, assume that a person would not look me in the face and shake my hand in commitment, yet honor neither! I always presumed another man's word was just as good as mine. If I make a promise, I keep it, whether it's sealed by a handshake or a signature. This became a very important principle as we put together my contract with the Nets and any contracts I entered thereafter. I was actually relieved to discover that after the initial back-and-forth, I was able to secure a great deal for everyone. It is just in neither side's best interest to walk around feeling that they are being taken advantage of. I finally came in touch with the necessity of asking for what I want and then putting that in writing. After all, what is the harm of memorializing in writing what others are swearing they will do? Asking for conditions to be in writing for whatever I want, or what I am being told, is not questioning the other's integrity or character. I could still trust them, but it's like the poker player says to the dealer: "I trust you, but can we cut the cards?"

THE CAPTAIN

One morning, following our practice session at the Meadowlands, Willis said we needed to drive across the river into Manhattan to pay our respects to a long-time NBA executive who had just died. We found a parking space and began the walk of a few blocks to where the wake was being held. As he and I walked along those crowded city sidewalks, I had one of the most unusual experiences I have ever been a part of. Cars slowed down and, in some cases, stopped for him. People waved, some honked their horns, while others called out, "Hey, Captain!" And those in closer proximity to Willis squeezed his hand

and reached for scraps of paper for an autograph. Willis had coached the Knicks for a season, but his greater fame had been as the captain of the fabled team of the sixties. Some would begin to recount to him some now-glorious night in "Da Garden" when this thing or the next had happened.

The popularity of some athletes is soon forgotten or as the Bible says, "it came to pass." Then there are those persons and events that are forever pressed into the hearts and memories of the faithful. They were right there, saw it on television, or heard it on the radio. I had heard the phrase that such-and-such-a-person could stop traffic, but for the first time in my life, I witnessed that firsthand. Willis Reed proved that right in the middle of Manhattan and New York City as he led the parade. The spontaneous show of enthusiasm and respect shown to Willis was incredibly genuine and generous. I was proud of him and proud to be along with him for his ride. I was reminded of Sinatra's, "New York, New York, if you can make it there, you can make it anywhere." What that must be like to still be the toast of the town all these many years later. Little that happened before or after matters; New York fame appears to be eternal.

When the season begins, everyone is great on paper because no one has played a game. Every team in the league is a winner at the opening of the basketball season. We all have a clean slate. This is a time when everyone is filled with enthusiasm and hope of what can be. That is before the reality of who everyone really is or is not begins to sink in. It is inevitable that the reality of everything missing will be amplified the further you get into the very long season. However, managing that harsh reality is different than simply rolling over for dead from the start.

I never accept a lack of talent or not being a playoff contender as an excuse for not being as competitive as possible. A team may have no control over the talent within it because you are who you are. What all of us have control over, though, is effort and honest intention. Perhaps that is part of the magic of each season and each night that a team takes the floor. No one truly knows the final outcome, but you have to try hard every night.

Willis and I would probably be fine as a coaching unit, but what we did not have at New Jersey was a collection of necessarily skilled players to successfully compete night in and night out in the NBA. Teams with a shallow pool of talent will come up with a win here and there, especially early on in the very long eighty-two-game basketball season. On occasion, teams can rise above their lack of talent, but many wins are not possible over the course of an entire season if your team does not have the talent.

I'm not sure if my being a voice of calm for Coach Willis was part of our deal. If it was, I should have done better. One night, somewhere in the midst of a very rough patch in our season, Willis became frustrated. He had taken all he could take and was not taking any more. Willis was an old-school player straight out of a might-makes-right culture of a time gone by. In our locker room, during halftime, he offered a challenge to any player who thought they were better than him at running the team. All these years later, I cannot be sure if he really meant it or was just throwing something against the wall to see if it would stick.

He suggested that things had gotten to the point that "maybe we need to go in the room with one key." Continuing, he said, "If one of you can whip me, you can come out of the room with the key and take over this team. Back in the day, this is how we did it." If that was not enough, he added that he was the type of guy that hunted and killed animals in the woods and that he did not understand anyone that was not for that. My eyes were big as saucers as we all stood still, not wanting this thing to escalate, if escalation was even possible. All in attendance agreed, judging by the lack of takers for this he-man challenge. Fortunately for us all, time ran out, so we had to return to the floor for the second half, and all keys remained in their rightful pockets. There was no fight then, nor did we prevail that night on the basketball floor. After a while in the NBA, I just grew to keep my belt buckled because I never knew when something crazy could occur, followed by the next crazy event.

Another example of our frustration occurred while playing on the road one night against Boston. We had struggled from behind and finally taken a one-point lead with eight seconds to play—our ball, backcourt, with our opponent pressing. All that was needed was to run the last seconds off the clock. We made a good pass to our rookie at mid-court, who quickly dribbled into the front and shot a terrible, off-balance shot. Boston rebounded and immediately called a timeout. They advanced the ball to mid-court, drew up a last-second shot, made it, and we lost a heartbreaker in Boston Garden. It was always heartbreak for the New Jersey Nets as we snatched defeat out of the jaws of victory. The next day, as we were waiting in the airport to board our plane, our coaching staff discussed our last possession and were puzzled as to why our rookie would take the shot. It was decided that I should ask him if he knew the time and if he would shoot that shot again in that situation. The rookie's response was yes and yes.

Willis would eventually move as they say "upstairs" to administration.

While attending the yearly NBA League meeting in California, I happened to be seated next to Del Harris on the bus that shuttled us from place to place. Del was the head coach for Milwaukee at that time. I'd known and respected him since our college days when he was at Earlham and I was at Transylvania. He asked me about my job situation with the Nets, and I told him it was up in the air. He said he had a position open as personnel director and invited me to fly to Milwaukee and talk to the owner of the team, Senator Herb Kohl. I did and was offered the position.

MILWAUKEE BUCKS

I CAME TO my new position as director of player personnel with a unique set of skills I had acquired over the years. I would be employing a range of lifelong experiences from playing with Taterbug on our homemade basketball court to most recently being a coach in the NBA. By this time, I had even spent fifteen years in charge of the coaches at the NBA Summer Pre-Draft Camp. This camp had given me invaluable exposure to all the top college and European prospects invited to Chicago. Director of player personnel felt like one of those moments when you feel that everything you did before prepared you for this moment.

As the director, I worked closely with the head coach and general manager. They gave me the freedom to make my own schedule and encouraged me to look in Europe, the summer leagues, and virtually anywhere else, I might find basketball talent. I would write reports on all possible college prospects, provide lists of updates on those outstanding prospects, and keep them abreast of my progress. My search involved traveling throughout the United States and Europe to evaluate these players. In 1992 twenty-one foreign players were on NBA rosters, and teams began aggressively seeking to increase that number. Consequently, scouting internationally became a natural extension of everyone's recruiting and evaluation efforts.

There had been some talk that NBA teams were scouting foreign players because the league and fans wanted more white players in the majority-black league of basketball players. The impression by some was that the NBA and its member teams were going outside the country to find the white talent they could not find inside America. I am not convinced that that is so. I was never a part of any meeting discussing race and ethnicity. I did not feel that way, nor did I ever hear that sentiment from others in Milwaukee, nor from others in authority throughout the league. My observation of this group of foreign players was they were capable, and I liked their playing style. Their guards seemed hardnosed and aggressive, and their forwards were legendary for being prolific shooters on the wings. I am unable to defend or advance others' perspectives, but that is mine.

Del welcomed me to the Milwaukee Bucks by personally showing me my office and introducing me to my secretary. Working with Del, and the general Milwaukee situation, was one of my better experiences in the NBA. We had mutual respect for each other. He left the personnel scouting completely up to me and respected my evaluations. I enjoyed his willingness to give me important issues to work on and then leave me to my process.

Seventeen games into the 1992 season, Del transitioned to front-office duties and away from the bench. Frank Hamblen, Del's first assistant coach, took over as the interim head coach and asked me to be his first assistant. We finished the last sixty-five games of that season together. Then, Senator Kohl decided to bring former player, Mike Dunleavy, back to the team as the general manager and head coach. Senator Kohl knew and was very comfortable with Mike, who came to Milwaukee on the heels of being the head coach of the Lakers. He had most recently taken the Lakers to the NBA finals, which lent a certain enthusiasm to his arrival. While I had spent some time with Del and Frank on the bench, at this point, I was made vice president of player personnel and settled back into that job upon the arrival of our new head coach.

THE SENATOR

Senator Kohl was, in a word, a gentleman. I found him to be soft-spoken, kind, and a reflective person. He was in Washington D.C. most of the time, in service to the United States as a senator, representing Wisconsin. Whenever he was in town, we always had coffee together. We would catch up on team details, and progressively we began to engage each other as friends. As our relationship unfolded, he came to me and said that since I was going to have to be traveling a lot in Europe, I should take Elo along on my longer trips. I was gratified that he had witnessed something about us as a family that led him to that decision. He knew that she and I loved being together and traveling to all of these places, and so he made that gracious offer. We accepted. I am eternally grateful to the senator for his generosity. I believe he thought the world of Eleanor and me, and we felt that way about him.

Putting together a successful team on the NBA level is like putting together a series of puzzles. Each puzzle then needs to be incorporated into a larger puzzle. After I put my puzzle together, I then collaborated with the owner, general manager, and head coach. As the director of player personnel, I would set the table for all this coming together with volumes of information and recommendations. From there, everything was driven by the power share of the general manager and the head coach. It should go without saying that the team owner is truly the biggest boss and will always have the final say.

There are a variety of owners and bosses throughout the NBA, each with their own details and distinctions. Some are remote and fairly detached. Back in the old days, a team owner like Franklin Mieuli would literally go sailing on his boat for long periods at a time, only to return long enough to be told what had been done while he was away before off he went again. Then, there are owners who are very involved, perhaps too involved at times, given their understanding (or lack thereof) of basketball. Perhaps one of the favorite owners for staff is that owner who properly staffs and funds a team, then joins the other fans courtside with popcorn and enthusiasm. However, we all have to accept that while the boss may not always be right, the boss remains the boss. Our organization was fortunate in our relationship with Senator Kohl, as we found him to be reasonable. That may not be the same thing as saying I agreed with every one of his decisions, but he probably remains my favorite team owner.

WHEAT FROM CHAFF

Trades and free agency have been the common way for a team to instantly change its composition. For as big as the headlines are around trades, headlines would be even more spectacular for all of the deals that do not quite occur. Try to keep in mind that when your job is to do deals, you are constantly looking for one—every hammer is looking for a nail. When you are a director of player personnel, general manager, or coach, you are constantly shopping. Sometimes, it is just a wish list that will never happen—things like injuries or just a change of heart for the dealmaker can make everything come undone. I would add that it appears that the best trades are often done in the offseason. That allows everyone to get adjusted after the dust settles. You get to go into training camp as a unit.

In high school, there are try-outs; in college, they recruit; and in the NBA, we draft. A major challenge in our process is when one ranking staff member likes a particular prospect and another administrator prefers a different position player. A particular rub for me was that I felt most prepared to make some of these larger decisions but was not always granted the authority to do so. Somewhere in the fine print, between the lines, was that the final decision making would not necessarily rest with me. Over longer periods of time, that detail can be a bit frustrating. In fairness to the people I worked with, not accepting my strong recommendations did not make them bad. It just felt like a series of missed opportunities.

My biggest regret in Milwaukee was my inability to convince our staff to draft Michael Finley in 1995 and Steve Nash in 1996. I did my best to persuade our staff to draft future standout Nash, but they could not be persuaded. Nash went to the Phoenix Suns at the fifteenth pick. This two-time NBA Most Valuable Player, eight-time NBA All-Star, et cetera, may be recorded in history as the most phenomenal player ever picked at that low of a spot. In my position, I would see player prospects ten times at a minimum throughout the year. It would have been ideal for me not only to put in all of those hours of evaluation of this superstar but also be empowered to make the final decision as well. I naturally felt that the person with the most information on the details of any player should have the leadership on the final selection. The head coach or general manager would only see a player one time, yet they might have the final thumbs up or down on our ultimate selection. Heated discussions would sometimes follow until the general manager, other scouts, coaches, and even owners came together to resolve the issue. The final decision on these matters can be the difference between success and failure. Historically, successful teams have been successful at player selection.

In fairness to all parties involved, we will never know what would have happened if those draft picks had come our way. Some players may come to you fully formed, while others will be diamonds in the rough. The challenge with players and team composition is that everything and everybody is connected to everything and everybody else. Perhaps it was Nash's great fortune to be paired with the team and teammates that he had in Phoenix. Had he gone anyplace else—including Milwaukee—his fortunes may have been different in some way. Or, perhaps, he would have been as spectacular with us as he was in reality. None of us will ever know for sure.

I was deeply involved with decisions around trading and cutting players. Most coaches and personnel in charge of trading or cutting a player find it difficult to do. Delivering the news to a player that they have been traded is difficult, and even more so, the news that they have been cut from the team. In sports talk, players are trained to believe that the team is their family, but if you're cut or traded, then your family is kicking you out. It is emotional for everyone involved. Whether trades will end up good or bad is difficult, if not impossible, to predict. Team culture and talent dictates so much of whether a trade will ultimately be judged successful or not. Much of it revolves around how all these different and similar chemicals come together. Do they soar, explode, or just lie there?

Very marginal players have done quite well for themselves when placed in a perfect scenario for them. You might have a player who ordinarily cannot create a shot for themselves on offense. All of that can change if you have him come off a pick set by a strong man for an automatic shot. Then there are players who are considered finesse players or "soft," who can do quite well if they are surrounded by players of brute strength. Let the brutes beat up other players and let the finesse player provide truckloads of points on the scoreboard. The great George "Iceman" Gervin comes to mind. The world would have missed one of the all-time-great offensive performers if he had been required to play out of the position of his natural greatness. San Antonio expected him to do what he was best at, and he did that all of the time.

Sometimes, a team has to go outside in order to create the desired situation. Free agency is often a tool they use. I like the possibility of free agents enough, but the situation has to be near-perfect. Instead of participating in a contest for the prized free agent at the fair, I prefer to do team development through careful draft selections and player development. Some teams can lose sight of the talent they have as they are in a constant hunt for greener pastures. It feels to me that sometimes these blockbuster deals work out well, like when Moses Malone provided the missing piece to the Philadelphia Seventy-Sixers' puzzle in the eighties. I recall one of the camera shots after they had won the championship—Moses pictured with an oversized check and caption reading "paid in full." Then there are teams and players that never fulfill their promise. Even that very Philadelphia team had put together a superstar squad at every position a decade earlier that did not live up to its billing. It is just that way. One plus one sometimes equals less than two. To paraphrase the movie character Forrest Gump—it's like a box of chocolates, you never know what you have until you bite into it.

ONE AND DONE

Over the years, there was all this controversy about players leaving college early to pursue professional careers in the NBA. In the earliest days of the NBA, the league established a rule that a player could not make himself available for the draft until two years after his high school graduation.

The first major challenge around free agency arose with Spencer Haywood. The case eventually reached the Supreme CourtU.S. Supreme Court, which issued a 7–2 decision in Haywood's favor in 1971. After the decision, the NBA allowed players to leave college early as "hardship cases," which essentially meant that the player had to prove financial hardship and then would be deemed eligible to enter the NBA. The old hardship rule has been informally replaced with the one and done—one spectacular year of college and then on to the pros.

For all of the criticism a player receives for leaving college before his graduating class, I doubt really that any of us can begrudge any of them for the prosperity they seek. In this modern culture, it is a foregone conclusion that the player will leave college for the bright lights and fortunes of a professional basketball career. I suppose that at some point, everyone just gave in to accepting a thing for what it is. College basketball seemed to evolve into the minor leagues for the

NBA. Just a stopping-off station before a young person reached their ultimate destination.

Who can know for sure? Maybe players should seek their education later in a calmer and more focused time when they are not distracted by all the noise that a college athlete is surrounded by while trying to be a student. The amount of money that a very young person can earn in a very brief period has to be weighed against whatever benefits they might gain by spending a full term in college. A player could always return to school later to get a diploma. He can even pay his own tuition with some of his riches. In some ways, I wonder if some people are actually jealous that these young men are making "all that money." Who among us would turn down a million dollars today and accept the potential risk of injury, misfortune, and any number of unforeseen calamities that the future might bring? In some way, if the public were truly disturbed about these young men potentially not getting an education, perhaps that concern would extend to all young people.

Who could know when a young person is ready or not to professionally compete in two practices a day, training camp, nine preseason games, eighty-two regular-season games, and potentially a playoff schedule? They can look ready athletically, but deep down, there is a question of whether they are up to the emotions of living and fighting among grown men night in and night out.

My greater concern about an early departure from college is for a young person's long-term mental, physical, and skill preparedness. I often wonder out loud if many of them are prepared for the task at hand. Professional basketball, beyond the headlines, glamour, wealth, and fame, is a really tough place to be somebody. The game can be the best thing that ever happens to a young person and their family, or it can be their worst nightmare. You can end up ill-prepared and walk away with the post-traumatic stress of an unsuccessful battle. Coming into the league is like making the transition from baby formula to red meat—very tough red meat. No one can really be prepared for this thing. All of the preparedness is in the doing. Yes, a player may have been a star in high school and on the college level, but that is a mild indicator of what lies ahead in the National Basketball Association. You start with the harsh reality that there are so few positions for so many applicants. For someone to enter, someone else must exit. Fortunately, for players in the NBA, there are guaranteed contracts, so at least some players and coaches are left with hurt feelings but not financial devastation to add to their difficulty.

I still struggle with the concept of one and done. I am just hopeful that the young athlete's formula for success includes a college education and diploma. Education is about learning, developing a world view, interacting with other students and professors, and being exposed to the diversity of ideas that comes in the forum of a classroom and the culture around it. We see all too often, young men enter the professional world of sports when they are not prepared in any way to interact with the world beyond the basketball court and their hotel room.

THE GOAT—GREATEST OF ALL TIME

There are certain questions that follow me wherever I travel. If I should introduce myself as the director of player personnel for the Milwaukee Bucks, some will break out the shortlist of their favorite questions. They open up their can of a lifetime of questions and curiosities about big-time basketball. Depending on the circumstance, I might even offer the conversation unsolicited—after all, I am a fan of basketball beyond my professional relationship. Basketball is not only how I make a living; it is also part of what I have lived for. The sports part of me is not something that I shy away from. I feel secure enough in myself that I can hold this passion for basketball, but that is not to the exclusion of all the other aspects of what, for me, is a full and whole life.

People alternate asking me who my current favorite basketball player is and who I believe is the greatest of all time—the GOAT.

Answering that question tends to be a reflection on where you were and how you were feeling at the time. Like many subjects, it comes down to personal taste in the end. The most anyone can learn from the answer to this question is the personal likes and dislikes of the person answering the question.

This is always a fun question with no clear objective standard to come to a clear conclusion given the sheer volume of players over the ages, and that does not even include the players who we do not have much film on. A lot has happened since 1946 and that inaugural group of eleven teams that has become what we now know as the National Basketball Association, with thirty teams. Each player, over that time, was part of a generation with its own definition of greatness.

Certainly, players like Bill Russell, Michael Jordan, Larry Bird, Oscar Robinson, Wilt Chamberlain, and Pete Maravich, have to be considered when answering that question, but so does a whole group of other players who have pounded that hardwood for over seventy years, let alone the great talents of the college game. The topic is wide open, and the determining factor becomes: what are the criteria for greatness? Answering that question requires context. In what era did the player compete? Are we discussing individual talent or team impact? Even teammates must be included in that calculation. Championship players like Bill Russell, with his eleven championship rings, could be my answer. It is hard to argue with that kind of success. Then there is Michael Jordan, a winner who did it with a certain style not known before his time.

How can anyone honestly choose one player across all the generations of players that have played? Even in this very modern version of that conversation, I am challenged to be specific. I liked Steph Curry when he was a child, tagging along with his dad, the great shooter Dell Curry, while I was with the Charlotte Hornets in the 1990s. I liked him even more as this three-time champion with the Golden State Warriors. Save for his family and friends, how could anyone have predicted that this small man (by basketball standards) would be such a dominant force in any contest? He is listed at 6'3", but often appears smaller than the other players on the court. He acts in some ways as a magician, performing sleight of hand as he scores around players larger than himself, sending the defender one way and going another. He is so good that rarely is there any mention of his potential size disadvantage.

Lebron James is another talent that just cannot be denied. One of the few over-the-top success stories of a young man straight out of high school. Entering the NBA draft without going to college, he never looked back as he charged toward greatness and distinction. He acts like a man among children, dominating both ends of the court. His greatest challenge might be the effort that he makes to include his team in his success. Lebron is such an extraordinary basketball player; you just know that if he chose, he could pad his stats with scoring by being selfish, but he seems to value team goals over personal statistics.

STYLE AND SUBSTANCE

We all love a slam dunk or a blocked shot sent flying into the stands—spectacular plays have their place in the entertainment part of basketball. I prefer it when a defender blocks a shot, but keeps it in play, resulting in a possession and, therefore, creating an opportunity. If a team creates enough opportunities for themselves during the course of a contest and executes well, there is success. Slam dunks are even more impressive when they occur at the end of a well-executed strategy. Fans the world over would come to the stadium to witness the breaking of a backboard, but I prefer to keep the backboard intact and win some games. When Herb Williams broke the backboard in Lithuania, the crowd was delighted, but it took forever to sweep up the glass and continue the game. I even enjoyed the sight of it all myself, but I am not sure how much it helped our effort. I would trade that one big play for a series of less-impressive but well-executed plays by team USA instead of the struggle that we experienced during the competition.

Rather than talk about who is the best of all time, perhaps we are better off examining what qualified them as great. There are many reasons many of us remain fans of the greatest in another sport— Muhamad Ali. Chief among them was his gift for not only talking trash with flair and color but, even more importantly, how he backed up what he said with performances we are still talking about all this time later.

During my time managing the Development League, in one practice situation, a couple of players began shouting at each other, disrupting the entire practice. I felt that the coach let it go on too long, and that night at dinner, I asked him what that was all about. He said, "Oh, they were just doing some trash-talking." He followed that by asking what I thought about that. I said that he didn't have a player good enough to trash talk and that if I were in his position, I would let the players know that. I believe trash-talking is reserved for after you have successfully executed and won the contest.

Given that we were talking about players in the Development League, I was suggesting that however good they were going to be, they were not that yet. I wanted them to put their trash-talking on hold until they truly had something to talk about. The next day at shoot-around, the coach called the team together and gave them this perspective. There was no more trash-talking, and the suggestion improved team morale. It was perhaps a small suggestion, but one that made a world of difference in player relationships.

CHARLOTTE

WHILE SUPERVISING THE Chicago NBA Draft Camp in 1995, my friend, former head coach and general manager of the NBA's Charlotte Hornets, Bob Bass, asked me if I'd like to get back on the bench as a coach. My most recent activities were more on the administrative and player personnel side of the business. Bob said he was considering hiring former Boston Celtic great, Dave Cowens, as head coach and was interested in me as his assistant. I was intrigued and said yes to a meeting with Bob and Dave.

Hall of Famer, Dave Cowens, was sometimes known as "the redhead" because of his red hair and his intense style of play. Subconsciously or not, the team was hoping that Dave Cowens would bring them some of the luck of the Irish to their new task. Perhaps all of the glory of a time gone by might rub on the rest of us. That all sounds like a great fit if you ignore some of the realities of the details of this heavy lifting.

A meeting in Bob's hotel room was set, and the three of us got together between camp sessions. Bob introduced us and then let Cowens ask all the questions. When Cowens asked, "Why would you want to coach in Charlotte?" without a moment's hesitation, I said that I had a son and grandchildren who live in Charlotte. His reply was, "And that's a good reason?" I responded immediately, "Yes, that's a good reason for me." So began our five-year adventure.

COACH LEE ROSE

In addition to returning to Charlotte, I believe Bob brought me in because he probably wanted me to become the coach whisperer. Perhaps, I would be able to share some of the practical details of my coaching experience with Cowens, a great former player, as he further developed his career as a head coach. I would provide calm and structure, and the player-turned-coach would provide everything else. In addition, it has to be irresistible for a team to marry a formerly successful player with an experienced coach.

Charlotte is a centerpiece to my coaching career. I have served the University of North Carolina at Charlotte, the Charlotte Hornets, and the Charlotte Bobcats. Over these many years as coach and coach's assistant, I have seen and experienced much. In some ways, I am a natural fit with these often younger and inexperienced men, who had bravely fought many wars as players but not as many of the coaching kind. They had been excellent soldiers, but now they were being called upon to command the entire squadron into battle.

When Cowens became head coach, he had had minor exposure and success as a coach. We became acquainted by way of questions he posed to me in our meeting. He wanted to know what I thought his biggest challenge would be as the head coach. Without hesitation, I replied that I knew what his biggest problem would be, and I would share it if he wanted. "What," was his flat and immediate reply, with a bit of skepticism. I said that he had been very talented, hardworking, self-motivated, and successful during his celebrated career as a player. The players he would be coaching would have salaries many multiples of what he had made as a player. When some of them did not measure up, it would frustrate him to death. He responded that that was BS, and my response was, "We'll see," and we did. The great ones transitioning to coach after a spectacular career as a player are destined to become frustrated when their young charges just don't get the difference between being good and great, and how to get there—and moreover, how to do that every night. I am not sure why. Perhaps that level of greatness cannot be communicated.

CHARLOTTE

There is a divide that exists between coaches who played at high levels of NBA championship and glory and those who did not. The most simple-minded explanation may be that former players hold over a certain pride from their glory days, especially when their glory does not serve them very well as a coach. Their fallback position is how great they used to be or what they did back when.

One of Dave's often-repeated notions was if you didn't play in the league, you shouldn't coach in it. I am not certain where this came from, or if he truly believed it, but I have heard it said enough to convince me that it holds some meaning for former players. Another layer to this hazing that sometimes occurs is what I simply referred to as the player trump card. He would ask for suggestions, and before anyone could respond, he'd say, "When I played in the NBA, we did so-and-so." This tended to silence the entire staff. This especially occurred where the assistants had no playing time in the NBA.

Here was this relatively new NBA coach, who had never coached a championship team, who, for some reason, felt comfortable putting down non-former players. But just look at Chuck Daly, Gregg Popovich, and Erik Spoelstra—none of those men ever played in the NBA, yet between them, they had coached and won nine NBA Championships. His comments stung a little for coaches that come to the game fully prepared with coaching credentials, but very little, if any, experience as a basketball player in the league. Deep down, perhaps a coach does wonder if he is missing something having not played on that hallowed ground as an NBA player. Every now and then, I have wondered what Cowens and others are talking about; however, I never felt that I was less of a coach because I didn't play in the NBA.

Coaching, at its core, is teaching. Being a player may enhance your teaching skills, but it does not create an ability where none existed. Even if you understand the game in some special way that made you a phenomenal player, that is so different from being able to communicate that genius. I would go even further to say that having genius may create frustration when what came naturally to you is not computing with your student. On most days, these and other water drops roll off my back, but on occasion, I want to bring to their attention what goes unnoticed for some of these former superstars. I would have them be aware that I have an equal amount of confidence in myself and accumulated experiences on all these levels of basketball. Just as they had stuff to point to with pride of accomplishment, so did I. So much so, I doubted that it had to be stated in either of our cases. I could never be certain if they just once again wanted to stand in the glory of yesterday, or if that was all they had. I was coming from the perspective of congratulations on all of that to both them and myself, but, "That was then, this is now"—let us get on with our future.

I remember being in a coach's conference with NBA Hall of Fame basketball player, Larry Bird. At that time, he was transitioning into coaching and basketball operations after his distinguished career as a player. After yet another long afternoon session on one coaching topic followed by the next, Larry looked me in the eye and stated in no uncertain terms that "coaching is overrated." I was not sure how to interpret that statement coming from this great former player. Perhaps he was just wondering out loud in a question more than a statement, but he said it nonetheless for me to figure out. I was never sure if Larry understood that his words were being spoken to one who was very proud of a long and fruitful career as a coach on many levels of competition.

Certainly, some of his comment could be assigned to Larry's trademark of an at-times salty personality, but it is understandable that someone with his intuitive brilliance may not fully understand all of the many nuances of basketball strategy and organization from a lifetime coach's perspective. I use Larry as my illustration only in part, because he may not be the best example to prove my point. After all we are talking about a former player with a near perfect vitae as player and later as coach and front office professional. Whatever his perspective, I am obliged to offer that none of that would truly render coaching overrated. The results have been mixed for some of the more phenomenal players as head coaches. It would seem that they would be able to just spread that greatness all around, but teaching is more involved than that. In theory, talented players should be able to teach talent and coach a team, just as jump shooters ought to be able to teach a player how to shoot the ball better, rebounders to rebound, and so on for each detail of the game. There is a difference, though, between knowing the game and being able to transfer what you know to the uninitiated.

Perhaps Larry was really reflecting on his lack of understanding, or maybe his personal reflection on the layered complication of the role of coach was much ado about nothing. As a player, he appeared to be in control and have a deep understanding. That is fine for a great player and his responsibility for a personal performance, but what happens when you are that person responsible for everybody?

Despite some of the philosophical differences about coaching that Cowens and I had, we actually got off to a pretty good start. More than fifty wins in an eighty-two-game regular season is what every team wants because that means enough to get you into postseason play. Also, you have won enough games to be thought of as a winning team, and the world loves a winner. The challenge with fifty wins in your first season is that the statistic can be misleading. Instead of it being the beginning of something to build on as you move to the next level or even the markings of possible championship play, it could be just a high watermark. Unfortunately, our early success didn't last. Instead of the beginning of something special, what looked like progress turned out to be the best that it was ever going to get.

After two successful years, Dave ran into a bad spot that resulted in his resignation, in part because the team had gotten off to such a horrible start in year three. In another part, Dave was in a contentious contract negotiation with the front office. It can never be clear when contract talks break down if the parties are just sincerely that far apart or if it is by design. Sometimes, contract talks are just an opportunity for the team to part company with a coach or player that management finds difficult and no longer wants to deal with. The converse certainly can be true as well, whereby the talent in question may be ready for a change from management. At any rate, Dave resigned.

FURTHER ON

When Cowens departed Bob Bass offered the head coaching position to me with the condition that I have Paul Silas act as my assistant. I had a deep feeling that would not work. My response to Bob's generous offer was that I would accept being Paul's assistant but not the other way around. Paul and I had worked well enough as assistants under Dave Cowens, but I was not encouraged that he would fully accept my leadership as the head coach. Perhaps I should have negotiated harder on the details of this offer. If I had, I could have prevailed as the head coach with my own staff and team, but I did not. In some way, I just wanted us all to play basketball and get on with it—whatever the configuration. My counter was accepted, and I began my tour of duty in Charlotte under Paul Silas.

Paul, as head coach, was a bit complicated. He had been a very successful NBA basketball player. I did not know Paul in his player heyday, but as a leader and a coach, he seemed to create a highly charged and what felt like a chaotic environment to a person and coach like me. Some of this is common for most teams but a challenge nonetheless for someone who prefers to focus just on basketball. Even the basketball stuff could be twisted into personal and political layers. It reminded me greatly of my childhood environment with my mother and her sisters with their frequent, high-pitched, heated drama in the kitchen. High volume seems to me to be what a person does when they can't do anything else. Those were times that led me to want to be outside playing ball or any place else but there. I see myself as non-confrontational, and therefore my response to shouting and railing against one another is to retreat.

CHARLOTTE

Unlike those times long ago, when I would go outside to get away, in this professional basketball setting, it was my job to be present and do what I could. Sometimes, it felt there was no true interest in a solution if I am to judge by the response I received to my recommendations. It was like he was obliged to hear me out in most instances, but rarely was I left feeling there was any sincere interest in my contribution. I just wanted to coach basketball and help out the best I could, but we always seemed to be on different pages. In some instances, I imagined Paul rolling his eyes as he turned his back to walk away—he probably did not actually, but that was how I felt. My comments were used more like traps or fertile ground for the next donnybrook or some future dressing down of the low man on the totem pole. At some point, it seemed like we all had become children of a fairly dysfunctional and chaotic family. We even had the great distinction of returning to the locker room one night after a hard-fought game with one of our assistant coaches thinking we had lost a game that we had, in fact, won.

As an assistant, I was, at times, responsible for being the bearer of unwanted news. I was confounded by how Paul would turn his frustration at what I had just told him toward me as though I was the culprit instead of the messenger. When I reported to Paul that our star player had refused to accept a certain defensive assignment, he responded as though I was telling him that I was refusing to implement his instruction. Having players tell coaches what they will and will not do is not so uncommon in the NBA. Some of that probably turns on the reality of adults instructing adults and said adults having the leverage of big, guaranteed contracts. At some point, some players discover that they are richer and "weigh more" than the coach. Wanting to avoid drama and conflict, I would often just endure Paul's wailing, then try to figure out how we could move forward in a more constructive manner. These thousand tiny cuts were further aggravated by the fact that we were in the midst of a horrible losing record. Losing reveals a multitude of sins.

I guess, in some way, all teams will have their share of drama.

It would be unnatural for fourteen adults' lives to intersect with so much on the line without a collision. It is unreasonable to have that many moving parts and not have something bump into something else. However, in Charlotte, it just seemed there was always one thing followed by the next. It was like I had my own reality television show, except it wasn't television—it was my life and career in real-time.

BEHIND THE SCENES

There was that one year that our then-owner, George Shinn, had a very public ordeal involving alleged sexual misconduct. Many of us had grown used to this type of drama with players and sometimes even staff, but having the big boss as the subject of the controversy provided us a different variety. To add fuel to the fire, the Shinn trial was televised for all to witness with all of the details that none of us should really want to know.

I was even a referee of a fight between two players. First, you must understand that it is rare that a real fight happens between basketball players. It is mostly saber-rattling and barking at passing cars, so I was never in any true jeopardy in my role as a peacemaker. Yet, there I was, positioning all of my five feet, nine inches between these two massive human beings as we moved toward our locker room in the midst of them going at each other. Some observer probably had a good laugh at my trying to separate two people, each of whom was taller than me by nearly two feet!

Tragedy struck in Charlotte when we lost one of my all-time favorite players and people, Bobby Phills. I had met Bobby back when I was at Milwaukee, when I scouted him as a potential high draft pick candidate out of Southern University in Baton Rouge. Now he was playing in Charlotte, and that was a good thing. He had been impressive from the start. Bobby told me in his interview long ago that he wanted to give basketball a chance while he was young, but his ultimate goal was to study medicine and become a physician. In what can only be seen as a lapse of otherwise intelligent judgment, one morning he decided to drag race with some other guys after practice. It ended badly. As many of us rushed to the scene of the accident, the police officer in charge begged his young bride not to see him in the aftermath of the horrible crash. He encouraged her to hold on to the better memories of her thirty-year-old husband.

A season can be lost as a result of a failed collective bargaining agreement, whether it is the owners locking the players out of the facilities (a lockout) or the players collectively refusing to report to work (a strike). The NBA and other unionized organizations have routinely threatened lockouts and strikes over collective bargaining stalemates, and we finally had one. That resulted in a fifty-game season and no all-star game that season. All of this is strange for everyone involved because we just don't associate the fun of sports with the seriousness of collective bargaining, health care, and pensions. That is until you realize that there are adults, families, and futures that need to be tended to.

AN ENDING

Following a playoff loss to Milwaukee and thus the end of our season, we headed back to Charlotte. As we boarded the plane, one of the managers informed us that Paul Silas wanted everyone to report to the office at 9 a.m. the next morning. I arrived on time and was stepping into my office when Paul stepped in and said he would like to see me in his. I went in and sat down, and Paul immediately said he had decided to go in another direction and would not need me anymore on his staff. I stood, extended my hand, said good luck, turned, and left. I had been released or fired before, but this was that rare instance where it was done in person.

For all of Paul's shortcomings, I will have to give him credit for firing me to my face. So often, my employment status was provided to me through the media or unreturned phone calls. I cannot know if this was a sign of character on Paul's part or if he got some satisfaction from delivering the final blow in person.

Bob Bass met me as I was getting ready to leave and assured me that I could stay within the organization and scout state-side and in Europe. Somehow, I immediately knew that I could not imagine doing that. From a practical perspective, I had completed my fifteen years in the league, which was the required number for a full pension. Emotionally, in one way or another, I felt that though I would miss coaching, I was not going to miss most things about my raucous five-year stretch with Charlotte.

The players were the primary thing I would miss. Teaching and working on the strategic parts of the game was what I had loved most. It is the grist for my mill. Departures from the grand stage of professional basketball rarely place a period at the end of the sentence. There are rarely, if ever, happily ever after, endings, all neat and tidy, when anyone is exiting stage left. Perhaps there are too many unreconciled events and emotions to put a shiny bow on it like that.

GOLDEN YEARS

I WONDER IF anyone really retires to a life of inactivity. Perhaps we just recreate ourselves on our own terms. Retirement for me did not mean inactivity and retreating into nothingness. Retirement meant that I would now determine what was important to me, especially when money was not the issue. All of this time, Eleanor and I had become good stewards of our assets and resources, which granted us choices as to what was next, beyond the money question.

As I began to wind down and out of basketball as a full-time coach, I remained interested in doing something but maybe just a bit less intense than what I had been. My retirement from the intense rigors of coaching was not the same as saying that I did not want to do anything. I just wanted my future activities to be my choice, not out of the necessity of needing a job. The NBA's Pre-Draft Camp and the Development League were places that I believed I could help. I suppose that they became my way to stay in the game and at the same time, give a little back to something that had given me so much.

In 2001, I directed the Chicago Pre-Draft Camp as I had for many years. Pre-Draft Camp is the place where college players have an opportunity to get a second look from NBA team officials in anticipation of the coming draft. The very top players have already been decided on—the Pre-Draft Camp is for everyone else. Since this event was technically during the NBA off-season, for many years, I was able to do both because their calendars did not conflict. That was perfect for me because I really enjoyed participating in this phase of these young men's journey as they answered the call of what was next.

When the camp ended, I was approached by an NBA representative who asked if I'd be available to oversee the players and coaches at the Development tryout in Atlanta, Georgia, in the next couple of weeks. The Development League became a place where 120 players already in the NBA's system were given further opportunity to make an NBA team. This was for those players who failed to make an NBA roster the first time around. The D-League, as it is known, became a pathway for players and inexperienced coaches as well, to grow, develop, and improve their games and in many cases, get another NBA tryout.

I was interested in the job and flew to New York to meet with the NBA staff. Karl Hicks was responsible for overseeing the entire D-League tryouts. My role would be as the director, the same as what I'd done for the NBA Pre-Draft Camp for many years—organizing and creating systems. There would be a draft by twelve coaches, and I would oversee the drills and scrimmages each day. Karl was great to work with, and we had a great experience. I signed on for a six-year term.

I admired the mission of the Development League. I feel very strongly that the D-League worked hard to prepare its coaches and players for the NBA and that they were successful in doing so in many instances. The NBA was stepping up and lending a hand for what is a difficult time for retired basketball players who wanted to enter coaching and for young, inexperienced players starting out. In the past, these guys were out there in the wilderness, alone. Now at least they had a jumping-off point. For the new players, the D League gave them that second and third look that justice requires for a young person who is on his last leg and possibly at career's end.

During my tenure as the director, I had the pleasure to work with many young coaches, such as Alex English, as they developed their coaching style and perspective. Alex was a Hall of Fame, former NBA scoring leader, and all-star player. He and I spent long hours on my summer porch discussing whatever I was able to share. Being an NBA superstar rarely prepares a player to be a coach, so I was pleased to work with those willing to learn. It is like they are an expert at a particular part of a much larger scheme. When you become a coach, you now have to gain full knowledge of how all the parts come together as you are responsible for that union. While hard work is certainly part of most great players' equation for success, there is an equal portion of something intangible, often unexplainable, that is required to make anyone a remarkable coach. A coach has to see the entire floor, all the players, and the clock at once. This high requirement is not lost on the guys that go on to be successful.

My participation in the D-League was my opportunity to "pass it on," by helping young coaches make their transition from expert players to rookie NBA coaches. I am encouraged when I see some of these guys walking courtside during basketball games as college and NBA coaches in a variety of situations. In addition to Alex, I worked with Paul Mokeski, Doug Marty, Robert Werdann, Sam Vincent, and many more, providing recommendations and guidance where I could. They still check in with the old coach from time to time. They are the next generation of coaches just as I had become the next generation to Adolf Rupp, C.M. Newton, and Tay Baker. That is so hard to imagine that anyone can truly succeed the great coaches of a particular era, yet they do. Each generation puts its own gloss on the game, but at the core, it remains basketball, and the game moves forward with us or without us. However rich the legacy of a player or coach, we only come to pass. Like a good song, every season has its end, and so do careers.

Following my sixth and final year of my contract agreement, I decided to step back and turn it over to a younger NBA assistant coach. The travel began to be more than what I had signed on for, but I am pleased to have been a part of this league and its beginning.

As the Development League grew, many of the teams were purchased through private ownership, and their locations expanded across the map. By 2014, the NBA Development League had seventeen teams, stretching from Maine to California. They remain devoted to developing players, coaches, referees, and front office staff.

FORWARD IN THE FIFTH

In March 2004, *The New York Times* ran a series about economic classes in the United States. One of those very in-depth articles focused on Della Mae Justice. This feature outlined the demographics and culture of my beloved Appalachia, along with the poverty and literacy rates that were tragically among the worst in the nation.

Della Mae was a young woman from Pikeville, Kentucky. She was left without parents at age fifteen when her mother died. She was placed in a foster home and then went to live with an uncle. Amazingly, Della Mae graduated from Berea College and finished fifth in her class at the University of Kentucky Law School. Initially, she had worked for a large Lexington law firm, married, traveled extensively, and lived in a beautiful home. It would appear that she had it all compared to her tragic start in life, but something was missing for her. Della Mae chose to return to Pikeville, where she practiced law in her uncle's small law firm. She also took in another family member who was headed to foster care as she had been many years before.

That story stopped me in my tracks. It resonated with me on many levels. Like me, Della Mae was from Kentucky, had been poor, and had lost a parent at an early age. Della Mae inspired me to want to do something for the folks back home. For all of our ambitions along the way, each of us will meet a time for giving in the midst of all of our getting and receiving.

I began contacting agencies in Kentucky about being involved in some sort of literacy program. Literacy is this grand passport that allows us access to so much and so many places. I continue to be amazed at all the places I can go simply by turning the page of a book. My core message would be centered on the power of education and making good choices. In particular, I wanted to tell them to stay in school so they would have choices. I knew firsthand the value of a good education and the development of proper attitudes in my own life, and I wanted that opportunity for them as well.

I had no interest in building a program from the ground up, so I decided to find an existing program that was geared specifically toward Appalachia. I wanted to work with young people, in particular, students. I believed there would be some value in sharing my own story of being from where these young people were from. I knew and understood their story for whatever that was worth to them, and I wanted them to know that it could get better if they were motivated to invest in themselves.

I spent several months trying to find an existing program addressing the issues facing the students in these remote, mountain areas of Appalachia. My partner of choice was named Forward in the Fifth. This non-profit was formed in 1986 and covers the fifth congressional district of Kentucky in support of poor families in the region. This district encompasses forty-two counties in Appalachia. What I wanted from Forward in the Fifth was their help with scheduling and contacts within the schools. I would give in return my time and energy as a former athlete, educator, coach, speaker, and if I place modesty to the side—local child made good role model.

I spoke to educators and administrators about which students might benefit the most from my message to stay in school. The consensus was that the most at-risk students are those in middle school. One of the administrators informed me that kids who fail one or two classes in middle school have a 50 percent chance of dropping out of school before graduating, and the wretched cycle continues. As our alliance was developed, Forward in the Fifth sent information to all the middle schools in the forty-two counties, asking if they would like to have

COACH LEE ROSE

Coach Lee Rose come to their school and talk to students about staying in school. The response was strong as principals, guidance counselors, media specialists, and coaches from various schools seemed to stand in line requesting that I visit. Our agreement was that they would assist us in scheduling the school visits and outreach, and my family would be responsible for all the associated financial expenses and of course, our time.

In April 2005, Elo and I drove from our home in Charlotte to Kentucky to begin the first of our two-week trips. We visited ten schools in ten days, drove over three thousand miles, and spoke to approximately 1,800 students. At first, I was a bit concerned about how well middle school students in 2005 would relate to a white-haired coach who was more than fifty years older than they were, but I should not have been. I realized that the most important connection that I made with the students was that I could speak their language. I could relate to these students who lived in tiny towns surrounded by mountains stripped for their coal.

I needed them to know that I grew up in the insulation and desperation of a small-town, mountain community. I shared with them that my great-grandfather had lived in Letcher and Owsley counties in Kentucky; the tiny town of Hyden, Kentucky, had been named for his great-grandfather, John Hyden. Even my middle name was Hyden, as well. I told them that I was born in West Irvine, had walked to school, and had soup beans and cornbread as standard fare. By the way, the beans and cornbread may have made me seem a little fancy to a community of children that, at times, went without a warm meal. As I shared my story, I could see and feel the barriers being broken and walls coming down. I believe that because I had been where they were, it drew them near to want to listen to me. When I finished talking, I always made enough time for the students to ask questions and have an open conversation with me. The young people thanked me for coming and for sharing my time and thoughts with them. It was especially heartwarming when they expressed their pride in my achievements as a coach. They added that they thought I had a good life, which I found mature and precious coming from children.

I continue to be amazed at how mutually beneficial working with children in need can be. All the time, while I am helping them, they are helping me. Sometimes, hearing myself promote values of character, integrity, and hard work has compelled me to continue to make that my truth as well. It is a good feeling to be in service to others, especially meeting a person in their moment of need. With each declaration that I made to these young people, it stood as a reminder of the person I should always try to be. Every school had a story, and without fail, someone tugged at our emotions and inspired Eleanor and me to load up and do it again, no matter how weary we had become.

On one trip, we passed abandoned mines and shuttered storefronts as we followed the directions to this one-story school just off the side of the road. When we arrived at Kimper, there was an outdoor sign saying, "Welcome, Coach Rose." Kimper also tugged at us as we were thanked over and over for coming and were told, "no one ever comes to Kimper." I mean, you just don't drop in on this school, which had taken us almost two hours to get to that morning on a winding road from Pikeville, Kentucky.

The facilities were destined to be poor throughout these counties due to the uneven distribution of resources in the community and the lack of a wealthy tax base from which to draw revenue. Everything seemed makeshift and in repair. Students had to use half of the cafeteria for their physical education classes. There is also a talent drain in many of these communities. So often, those who can leave, do, taking with them their talent and resources, leaving behind mostly those who have little or no choice but to stay.

The principal at the Happy, Kentucky, school said that drugs are just terrible and getting worse. The concern about drug use was a chorus that we heard from almost every school. Many of the kids are right on the fringe. These are sixth, seventh, and eighth graders, many of them living in foster homes or with extended family for one unfortunate reason or the other. In this small school, three kids' parents had died recently because of drugs. Many of the students live with grandparents as a result of parents being absent because of drug deaths, incarceration, and other fallout of poverty and decay.

So often in America, the face of poverty and the dispossessed are illustrated using urban dwellers, housing projects, and people of color. Witnessing the devastation in these communities, and knowing there are so many just like them, gave me pause at just how bad the problem is. It makes me wonder if it would be helpful in our campaign against poverty if some of these mountain people were included in that sad collage. Would a more realistic image of who is suffering generate deeper compassion and an urge to fix it?

These were good people, all. One story followed by the next left us feeling that we needed to hold onto something to keep from falling over as we heard the details of lives that were so far removed from our present ones, yet lives we remained very sensitive to.

We stayed at The Holiday Inn Express in Harlan, Kentucky, which was almost always filled to capacity. Many traveling men stayed there. Many of them were doctors who came in for several weeks or months at a time to lend aid because of the shortage in the area. The woman who worked the breakfast area at the hotel told us of an anesthesiologist who was supposed to be on temporary duty at the hospital for a year but could not resist coming back time and again because the need was so great. This brought to mind the international medical group, Doctors Without Borders, that traveled through third-world countries, providing aid to the poor and disabled. Harlan is not some poor, remote village in a distant foreign land—this is America, and the people are Americans.

We drove deep, deep into the mountains to Beaver Creek Elementary School. Remote beyond remote. We had two groups that morning, eighth-graders and then seventh, with about thirty-six children in each group. Bill Hall, the principal, and one of the good people of the Earth, had been at the school for seventeen years.

His eighty-four-year-old father was there for my presentation to the students. The father had finished eighth grade and then worked in the coal mines for thirty years.

Bill told me that none of the students in that school had a newspaper in their homes because there was no carrier in the area. He got the Lexington paper via mail, and it cost him $400 a year. I asked about the fact that we used to see papers in those schools in the library, and I thought they were free from the newspaper publisher. He said that was true, but since there was no carrier in that area, they stopped providing it, and also, all schools now needed corporate sponsors to get papers. I also do not recall seeing computers in the school's library.

Many housing conditions we drove past were sad and unfortunate. Our travels took us through places that felt like something from a Stephen King supernatural novel steeped in despair, but this was real, not fiction.

Some of these children looked so much older than their years. When I asked what they could do to earn some money, some offered that they could clean houses, mow grass, and babysit. The question had been intended as my opening for how hard times were for me when I was their age, but the house-cleaning job was probably the closest to the farm work I did. I asked if any of them had ever milked a cow, and one little boy said, "No, but I have milked a goat!" Rarely did anyone raise their hand when asked if they liked to read recreationally. Not many played sports, but several played the guitar. I would really have liked to hear one of these kids play their guitar. We were told later that the fifth-grade class was one of the roughest across many schools. Many of them were physically and sexually abused. A couple of them put their heads down on the table and went right to sleep at the beginning of our visit. After I put my hurt feelings aside, I realized that this might be the only place they could get peaceful rest.

Part of my presentation involved the throwing of a basketball between my listeners and me. Whoever caught the ball became the star of our show. They seemed to really love the interplay with the ball. Back then, I used Lance Armstrong and his cancer as a lesson in overcoming the odds, but given the revelations that followed Mr. Armstrong's "cheating," I feel like I should backtrack and place an asterisk by his accomplishments for the children.

There was always some child's face I could not get out of my head for one reason or the other. Sometimes it was for a joyous reason around how bright and engaging one might be—but often, it was when I asked into their backstory and discovered that this child or the next was a survivor of abuse—physical, verbal, and/or sexual. For example, I can never get Brittany out of my head: she was slim, with blond hair, and had a conspicuous overbite. She waved her hand high when I asked if any of them had milked a cow or worked in tobacco. Her jeans were torn—perhaps from wear and tear, or perhaps they were hand-me-downs—but not necessarily in an unfashionable way. Elo told me later that Brittany reminded her of the little girl that her mother had brought to their house when they were a military family living in 1947 Germany. Omi brought the child in to bathe her, wash her hair, and give her clean clothes but had to allow the little girl to go her way afterward. Brittany's eyes were red as though she lacked sleep. She had already wrapped herself around my heart, and then I discovered later that that little sixth-grader had probably the roughest home life in the school. Brittany wanted to help carry stuff down to our car with us as we were leaving. She left me with a strange feeling like she wanted our exchange to continue, or even hoped it might be possible for us to take her away from the horror she knew. After one talk, a young boy came by to speak to me while the students were leaving the library. He slipped a note into my hand. Written on it was his email address, "just in case you need to get in touch with me."

Our tour of these middle schools in Appalachia was one of the highlights of my career anywhere. There we were, in our force of two. Elo took notes and helped with my organization. She also helped pass out the bookmarks we provided and gave cough drops for what at times seemed to be a chorus of coughs from the students. Elo shared with me the empathy she felt at meeting these students, interacting with the teachers and principals, and learning so much about a culture that is completely unknown to so many in our country. Meeting the people, watching the kids, taking pictures, and witnessing this culture up close and in person was a powerful experience.

That first trip brought back memories I didn't know I had forgotten, like the word "wide." As my mountain vocabulary returned to me, I realized that the gentleman saying "wide" actually meant "white." We were discussing our next trip when he suggested Elo and I return in the fall when "it is not quite 'wide' yet." It was unanimous. We would plan to visit again in the spring or early fall before the winter roads became "wide" with snow.

THE LONG GOODBYE—LEE

THE WORLD IS truly a mysterious place. For all of our personal plans and designs, some things will happen for which none of us could have planned.

I am now in the early stages of Alzheimer's, according to my brain scan and my doctor. I have begun my battle with this progressive disease. No matter how slow it turns, the die has been permanently cast because there is no present cure.

When an illness strikes, you are confronted with a decision to remain private or to make a public disclosure. I am choosing to speak in the public square on my circumstances as my contribution to raising awareness of this disease. Perhaps what I have decided to share here may be helpful in some way to the reader of my words—for those in the middle of this struggle and for those to come. It also seemed fair to members of my family and me to help explain in advance to others why I am not always the person they have known me to be. Unless I were to live as a hermit, it would be obvious to others that I was just a step out of line at times.

Alzheimer's disease is an irreversible, progressive brain disorder that slowly destroys memory and thinking skills, and eventually, the ability to carry out the simplest tasks. I read this aloud to myself, to continue my process of realizing what is happening to me. The data tells me that as time passes, I am scheduled to slide gradually toward complete dependency. Alzheimer's patients who do not die from a stroke or myocardial infarction (heart attack) are likely to transition slowly into a vegetative state. At that point, all higher physical and mental function is lost. My reality is that I could lose my sense of judgment as well as my ability to walk and even swallow. This is news that no person wants to ever receive. It is not that I never thought that this could happen to me—perhaps more accurately, I just did not think much about it for myself, even though this horrid disease is not new to our family. Eleanor's mother, Omi, lived with Alzheimer's for ten years before her passing. My father-in-law, Opa, was her primary caregiver. Since they lived in another town, I mostly experienced it at our family visits and gatherings—until now.

I first recognized that something was wrong when it felt that I was losing a bit of my edge. I have lived a life of details; it is what I do and who I am. When details began to escape me and were not at my grasp as they had always been, it got my attention. Now, even when I read the details that have been written down, I sometimes do not recognize them with meaning. After a life of being responsible for shepherding groups of men across the continent, I am sometimes now challenged to recall if I am in the process of standing up or sitting down. The simple chores that each of us performs without thought throughout our day are becoming a challenge for me. Early on, I had accepted my symptoms as just the challenges of aging. Regardless of age, many of us experience lapses in memory and are likely to have certain physical challenges. Aging is a bit precarious for any of us. In a large way, we are still kicking, just not high kicks. What may be different for those of us diagnosed with Alzheimer's is that we discover our ailments are recurring with greater frequency and tend to be more profound. This condition is even more problematic as I manage unrelated back surgeries, knee issues, hearing aids, oral challenges, and other health issues that at times, feel like a roll call of what could go wrong within the human form.

We are all scheduled to pass from this life—that is a clinical reality tied mostly to our biology. As an intellectual concept, all of us are shackled to *when*, not *if* we will die. We know that there will come a day that we will be no more. Each of us is scheduled for some event in our lives that changes everything. While health challenges can happen at any age, some of us accept that they are more probable at a later age. Things like illness, death, and dying are intellectual concepts until the substance of those words is staring us in the face and we are the subject. I get that; I just was not planning around this thing that I now know exists. My emotions still must settle into the very harsh reality of my medical details, if that is possible. It is impossible to describe fully this season of my life. I have always tried to be pragmatic. Embracing the truth is the part of pragmatism that allows me to manage the fear that often accompanies bad news.

This thing is acting like a thief—first a thief in the night because it is so subtle, unannounced, and creeping. Alzheimer's is just like that. In time, and at different rates for each affected individual, this thief becomes ever increasingly bold and arrogant, coming into the light of day, stealing and taking what is not it's to take, but doing so anyway.

The further insult to the injury of Alzheimer's is that everyone's sunset is different. The disease affects each person differently, each with their own timeframe. It comes uninvited, then stays for as long or short of a time as it will, creating chaos and pain all along the way until the victim's regrettable end.

Presently, I have more good days than bad. I am writing this on one of my better days. There are times when I am fully aware, and other times I am challenged to keep up with a conversation when it shifts gears even a little. I am sure that those around me are amazed that I can have these moments and periods of clarity, followed by confusion and chaos. I feel fortunate to have maintained a journal and notes for so many years. Some of my writings were intentional for some unknown-at-the-time future use, and some were just my way of maintaining the order that I prefer. Unrelated to my condition, I had begun some time ago to collaborate on composing my memoir with Elo, and Joe, one of my former players, now a friend and the publisher of this book. We discovered that what would become this book had already been written by me in my many journals and notes. The task that followed was to arrange the miles of content into memoir form.

Eleanor and I now use whiteboards as an aid to help me organize and remember things. The slick white surfaces are familiar to me from when I wrote game plans and notes for players. Coaches use whiteboards as a tool for instruction like teachers use blackboards. Elo discovered that there are smaller versions of whiteboards available, and there is one on our dining table most of the time. She keeps it up to date with information about caregivers and schedules for that particular day. Those written details help keep some order for me when facts and unwritten details seem to fly away from me. More frequently, I have to refer back to the whiteboard throughout the day. After a life of being responsible for an entire athletic department, I am sometimes challenged to hold onto details even if something is written on the whiteboard. I wrote two technical books about basketball and used my computer to do so. Now, even retrieving my emails is a struggle.

Fortunately, I have Elo.

THE LONG GOODBYE—ELEANOR

I AM ELEANOR Lollis Rose. I have been married to this wonderful man, Lee Hyden Rose, for more than sixty years. Our life together has been full and bountiful, a feast even. I cannot imagine a better husband, friend, father, grandfather, or person than my companion of all these many years. I would like to share a letter I wrote to Lee some time ago.

Dearest Lee,

When we first came together, we didn't speak of falling in love but very quickly realized that we were. I remember one spring evening during one of our dates when we parked at Calumet Farm there in Lexington. I got all teary. When you asked why, I said it was because I couldn't imagine my life without having you in it. That was how I sincerely felt at 17, and I feel that way today. For all these years, it has been a bit of a joke that shortly after we met, you told both your roommate Bob and my girlfriend, "I have met the girl that I am going to marry." I remember early on after we first met that I broke a date at the time with a nice guy simply because I knew I would rather spend time with you. You had basketball practice that didn't end until late, but I remember being so comfortable with the decision I had made to just wait on you. You came to the dorm when you finished practice, and we had dinner. We talked for a long time about our lives and the families that we came from. We have always naturally enjoyed each other's company.

I remember when we walked over to the historic Old Morrison building on the Transylvania College campus and sat on those grand, historical steps. I can still feel the joy and satisfaction I felt as we talked about our future together. We spoke about how *we would do things, not* if *we would. We never really had a formal engagement; we just knew we were going to get married. We knew where we were going and were convinced we were going there together.*

How could either of us ever have known all those many years ago when we sat on the back steps of the women's dorm at Transylvania in 1957, all the places we would go! And we could never have known how solid a foundation we formed during our early moments and times together. And, oh, how we have built on that foundation through these many years. We had a magic that comes with young love, and without speaking of our values and respect for each other, we simply had the same values and respect.

We wanted to be together, and that was reflected in job decisions down the road and on trips that were taken when you were a coach. I loved going with you when you refereed games when we were first married as I sat in the stands and studied. I loved going with you because we were together on the ride over and back from the game—wherever it was. When you always asked me to go with you, it made me feel I was very important to your process. As I reflect on those early moments and meetings, I think of all the glorious places we ended up going in our life together. When we were in NYC for that magical 1976 NIT the first time with UNC Charlotte, as we were running up to playing in the final game. After the semi-final game and win, you, me, and a group *of our friends walked into that restaurant to celebrate the win, which was also our then 17th wedding anniversary. We danced and fell in love with New York, New York, during that time. There was an almost unbelievable dinner under tents at a castle outside Madrid, Spain; a lunch and long afternoon tour of Beaufort, SC with just the two of us and the great writer and friend, Pat Conroy, one of our favorite authors; the dinner in Caserta, Italy. I know the romantic side of you. I love you for pulling off a truly surprise 25th wedding anniversary party for us. The long walks along Lake Forest Drive in Milwaukee; and hours spent walking on our farm in Kentucky; trips to Venice, Pisa, Geneva, Budapest, Palm Springs, San Francisco, Hilton Head, Aspen, and Chautauqua—all so special and all together. For as fantastic as those settings were, in so many ways, what was most special is that we did it together. And we both agree that our longest and most memorable road trip was the one spent driving the back roads of Kentucky on and off for the six years when you spoke to the middle school children in the mountains of Appalachia, encouraging them to continue their education. That was indeed good work.*

One of the very first gifts that you gave me was a copy of The Prophet *by Kahlil Gibran. That small, black book was very special to me in 1958 and remains so as I write to you at this present moment. So much of Gibran's poetry in that book always felt authentic to our relationship. As I reflect on our love and this letter to you, I speak so often of our being together. And yet, there were great spaces in our togetherness that Gibran reflected in, "On Marriage."*

> But let there be spaces in your togetherness,
> And let the winds of the heavens dance between you.
> Love one another but make not a bond of love:
> Let it rather be a moving sea between
> the shores of your souls.
> Fill each other's cup but drink not from one cup.

COACH LEE ROSE

> Give one another of your bread but
> eat not from the same loaf
> Sing and dance together and be joyous,
> but let each one of you be alone,
> Even as the strings of a lute are alone though
> they quiver with the same music.
>
> **–Gibran**

I knew without question that I could start a course at Columbia Seminary and be gone for the week at a time that it required over a number of years. I took jobs in different cities in the NBA league, working in a photography shop, in the kitchen of a great catering place, and took writing class upon writing class; and I knew you were supportive of any of it. You have always been so encouraging of my interests. You wrote your own brand of poetry to me—some of that has been lost in our many moves and a few perhaps because they were censored!

All these years later, when you are 83, I am 79, and we are close to our 60th anniversary, we are much the same in so many ways. We dance in the kitchen, love to hear live music, go to plays, and read poetry aloud. We hold hands—sometimes now for stability—along with the love that joined our hands so many decades ago. We have changed in the way that life changes folks. We have faced family crises and tragedies that we could never have dreamed of any more than we dreamed of the public part of our lives that were often quite glamorous. I love that you always felt I was "perfect E" and that I was and continue to be your girl. I am eternally grateful for whatever the spark of magic was that started our love and has held us together as we have wept, laughed, and stayed through the years.

Forever Yours,
Eleanor

THE LONG GOODBYE—ELEANOR

A CRUEL AND VULGAR VISITOR THAT WILL NOT LEAVE

Lee just can't have Alzheimer's! Not this man who I met when I was seventeen and married when I was eighteen. He was this great guy on campus: very handsome, a great basketball and baseball player, and had the best smile. Somehow, even at that time, with all of that talent and good looks, he was humble. He wasn't a big talker, but he swept me off my feet with his grin and our dancing after dinner. I don't even want to ask him now if he remembers, for fear that he may not, that special night that we drove off campus to one of the Kentucky horse farms with all of its beautiful columns. I could not bear his revealing to me that he does not recall such a precious time that we shared. At first glance, we were just two youngsters parked in this blue Plymouth hanging out, but what lay beneath that spring night with the moon overhead was so much more. I need him to remember that moment.

My first journey with this cruelty of Alzheimer's was with Mother in 1980, and now, thirty-five years later, it has returned to my family's door. We had all come to Alzheimer's brand new with our introduction being Mother's diagnosis. We had never heard of it and knew nothing about it. I adore Lee for many reasons, and one of those is how wonderful he was with my mother during her decline. I recall when we were all together at some family gathering or the other, and she would wander to the side of the room, where she sat alone. At times, when she became distant and disoriented, she would sit off by herself in this way. Lee would go over to where she was and usher her back to the group setting, speaking to her as one encourages a loved one. He would tell her, "Come on, Omi, you can't sit by yourself; we want you over here with us." The rest of us would follow his queue, always receiving her like she was what had been missing.

I shall forever admire my father's strength and character during this time that tested us all. Opa was quite protective of Mother; he never complained or explained her to anyone.

I bought the book *The 36-Hour Day* thirty-five years ago, while in the midst of my mother's ten-year battle with Alzheimer's. I recall the book telling about an Alzheimer's patient who would ask what time it was. After the information was given, she would ask again and again. The explanation for this is that Alzheimer's impacts short-term memory; there is not what is referred to as "hooks" on which to hang the prior fact of the time. There is no point of reference to support the memory that if it was 10:30 when the question was first asked, it might be 10:45 now. Those of us whose brain cells touch and connect with the cells around them can remember the first telling of the time, and thus we make certain deductions as to what the time is now. Those whose brain cells do not touch and connect well are stuck. They are stuck like the needle of a record player in a groove, unable to continue to the next tiny groove. Such beautiful music can be heard when the connection works; when it doesn't, the same two bars of the music repeat over and over until someone picks up the needle and helps—or tries to help—it to the next groove. For a while, we could help Mother move on to the next groove into whatever narrative we were in. But as the cells get farther away from each other, as they become more brittle, it becomes impossible.

The very harsh reality of this condition is that it reaches beyond just the memory for time of day. At some point, it will adversely affect other aspects, impacting organ function, and ultimately leading to organ failure. My mother died of the disease she fought for ten years, a decade that was emotionally and physically painful for her, my father, the rest of the family, and me. In some way, I may have believed that the long bout that we all endured with Mother had perhaps immunized any of us from dealing with it again. But, thirty-five years later, it returned to my family's door. And now, I want to write without mention of the fact that Lee has the same diagnosis. Perhaps, I write this way because I don't want to write stories about how Lee is beginning to lose his way in the grooves sometimes. I knew in my being, before the definite diagnosis, that he had this but just did not want to believe that it was happening again.

In fall 2014, I began to notice behavior in Lee that was just off-kilter for him. There were small instances of not simply forgetting a name, but also instances where it seemed that a chunk of time disappeared for him. It wasn't just something small like the name of a player that he was unable to remember—there have been so many players it would be unreasonable for him to remember all of them. But now, Lee seemed unable to place whether he had coached at one school before or after another one. Early on, I was able to provide him with prompts of facts and details that seemed to get him right back on track, but getting on the right track became less effective and didn't last as long. I tried not to dwell on this. I was ever vigilant not to have my imagination get the best of me. However, things progressed, and when the screen on his laptop computer, which had over the years been second nature to him, became a foreign element to him, I knew.

In our family, we speak of someone's having "earned opinion," which generally means that because of that person's experience, they should be granted authority to speak on the subject at hand. In this case, I had an earned opinion based on my experience with my mother. I knew where this was headed—I felt in my bones that Lee had Alzheimer's, and additionally, I believed he was fully aware of something being wrong with him. I suppose that there is really no perfect time or good way to discuss bad news. One day, when things were not clicking for Lee mentally, he walked upstairs to my office, sat down in the chair, and was quiet. I turned to him and asked what was on his mind. He said he didn't know if he could say this or not. That he loved me so much and was sorry that this was happening…again. There it was. Our cat was out of the bag. In actuality, the cat had been out of the bag for some time. Perhaps we were just accepting that not only was it out, but it was also walking around, and we were both seeing it.

With our reality firmly in place, we both recognized that it was time to seek professional help. In the spring of 2015, I discovered that there was a Memory Center here in Charlotte, which specializes in Alzheimer's care. I arranged a consultation with the founder, Dr. Charles Edwards. In this first appointment, I went alone, to get a feel for what we were up against, or maybe to allow myself to ease into the water. Following my private meeting with Dr. Edwards, Lee and I met with him together a few weeks later. Lee had some testing done, including a brain MRI. During our next meeting, Dr. Edwards was very encouraging as he told Lee to be confident and continue to finish up the memoir that he had begun. He showed Lee where the testing and MRI indicated that his mental loss was mild. He even had Lee read the word "mild." I imagine the use of the word seems like it should have softened the blow, but that can only be so if the listeners have no understanding that mild is followed by something progressively more cruel and unusual.

The next day, I called Dr. Edwards. I had one question: What did he write on Lee's medical folder that Lee's condition is? Dr. Edwards asked me if it was important to name it. I shared with him my feelings that in order to keep things open and honest, not only between Lee and me but with our sons and their families, I felt that it was important to name it. There is really no perfect time or a good way to deliver bad news. But for us, it helped to name the opponent, to begin to let it settle into our beings. I needed him to name it.

He said that Lee had early Alzheimer's.

Lee had known that something had gone terribly wrong long before we put a name to it. He may not have known the full detail of his diagnosis, but he knew that something was wrong. Having our suspicions confirmed was another matter. Hearing this out of Dr. Edwards's mouth was hard to process, even though I had felt strongly that this was likely the answer to my question. Hard as it was, it was also best for our sons and their families to know. Knowing was the only way we could all begin to come together, rally our group around this, and begin to formulate a plan. The time had come for all hands on deck.

A writing instructor told me once that I needed to take some of the heavy emotions out of my writing. I absolutely know what he meant, but that is hard to do. Ignoring the harsh reality of life does not eliminate it. The harshness of life will continue to impact our lives, whether we acknowledge it or not.

Lee asked me to watch a PBS program on Alzheimer's with him. I tried to relax totally and just stayed with him. I felt it a sign of his beginning to accept, to know, to acknowledge that, in fact, the diagnosis is correct. Until then, he had never said Alzheimer's in connection with himself.

I had wondered how Lee related to Alzheimer's; just exactly how he processed it. I discovered a bit of that when we went to a gathering for the new location of The Memory Center. I was more than surprised that Lee wanted to attend. But attend we did one chilly evening. The space was quite full of people, and the noise level was a concern for me as that seemed to jar Lee a little. At that time, he was still standing, not in a wheelchair. He was talking to a gentleman, and I slipped off to speak to one of the staff members there—making it a point to tell Lee that I would be right back. When I returned, he was still talking easily with the same man, and they were quite engaged in the universal language of sports! As we drove home, Lee told me that the gentleman asked him how he knew Dr. Edwards. Then he stopped. I said, "Well, what did you say?" Lee said, "I told him I was a patient of Dr. Edwards. That is what I am." That was the first time he had publicly stated his relationship with Alzheimer's—acknowledging the disease was his. I asked how it felt to say that. He said he wished he didn't have to say that, but it was the fact. It was no surprise to me that he approached it head-on just as he has done with everything in his life.

Very shortly after Lee realized that he was losing part of the details of his life, I asked him what he felt about that. He hated this because with the memory loss, coupled with mobility loss, he didn't want it to be a burden for Mike and Mark and their families, but his overriding concern was for me—his greatest hurt was for me. For years now, I have looped back in my mind to that statement.

He also said he was disappointed. Disappointed feels like such a strange descriptive for this situation. It doesn't feel like what I would say aloud, but it is what Lee felt. He was disappointed more as the losses settled in as he couldn't go to see his grandchildren in the marker events of their lives. That meant not going to football games where Mike is coaching or traveling to Florida to enjoy our grandson Zan's high school baseball games. The heartache also comes when Lee is unable to fly to see our grandson James in a play in New York City. That is where some of the heavy emotions land with me. While Lee's pragmatic response is asking me to take lots of pictures, it begs the question, how do we substitute for the real thing? We take the news and don't let it ruin our lives. He tries very hard not to allow his challenges to overshadow every other part of our lives.

There are stretches when he does great with facts for a short period of time before he returns to unknowing, to the days when he can't process getting to the "in-box" on his computer, figuratively and literally. We are both aware of these shifts. It is important for me to remember that it is the illness that is upsetting him—not me. But when faced with what would otherwise be irrational situations, remembering this isn't always easy. Sometimes people will say with all the best intentions that we should "live in the moment." I scream inwardly, "How can we live in the moment when Lee can't remember the moments?" I often catch myself not wanting to ask if he remembers something, for fear he will not. This is where the wear on the caregiver comes into play; I was beginning to *live* the pages from *The 36-Hour Day*.

At our meeting the other week with Dr. Edwards, he said we must plan things for success and be wary of fatigue and pressure. Good food and sleeping well are so important. He told us not to miss the joy in each day. He reminds Lee to be confident and write his book. I always enjoy and am impressed when Lee rises to the occasion. At a recent dinner, Lee was relaxed and good. He told many stories. While he got lots of facts wrong, they were still good stories! The joy these days comes as unpredictable as the sorrow.

> *Please don't leave me*
> *Don't go to that dark place*
> *Where you can't find your memories*
> *And I can't find you.*
> **–Eleanor Rose**

An added layer of difficulty in an already difficult situation is other competing and unrelated illnesses. Within a year, Lee and I went from doing yoga on the beach in Hilton Head to a rather abrupt navigation of our lives with Lee in a wheelchair. Not only are we learning to live with Alzheimer's, but the addition of him being wheelchair-bound has also been very hard. We've had to manage other issues such as back surgery, a pacemaker, and fragile bones. Just six months after the diagnosis of Alzheimer's, Lee fell and fractured his spine, requiring surgery. He did well with that and the rehabilitation, so he went forward with a much-needed knee replacement. Six weeks later, he fell in our home and broke his femur on the same leg. He was unable to bear any weight on that right leg and spent three weeks in a rehab facility. He left the facility using a walker very tentatively but relying primarily on a wheelchair. Two months later, he fell again in our home. The very next day, I could tell that Lee was unable to help me in getting him from the wheelchair to the car, and the in-home physical therapist said she noted the loss of strength. We went to several spine specialists and surgeons for testing. The results revealed severe spinal cord damage and we were told there was a very low-percentage chance of successful surgery.

Lee's multiple major back surgeries had left him with a ton of metal, screws, and pins along his spine. In addition, his reaction to anesthesia had gotten increasingly worse. Following the femur surgery, he spent several days with severe hallucinations and delusions, seemed to be fighting for his life, and was certainly fighting to regain any semblance of mental cognition. It was a scary time for our family. About ten days later, he seemed to snap back into reality but had absolutely no memory of anything that had happened during that week. It seems that advanced age combined with long periods of time under anesthesia are a bad combination. Our conclusion was that the combination of Alzheimer's and the negative effects of anesthesia for yet another seven hours of spinal surgery would be a terrible risk to him.

It is the physical losses that are so hard now. He has lost more mobility and feeling in both legs—he cannot feel it when I touch his legs. They are cold. He will probably get much less able to help me or anyone else assist him from the wheelchair to the bed, toilet, or recliner.

We have always had great relationships with our grandchildren Lee, Kristi, James, and Zan. They simply bring joy to our lives. We've always treated them with great love and respect, and they've been a credit to their parents and us in that they've treated us with the same love and respect. We took them on walks through the woods across from our house when we lived in Milwaukee as they searched for deer, and the walks could always be prolonged as our calendars were cleared for them. We have gone to football, soccer, basketball, and baseball games, lots of wonderful plays, and played more card games than we can count—and loved it all. We decided that we enjoyed the kids so much not because we didn't have the ultimate responsibility for them, but because we genuinely enjoy each other's company.

One day, before Lee had become wheelchair bound, we were watching a game with our teenage grandson, also named Lee. Normally this is a time of discussions on points of the game or something related, but this time, Lee (the elder) was giving much more attention to his iPhone than normal. I asked him if I could help him with anything as he looked at notes on the phone. He said that he had not written any of those notes and did not know who'd put them there, but he sure didn't. He was very agitated, and his tone was not at all what I had always known. It is in moments like these that I recall Dr. Edwards's counsel that I should move toward Lee in difficult times. I understood the term "toward" as to embrace Lee where he is, not to require him to be where I am. As a practical matter, it would have to be that way because it is unlikely that he will move to where I am, or anyone else is. So, I moved toward him. As we stood there in the kitchen area, I tried to speak very softly with him to ramp the anxiety level down. He finally just said that he was very tired and went off to bed.

Grandson Lee was sitting on the couch through all of this. I turned to him and told him that I was so sorry for him to have to see his grandfather like that. He said, "It is just such a jolt, so hard to believe." His phrasing it all as a jolt is just what it is—jolt and jolting as in a shock to one's system. Such a jolt is so very hard to believe.

Changes have tumbled out quickly as the Alzheimer's moved forward. They happen at infrequent intervals that hit you from out of the blue, and hit hard, in a way that I have termed "jolts." To realize that Lee didn't know what Google was, for example, constituted a jolt, and just like all of the various jolts caused by this uninvited "thing" in our home, it was like a physical kick in the stomach.

While Lee doesn't direct his bad feeling necessarily toward me, I accept his "mood" as the natural frustration of what he is experiencing. Otherwise, I would feel completely alone in this journey if I thought he was mad at me. As it is, I am able to fix in my heart that it is still Lee and me against all things awful.

On another occasion we had a silly and fun day with our grandson, James. But less than a day later, a jolt occurred when I laughed and reflected on those events with Lee, and he did not remember them at all. It is impossible for me to make peace with the loss of moments that are so vivid, ones that he was so prominently involved in, not just something that I told him about. Yet, it was gone forever from his memory. This was simply (for me) the day after an event, not many years later. That variety of loss is so different from his not remembering that the moon was full that night in Hawaii long ago. There is an ever-increasing volume of these events steeped in this mixture of memory loss and frustration.

I feel my energy and effort elevated in a good way when Lee is doing well and in a great mood. There are times when he might do great for three days before he returns to unknowing. We both are aware there are seismic shifts, where everything was okay one moment, then not okay in the next. I remember trying to make my way out the door in a hurry to go someplace and do something as Lee asked me about the meaning of something he was trying to figure out. I innocently replied over my shoulder as so many of us do—"try Googling it." I had to take a beat and realize that yes, a person can Google whatever the subject is, if you can simply recall what Google is and why anyone is using the term as a verb. Wrinkles, wrinkles, everywhere wrinkles. What do I do with it?

Not rushing to be on my way with my list of errands to do, I just relax and realize he needs to see total calm from me. That is the gift I can give him. If I rush and indicate that where I am going is more important than standing while he works through the synapse of his brain cells that won't jump, it makes it worse for him, but it is also not how to show him love.

Dear God, bless Lee and me.
Help us to get through this part of the journey.
Help me to be patient.
Help me to relinquish wanting to make Lee understand something.
–Eleanor Rose

THE LONG GOODBYE—ELEANOR

A strange thing has happened over the past few months. At first, I couldn't begin to understand what was going on. Lee can be in bed; there is absolutely no way he can get out of that bed by himself. But at least three or four times a week, I hear him walking. Sounds from the floorboards tell me he is about to walk into the room; to smile at me, to walk over and envelope me in a hug. But he doesn't. Then I remembered the concept of phantom pain, which is when a person feels pain in a limb that is no longer there. I am not going crazy. I just miss the part of me that I had for over six decades. And I feel the loss and pain of it. How much more must he feel?

He wheels past and sees my tears. He does know the loss we both share. But as an Eric Clapton CD plays softly, we know that we cannot wait for the pain to be gone to enjoy moments. If we try to figure it all out, we miss it. Just as the person videotaping every move of a child misses the greater joy by trying to see it through a narrow viewfinder.

At some point in this progression of losses, we realized that we had a choice. We could sit and weep, or we could do as my British sister-in-law has often said about difficult matters—"You take the news and go to lunch." It is not part of Lee's DNA to sit and weep. His manner of facing losses and seeking solutions for what was wrong were very much the way he faced difficulties throughout his life. He had incredible persistence, determination, discipline, and an old-school code of doing things in what he felt was the right way. Not one for short cuts, he was always incredibly disciplined and focused on the task at hand. He could sit for hours and figure out how to contain the offense presented by a top-ranked team or an All-American player or how to beat the full-court press of number-one-ranked Michigan in order to get to the Final Four in 1977. He showed up every day for three years to write his book, *The Basketball Handbook*. He drew every drill in that book by hand. We read and reread every word of that manuscript aloud, and when I had a question about the correctness of a technical drill he had written, he would have me stand here and pivot to there. He always loved the chess game of assessing the talent of players, working on game plans that would "accentuate the positive and eliminate the negative," and he didn't mess much with anything in-between. But now, we are faced with a thing of greater consequences than a game loss or missing a publisher's deadline.

He now transfers all of those qualities into his approach to rehabilitation. Since he has no mobility in his legs, Lee has gone to physical therapy three times a week for three years. He works with a physical therapist who is a major part of our support team. His initial effort to move a leg ever so slightly with any control was almost too painful to watch, but his determination to keep as strong as he could is amazing as he moves through the process.

Tonight is the first time that Lee said to me, "I will never be able to walk again. And the problem is that I have left you with so much to handle." Unfortunately, he is correct on both accounts.

I feel myself in a season of vulnerability; Lee and I are both in need of support. Not sympathy just support. We want that version of support that communicates to us that others see us and not through us. We want to be welcomed in all the same places by the faces we know and recognize. I want friends, family, and others to look at us, not through us as something uncomfortable to bear.

Being in this situation is so hard because it challenges all that I thought I knew. Throughout much of my life, I have tried to outrun the fatalness as expressed in "The Darkest Truth About Love," by Alain de Botton. That poem is so full of one person's commentary on the futility of love and the inevitable loneliness that each of us is destined for when we care about others. De Botton is articulate in his interpretation of our human condition, which I do not want to be my truth. He emphasizes that there are events that can and will be heartbreaking in this life. I am resisting the part of this life experience that is robbing me of hope. Don't we all have to maintain an eye to a hope-filled future, come what may? I do not want to be eternally sad. I want to maintain an enthusiasm that moves me to continue to prowl for good books to read, different foods to eat, and to be forever questioning. Even this culture of being a caregiver can create accumulated fatigue that will amplify the shock and weight of it all. All of this leaves me physically and mentally drained. In his very dark treatise, de Botton concludes by suggesting "let's pretend that we do not know any of this." I counter with: I will not pretend because my soul knows better. I know all of this, but I am determined to move through it.

In a calm moment, I look over as Lee is sending a text to our sons on his smartphone and become concerned about what he would he do without me. He frequently requires computer help. Who would handle the home business? Not because he forgot or was unable to, but because that has been my contribution to him over these many years. Our lives were always intertwined in an inter-independent manner, until now. What was inter-independent is now dependent. Alzheimer's can become your jailer if allowed. What was once an artful separation of duties within our unit now stands as a matter of choreography in pas de deux—dance with a pair of two. I step in concert with Lee's moments and movements. I am constantly trying to answer for Lee when he cannot fully understand the how and when.

Now, I do the practical thinking for the two of us, plus dealing with the emotional toll of seeing everything fall apart. Almost every day, something falls apart. Sometimes the van's ramp doesn't drop down as it is supposed to; sometimes, a hard rain starts while we are out, and the ramp into our home isn't covered; sometimes, it is easier to stay home.

Frequently, I cry inside my heart. Almost every day, I lose him a little more. I lose us. However, I refuse just to say okay and go on, give up, and give in. I will not have that for Lee, and quite frankly, nor will he allow it. We are intelligent adults who have lived our lives at high levels of excitement and energy. So we venture out again, and an afternoon movie goes without a hitch! We make it to church when we can—and there are kind souls everywhere who step forward to lend a helping hand.

There are emotional issues to be resolved for me as the primary caregiver. The question for me early on was, "can a person die from a broken heart?" I was told that it is highly unlikely. But the fact was that several times in the first months after getting Lee's diagnosis, my chest felt that it would burst. Intellectually, I knew that this was brought on by the grief before the going really gets tough. And it is a grief that millions of spouses and their families go through each day with this disease. In our case, the closeness of our family heightened the stress at first as everyone had to handle their own emotional toll from this. Mike and Mark saw this, and it was hard on them to figure out how to best help both Lee and me while we all dealt with the grief and loss. The ongoing grief tends to isolate the caregiver. A large part of it was that everything about the reality was totally overwhelming, and I was tired. These facts became nearly impossible to explain to those who insisted that I "must get out and do something for myself." Everyone handles situations like this differently, but in my mind, what I had to do was to try to figure this out!

Taking care of one's self is very personal to the individual and will look very different for each person as it plays itself out. In a large way, I accept the wisdom of the airline announcement that each of us hears, the instructions on what to do in the event of an emergency. The wisdom is that you should always secure your oxygen first before you seek to aid others. Which makes a lot of sense to me when I recognize that if I cannot help myself, how can I help Lee? How can the wounded be successful in helping other wounded people? By carving out time for writing, workouts, and walks through the neighborhood, I am better able to be the point person for Lee and me. Within this moment, I continue learning to accept the full meaning of taking care of myself.

I asked Lee to tell me if he could remember how all of this felt to him during one morning conversation about his condition. He said, "I don't know how to get from point A to point B sometimes. And I don't know how to get into it or out of it. I asked, "It?" He said, "It is just hard to know how to get into or out of the situation, the conversation when I can't find the words. But sometimes it is more than the particular word; it is like I am just lost from the second part."

After our first big outing with the wheelchair, Lee said, "I miss dancing." Music was always very much a part of our life. We danced at the old North Lime Grill in Kentucky, when we were in college. This little joint was there within a couple of miles of Transy's campus. There was a jukebox, and we put in coins and danced. With the purchase of a soft drink and a coin, we created what was scheduled to be a lifelong memory. So now we improvise, and even with the wheelchair, we dance as best we can. I know that I have so much to be thankful for. For all of our fond memories of rich experiences, I just want a few more years of good health for Lee.

Lee has maintained a sense of humor about many things as we make our way through this very rough place. We continue to be amused by silly things and remain conspirators against those things that get in the way. During a meeting with friends, one of whom is our investment advisor, Lee fell into his regular pose of pretending to be haranguing over how much something costs and fictions of being set back financially. This is always amusing for all of us because Lee and I are not wanting for money. He had said, "All of this talk of millions of dollars, and I don't even have money in my pocket." This may be technically true, since a person does not usually carry his wallet if he is not leaving home, but that is so different than not having anything to put in said wallet. So, as we were saying goodbye for the evening, they passed him two crisp one-dollar bills and said, "Coach, take this. I want you to always have some money in your pocket." Lee laughed as he played along, though he held on to the two dollars.

Lee and I have been blessed with such love and care from family, friends, and former players. Something special happens between Lee and most of his players that is hard to explain fully, but I am glad it does. In 2018, I called the Charlotte Coliseum for assistance in securing convenient parking for the Andrea Bocelli Valentine concert being held there. Lee had coached in that same arena during his time with the NBA Charlotte teams. I knew there was underground parking available for staff, and knew that he was not on staff now, but thought it was worth a shot. I contacted the officials there just to see if we could get parking for our van, which has a ramp that drops down to let Lee in and out with his wheelchair. I received a pleasant surprise and the good fortune in the returned call when the office of Michael Jordan and his business partner Fred decided to provide everything we needed, including the best seats in the house. I was actually expecting to pay for everything, but they insisted on providing parking and a perfect pair of tickets. Michael had been on the team that Lee coached in Switzerland and then Yugoslavia for the 50th Anniversary of the FIBA games many years before. On that night, we experienced one of the most beautiful and elegant concerts ever, as Bocelli elegantly rendered "Vivo Per Lei" and then on to "Time to Say Goodbye." Rarely one at a loss for words, Lee leaned over and told me that it was the prettiest song, but he wasn't exactly sure what Andrea Bocelli was saying. I replied I was not either, given that he was singing in Italian. We both laughed and enjoyed the moment.

NORMAL?

Things have leveled off here and there a little, but does it or will it ever feel normal? Not really. How can it? Just when we get settled into a routine, another shoe drops. However, Lee and I have both adjusted, to a certain degree, to the reality that what he has is what he has.

THE LONG GOODBYE—ELEANOR

What was the loss that happened today?
What did he lose along the way?
A sock, the name of the book that he wrote, a memory of the blue formal she wore
that night, but not the love that he saw in her eye, he did not lose that today.
How will this play out?
We had such a great card game going—then someone
threw in a card that we never saw coming.
Never.

–Eleanor Rose

Strangely, we humans can adjust, even to offensive phrases like, "You just have a new normal." Surely, this advice is a well-intended offer of comfort to me, but it is not. It is not normal, and neither of us wants this ever to be normal. You will not have normal at any level of illness. That is like saying that God needed another angel; thus, your child died in a wreck. I expect to have adjustments, sadness, and joys, but woe unto the next person who utters that God doesn't give us more than we can handle. This is just not the time and place for platitudes. Almost anything that is said beyond, "I love you," will feel trite and minimize the enormity of what we are dealing with.

Part of the constant emotional fact of his losses is that both of us must process and learn to ramp the emotions down about the fact that he can't do much at all that is spontaneous. Lee can't stop by the grocery or decide that he will go to Barnes and Noble without someone taking him. He was on his own from such an early age. And now Lee is totally dependent on someone to do almost everything for him.

We are fully aware of our shifting realities, chief among which is that we may have to move in the future to accommodate Lee's ever-increasing needs. There have been suggestions for us to move from our home of thirty years into an assisted living facility. The suggestions are all given with great love to us, for us. If we chose that option, we would have the needed help to handle Lee's physical challenges around mobility and the Alzheimer's condition. We also know that things are not necessarily easier in another space. Early on, Lee told me that he would leave these decisions to me. I decided to accept counsel from a Bonnie Raitt song lyric taped to Lee's desk—"Life gets mighty precious when there's less of it to waste." I have discovered that I feel a certain kind of way about assisted living and nursing homes. I am left feeling that no matter how elegant their presentation, they assault my concept of quality of life. The day is likely to come that I, and we, will have no choice, but I have decided that day is not now. So, I shall kick that can down the road…for now. I decided that we will remain in our home until we cannot. I believe friends and family that I trust will give me a good talking to should I cross the line that separates far enough and too far. Until then, we will live here, surrounded by art, photographs, and our favorite foods, sounds, smells, and all of our other favorite things until we cannot. There is a famous line from a movie citing that a person has to know their limitations. I believe we do.

We go out to eat at least once a week, but sometimes the energy expended is better used to have the food come to our house. I would prefer that we go out for a quick bite and then back home before anyone knew. Or better yet, that we have one of those long evenings out on the town when we looked up and discovered we were about to close the place. What we so often have instead are our quiet meals here at home when we don't feel up to the process of wheelchairs and vans, lifting and tugging.

Lee and I know right now that we are on a hard road much of the time. I have gotten help from family and experts on moving some of the big rocks out of the road so that Lee and I can move forward more easily. We continue to live our lives with as much grace and dignity as traffic will allow. We know realistically that life is brief, and that adds to the continued desire to live it to the fullest as we have always done.

At present, we are in a good, if not preferred place. Our nights are, for the most part, peaceful. I am thankful for that. I know that

I have so much to be thankful for. My preference is that Lee and I would be going on very long walks, with even longer conversations on the variety of interests we share. Our reality is that on good days, we sit in the quiet of our home, reading, listening to our choice of music for the day as we exchange glances and comments over the tops of our respective reading glasses. We enjoy our quick games of Scrabble several times a week. Lee continues reading every night before he turns out the light.

On the subject of his reading—I thought I was tracking his reading progress as judged by the placement of his bookmark. He explained to me that he was much further along than I knew. He went on to discuss where he was in the book and shared some of his thoughts on what he had read. I suppose that I am not the only one who has created systems around our reality.

There are moments that will be that kind of funny that can only be so between the two of us. No one else could be allowed to enter that still-too-fragile, broken thing. The broken thing is that part of the card dropped into our deck that we were playing so well most of the time.

A TEAM

At times it feels like I am the only one, when in reality, of course, I am not the only one. I know—absolutely—that there are so many of us who walk together with Alzheimer's only the names are changed; so many that walk together with a partner who doesn't walk upright anymore. We are all just part of the quilt of humankind and must be ready to reach out our hands to help and our hearts to love ourselves, our partners, and others who have the same issues.

My father intentionally isolated himself from his community in part because he just didn't know or understand what was happening to his beloved Marge. I understand why my Dad tucked in: he didn't know how to introduce friends to the person my mother was becoming, and he never knew quite what to expect.

For the first time in my adult life, I feel the downside of having moved all over the country during our over-sixty years of marriage. We have dear, dear close friends that fill our contact lists and even my old-fashioned address book. But I must make our local list broader and more active. I must take the experience that I learned from those ten years that Mom and Dad lived with Alzheimer's and the time since Lee was diagnosed to continue to build on a game plan. That plan must include relationships because relationships are important. I have seen the troops rally around my friend Leah as she starts chemo for lymphoma, for our friend Mitch as he deals with severe spinal cord injury. Mary Ann's youngest son has rallied their family and included me in the loop of this dear friend's fight against lymphoma. I realize I have to maintain a team around the two of us too. A team that may choose to be active in our lives and knows what is going on with Lee.

I had let our children know what was going on in our lives, then a few relatives, dear friends, and our immediate neighbors. I sent an email to several of his former players. Our two sons and their families were instrumental in creating this team and helping us with this life transition. Ironically, for our family, the initial shock of Alzheimer's was almost nothing compared to the challenges we faced with Lee's confinement to a wheelchair, his immobility, and the need for assistance with almost all activities that we otherwise took for granted. Clothes, showers, bathroom, shoes, the fact that his office was upstairs all required assistance or change.

At the outset, Mark flew up from Tampa twice a month for six months, and we slowly tweaked the needs, helpers, timing, and processes, and he continues to help with that as Lee's situation requires constant tweaking. Lee and I stayed at Mark's home in Tampa for three weeks while our bathroom was being renovated to work for Lee and the wheelchair. Mike works in the insurance business and has immeasurably helped as we navigated our way through Medicare our long-term care policy, claims, home health care, and system upon system with their own specific rules and details. He continues to be helpful in handling the details of getting a wheelchair van, coordinating Lee's physical therapy, and pushing to get Lee's medical team all on the same page. Mike coaches football at Charlotte Christian High School, and about three years into the process, he started bringing his defensive unit to Lee's former upstairs office for their weekly film reviews. It is wonderful to have those young guys come into the house and visit with both of us before the films start. Mike also works out the logistics of seating and parking for us when we go to his football games. The availability of the disabled parking spot and a helper to get us to our seats is planned, not random, and all of the small details make a big difference. Mike visits weekly to talk football, basketball, or baseball with Lee and just sit and visit. Mike's wife and my daughter-in-law, Kari, and I continue our shared meals, and my granddaughter, Kristi, comes over with her smile that lights up the room. We don't have pets, but she often brings her dogs, and Lee responds so positively to them. Our daughter-in-law, Denise has a nephew who had been in a wheelchair for over two years from a spinal cord injury, and she was able to provide invaluable advice about the road that lay ahead. Grandson Lee coaches football in Poland, and the phone calls from Warsaw are frequent and priceless to us; he has always been very attentive to Lee. Grandson James is an actor in NYC, and my trips to see his plays (and bring back recordings for Lee) have been a breath of fresh air. Grandson Zan plays high school baseball in Tampa, and at seventeen years old is the stat man of the group and the knower of every sports fact.

Lee has become incredibly proficient with the wheelchair, and the construction modification we did has made our home easier for him to navigate. Things don't always click, but that is where Mike and Mark, and their wives and the grandchildren, are great with him; they respond to him and are able to bring an air of lightness and humor to the setting.

I needed professional caregivers in our home to assist Lee in order to take some of the physical weight off of me. The Memory Center was a wonderful source for finding these caregivers. At first, someone in our home felt like an intrusion on our space. There was definitely a learning curve to figuring out when and how someone could best help Lee or me. But we learned how to let these wonderful people help, and as the years have gone on, we now have three caregivers who rotate in and out of our home and are valued members of our support team.

We have dear friends and family who often come to visit us; we know that we are not on the direct path for many of these friends, but their visits are special and so meaningful. The special relationship between Lee and his former players is hard to explain, but I am glad it exists. They stay in touch. They visit. They call. They send texts and emails on special occasions. They connect him to special memories: games, practices, names, and places that are so important in our shared experience. Former classmates drop by to say hello and give hugs and support. Local University of North Carolina Charlotte and high school coaches visit to discuss basketball with Lee. He meets with a group for coffee and with his former grad assistant for lunch—not as often as in his life before, but when he can. Our weekly Saturday breakfast with our dear friend, Dot, is a cornerstone of consistency and joy in our week.

Lee and I have been blessed with great love and care from all of our family, friends, and former coaches, and players. Our choice to be open about Alzheimer's with our family and friends has allowed them to respond, and they have responded with an outpouring of love and support. We have worked hard these past few years and now have a team around us that is active and helpful, and understands what is going on with Lee. He will not win this fight against Alzheimer's, but a team makes that fact easier to face.

This disease is undefeated as it destroys. There is nothing out there in the medical world to beat this, but we must manage it. There are no current solutions. We can only hope that the disease will be slowed down in its forward march through our lives.

We have much to be thankful for and are grateful for the love and support of so many. We try to continue our journey with grace and gratitude, knowing that much is lost, but much remains.

WRITING A MEMOIR

It was during a visit one January night in Hilton Head when Joe Barry Carroll sat with us in our condo overlooking the ocean and said that he would help tie Lee's vast quantity of written material into a memoir and publish it. Joe has remained an important person in our lives since Lee coached at Purdue. We continue to make the transition from the relationship of player and coach to a friendship of more than forty years. Coincidently, Joe had recently established a boutique publishing house and seemed thrilled to add his old coach to the library of offerings. Thus began not only a shifting of roles for teacher and pupil but four years of work. The three of us had weekly phone conversations beginning in August 2015 to go over tone, facts, and flavor. We have exchanged written chapters back and forth since then.

To say it is difficult to wrap up and polish a memoir when Lee's memory is being wiped clean is an understatement. My habit of keeping journals and calendars filled with details has helped. The fact that I was with him on every step of his amazing journey helped. Emails, letters, cards, and boxes on top of boxes of newspapers helped fill in the facts as well.

Joe has shown great care in the handling of Lee's story. He pushed Lee to tell him and then tell him more about some of the material that Lee had written in his own journals and memoir rough drafts. Joe is constantly probing for deeper meaning and understanding. Sometimes we laugh at Lee's frequent response of, "What part of that don't you understand? Sometimes a person crosses the street simply to get to the other side. Why does there have to be a deep meaning to everything? Hell, Joe, I thought you knew that!" We all laugh as Joe digs in deeper for Lee to help him understand what, where, when, and the ever-present why. It was a gift of time and resources from him to Lee—his coach and friend. Perhaps this is a key example of the benefits of not isolating ourselves from those whom we care about and who care about us.

Dear God, bless Lee and me.
Help us get through this part of the journey.
Give us grace.
–Eleanor Rose

IN GRATITUDE

I AM PROUD to be Dad to Michael and Mark, father-in-law to Kari and Denise, and Grandpa Lee to Lee, Kristi, James, and Zan. They have given me more than I could ever have hoped for in our wonderful family composition. I am so proud of our life together, and their words and deeds of love show me that they share my love and respect for each of them. They show up in my life with their visits, telephone calls, emails, and other acts of caring. My wonderful family and career do not necessarily make me feel a whole lot better about this hand that I have been dealt, but I need to say out loud just how grateful I am to them and for them.

I am grateful for my life thus far. I have traveled so very far from that small, A-framed house in West Irving, Kentucky that my grandfather Hyden built with his own hands. I have enjoyed the company of a president, heads of state, and other important and good people. I have ushered young boys into manhood and witnessed them realize their potential as human beings. I remain grateful for all of that.

No one will ever have a more perfectly suited companion than I have had in Eleanor Lollis Rose as my wife for over sixty years. She has honored me to accept this journey that would have been impossible for me without her. Neither of us could have known where we would be today, but we have been flexible, adaptable, and willing to trust that our love and commitment to each other will make any situation work out.

www.ingramcontent.com/pod-product-compliance
Lightning Source LLC
Chambersburg PA
CBHW031102080526
44587CB00011B/793